VOLUME 17   NUMBER 1   2011

Rethinking Sex

Edited by Heather Love

INTRODUCTION

Heather Love

One of the first things I read in graduate school was Gayle Rubin's 1994 interview with Judith Butler, "Sexual Traffic."[1] It was an uncanny experience. In response to questions from Butler about the relation between feminism and lesbian and gay studies, Rubin reflects at length on her intellectual and political formation. She remembers reading "dirty lesbian novels" by "the Natalie Barney and Renée Vivien crowd" in the upstairs reading room at the Bibliothèque Nationale in the early 1970s for a thesis in lesbian literature; I read those same books in that same room in the summer of 1990, also for my senior thesis. Rubin also remembers how she came to rethink the politics of sex work and pornography in the late 1970s; I spent a lot of the early 1990s tracing the early history of the feminist sex wars. As for Rubin's discussion of sexology, the limits of psychoanalysis, the work of Michel Foucault, kinship, and the early history of "social construction" theory, these obsessions had not yet emerged for me, but they were about to. I spent the next decade or so working on these topics as part of an apprenticeship in queer studies. All that time, I thought I was just living my life, while I was in fact following in Rubin's footsteps—and, as I later came to realize, she had also traced out the path ahead.

As odd (and exhilarating) as I found this experience, my sense now is that it was not all that unusual. For those of us invested in activist histories, lesbian and gay archives, sexual politics, and queer feminisms, Rubin has a singular significance. She has been involved in the defining political events of the last few decades: working as a feminist, supporting sexual freedom and expression, arguing for the rights of sexual minorities, and documenting the costs of HIV/AIDS, urban zoning laws, and the rise of the New Right. At the same time, she has produced some of the most significant scholarship in feminism and gender and sexuality studies: her groundbreaking essays "The Traffic in Women: On the 'Political Economy' of Sex" (1975) and "Thinking Sex: Notes for a Radical Theory of the

GLQ 17:1
DOI 10.1215/10642684-2010-014
© 2010 by Duke University Press

Politics of Sexuality" (1984) set the terms for feminist and queer scholarship.[2] Moving between scholarship and activism, and between academic and nonacademic settings, Rubin has been an exemplar for many of us. By integrating methods from anthropology, sociology, Marxism, psychoanalysis and sexology, deviance studies, history, and urban studies, she has laid broad foundations for our critical and activist interventions. In her current work, she challenges us to move beyond our particular investments and disciplinary training to confront pressing questions of belonging, inequality, and survival.

This special issue is devoted to the work of Gayle Rubin. It emerges out of a state-of-the-field conference in gender and sexuality studies held at the University of Pennsylvania, March 4–6, 2009, "Rethinking Sex," which celebrated the twenty-fifth anniversary of Rubin's essay "Thinking Sex."[3] The essay was originally published in *Pleasure and Danger: Exploring Female Sexuality*, a collection edited by Carole S. Vance that emerged out of the Scholar and Feminist IX conference "Towards a Politics of Sexuality," held at Barnard College on April 24, 1982. A key event of the feminist sex wars, the Barnard conference drew together feminist scholars, activists, and writers to explore the politics of sexuality; it also drew protests by Women Against Pornography and allied groups that resulted in the confiscation of fifteen hundred copies of the conference *Diary*, a seventy-two-page booklet that was to be distributed to participants (excerpts from the *Diary* are republished in the *GLQ* Archive in this issue). In taking Rubin's essay as the occasion for "Rethinking Sex," we sought to mark her influence on gender and sexuality studies and to consider the future directions for the field that her work and her career suggest.[4] We also wanted to emphasize an alternate genealogy for queer studies, one that dates not to the annus mirabilis of 1990 (the year that Butler published *Gender Trouble*, David Halperin published *One Hundred Years of Homosexuality*, Eve Kosofsky Sedgwick published *Epistemology of the Closet*, and Teresa de Lauretis coined the term *queer theory*) but to feminist histories of the 1970s and 1980s. While my graduate training had focused on a philosophical and literary lineage for the field, my own experience, intuitions, and desultory reading suggested other affiliations and genealogies. Finally, in response to scholarly narratives about the decline of queer studies, we wanted to demonstrate the vitality and range of interdisciplinary inquiry in gender and sexuality studies in the present.

In my invitation to Rubin, I asked her to reflect on the original contexts of "Thinking Sex" and on the changes—both intellectual and political—that have taken place in the decades since it was published. The essay has been canonized—most notably in *The Lesbian and Gay Studies Reader* (1993)—as a point of origin for sexuality studies, but it has often been read without significant attention to its original context.[5] By organizing a general state-of-the-field conference around this essay, I wanted to test my hypothesis that the field as it is currently constituted owes an unacknowledged debt to feminism, and particularly to the debates about porn, S/M, and butch/femme in the late 1970s and early 1980s.[6] Rubin's presentation, titled "Blood under the Bridge: Reflections on 'Thinking Sex,'" drew an audience of nearly eight hundred people on the conference's opening night. This turnout, as well as the palpable excitement in the room during the next two days, offered ample testimony to the liveliness of the field of sexuality studies as well as to a widespread investment in links between the sex wars and queer theory and politics. Rubin's essay, a version of which is published here, traces some of these links by mapping the activist and scholarly milieu out of which "Thinking Sex" emerged. In addition to "Blood under the Bridge," this issue also includes short pieces that draw connections between Rubin's work (with a focus on "Thinking Sex") and live questions in contemporary queer studies. In addition, Regina Kunzel provides an account of the conference in her review, "Queer Studies in Queer Times."[7]

Unpacking the complex relations between Rubin's work and sexuality studies is the task of this special issue. There is no doubt that "Thinking Sex" has had a shaping influence on the field. For the past few decades, scholars have relied on Rubin's clarifying analysis of sexuality as a "vector of oppression," to be understood as related to but distinct from gender hierarchy.[8] Describing the regulation of sexuality through moral panics, antisex ideologies, and the scapegoating of sexual minorities and people with AIDS, Rubin called for developing "an autonomous theory and politics specific to sexuality" (309). The analytic separation that Rubin makes in the essay between gender and sexuality, as well as her insistence that resources are allocated according to a hierarchy of sexual behavior and identity, cleared space for the emergence of a conceptually rich, historically informed, and politically forceful field of inquiry.

If "Thinking Sex" seemed in many ways a clear choice as the basis for our conference, it proves remarkably difficult to pin the essay down to the year 1984. For one thing, since the collection *Pleasure and Danger* points back to the events of the Barnard conference, 1982 turns out to be an equally if not more significant date for the essay. Also, in her accounts of the germination of the essay, Rubin has consistently pointed to a broader intellectual and political context that put the roots of the essay several years further back.[9] In "Blood under the Bridge," Rubin describes the "dense intellectual and social network" in which the central insights of the original essay emerged.[10] Rubin has also insisted across her career on the long history of sexuality studies. That genealogy, as she has repeatedly described it, includes not only lesbian and feminist work of the 1970s but also gay history, sociology, and anthropology as well as work in deviance studies, Chicago School sociology, midcentury urban studies, and sexology.[11] If it is hard to fix "Thinking Sex" in 1984 because its historical roots keep showing, it can also be hard to fix it there because the essay tends to slip forward into the future. So much of the essay's influence depends on its republication. The most influential of these republications is its appearance as the lead essay in *The Lesbian and Gay Studies Reader* (edited by Henry Abelove, Michèle Aina Barale, and David M. Halperin). While this placement of "Thinking Sex" has secured the essay a place in the canon of lesbian, gay, and queer studies, it has also been included in anthologies in several fields.[12] The essay's influence is also an effect of its prominence in syllabi in gender studies courses as well as in courses in anthropology, sociology, and urban studies. Rubin's essay begins, "The time has come to think about sex." These well-known opening words point both to the essay's timeliness — its intervention in the historical moment of the sex wars — as well as to its potential reanimation across many times.

The short essays that make up this special issue speak to the significance of Rubin's legacy and her influence across several disciplines. These pieces consider a range of topics, including Rubin's history in sex radical cultures (Susan Stryker); the significance of her work as a model of social scientific method (Steven Epstein); the relation between "Thinking Sex" and black feminism in the context of the original event of the Barnard conference (Sharon Holland); the ethics of sexual variance in different historical moments (Joanne Meyerowitz); sex radicalism and crip sexuality (Robert McRuer); the significance of "Thinking Sex" as a conceptual model in different national contexts (Neville Hoad); social class and sexual subcultures (Lisa Henderson); Rubin as a theorist of heterosexuality and the significance of "Thinking Sex" to current debates on sex trafficking (Vance); and the history of Rubin's "passionate engagements" and the "affective surround" of the sex wars (Lisa Duggan). In adding to these powerful accounts of her work and her presence across the last several decades, I want to mention the points that I find most salient and energizing in "Thinking Sex" — the reasons I thought this essay made sense as the basis for a state-of-the-field conference in contemporary gender and sexuality studies. This list is not exhaustive but emphasizes what I see as the key lessons for contemporary scholars and activists, insights we have yet to absorb.

Sex-Radical Feminism

In the long run, feminism's critique of gender hierarchy must be incorporated into a radical theory of sex, and the critique of sexual oppression should enrich feminism. In the last section of "Thinking Sex" ("The Limits of Feminism"), Rubin suggests that feminism, despite its strength as a tool for analyzing gender, may not be the best tool for analyzing sexual practices and cultures. Reversing her emphasis on the "sex-gender system" in "The Traffic in Women," Rubin called for an analytic separation between sexuality and gender. Rubin's critique of feminism has been overstated and taken out of context. As Rubin points out in conversation with Butler, "Thinking Sex" "assumed a largely feminist readership" (97). The essay was not meant as a dismissal of feminism; it was a feminist argument, meant as a corrective to a reading of sexuality solely through the lens of gender and through a particularly rigid and literal understanding of gender hierarchies. Still, if we understand "Thinking Sex" as an immanent critique, we must also recognize that in its call for "an autonomous theory and politics specific to sexuality," it points the way toward the emergence of lesbian, gay, and queer studies as a field separate from feminism. In this sense, the essay marks a parting of the ways between feminism and sexuality studies but at the same time marks a connection between these fields; in particular, it binds sexuality studies to sex-radical feminism.[13] Although this genealogy of queer studies—out of lesbian S/M, butch/femme, and sex-work activism—is often forgotten, the sex-radical position staked out by feminists in the late 1970s and early 1980s was crucial to this history. The questioning of the subject of woman, the interrogation of the politics of desire, and the emphasis on complex intersections between sexism and homophobia were all key feminist topics that live on in the methods and preoccupations of sexuality studies. Insisting on these connections reminds us of the continuing need to develop a radical politics of sexuality that is attentive to gender hierarchy and to the social life of gender.

The Sexual Rabble

As a basis for sexual politics and scholarship, "Thinking Sex" offers a broad and inclusive vision of a coalitional politics of sexual outsiders. Although "Thinking Sex" considers the history of homosexuality and the politics of homophobia, Rubin's focus is on a much wider range of sexual minorities, what she calls the "sexual rabble" who occupy the "outer limits" of the graphic renderings of "the sex hierarchy" (see figs. 1 and 2). This group, exiled from "the charmed circle"

Figure 1. The sex
hierarchy: the charmed
circle vs the outer limits

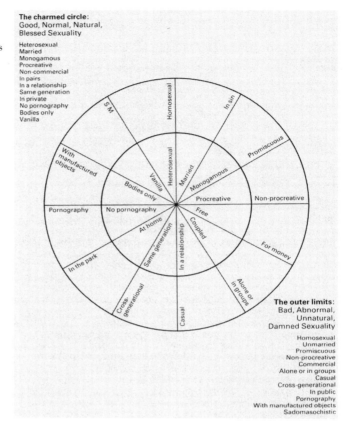

The charmed circle:
Good, Normal, Natural,
Blessed Sexuality

Heterosexual
Married
Monogamous
Procreative
Non-commercial
In pairs
In a relationship
Same generation
In private
No pornography
Bodies only
Vanilla

The outer limits:
Bad, Abnormal,
Unnatural,
Damned Sexuality

Homosexual
Unmarried
Promiscuous
Non-procreative
Commercial
Alone or in groups
Casual
Cross-generational
In public
Pornography
With manufactured objects
Sadomasochistic

of "normal" and "natural" sexuality, includes not only homosexuals but also sex
workers, sadomasochists, fetishists, and those who engage in cross-generational
intimacy or public sex. This coalitional model of sexual outsiders is, as Rubin
notes in "Blood under the Bridge," protoqueer. She mentions that this antinormative rather than identitarian basis for sexual politics is one of the things about
"Thinking Sex" that she is proudest of. At a moment when the antinormative
coalitions once imagined under the sign *queer* (and in earlier versions of lesbian
and gay studies) are increasingly vulnerable, it would be worth remembering
that Rubin's original call for a radical politics of sexuality that emphasized links
among marginal subjects and populations. While *queer* was supposed to name this
coalition of the marginal, it has not always lived up to this potential. In her 1997
essay "Punks, Bulldaggers, and Welfare Queens," Cathy J. Cohen describes how
queer has been used as another name for lesbian and gay; in the unlikely coalition
of her title, Cohen suggests how *queer* might function across categories of sexual
orientation to name the sexual marginality of poor people and people of color.[14]
Given the widespread commodification of the term, as well as its history of uptake

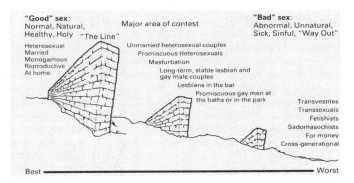

Figure 2. The sex hierarchy: the struggle over where to draw the line

in sexuality studies, it is not clear if *queer* can continue to do this work. Nonetheless, Rubin's essay stands as a crucial articulation of this possibility. Although the implementation of this model cannot be seamless—see, for instance, Hoad's discussion in this volume of the complexities of thinking Rubin's model in the South African context; Meyerowitz's account of the limits of both feminism and sexuality studies in addressing the range of historical experience, including what we might now call transgender experience; or Holland's discussion of the force of the black body as example and analogy in "Thinking Sex"—the focus on hierarchy and the real social effects of marginalization make this a promising model for a renewed politics of coalition.

Sexual Repression Is Real

"It is important to hold repressive sexual practices in focus" (277). In a critique of the reception of Foucault in "Thinking Sex," Rubin discusses a danger in overlooking the very real ways in which sexuality and marginal sexual communities are policed. She writes, "Because of his emphasis on the ways that sexuality is produced, Foucault has been vulnerable to interpretations that deny or minimize the reality of sexual repression in the more political sense" (277). Rubin strikes an exemplary balance in the essay between a Foucauldian account of the generativity of sexuality as discourse and an account of sexual stigma, legal controls on sexuality, and the granting of economic and social privilege to sexually normative subjects. Since Foucault's influence in sexuality studies has grown exponentially since the original version of this essay was published, Rubin's reminder about the ongoing repression of sexuality is relevant today. Throughout the essay, Rubin details how sexuality—on its own and in conjunction with other social factors—works as a vector of oppression; sexual minorities pay real costs for their position in society.

Rubin's attention to the specificity of sexual oppression—and its effects on all sexual minorities—is also important to recall at a time when critiques of the mainstream gay community can take attention away from the ongoing significance of "repressive practices"—particularly homophobia. In her account of the sex hierarchy, Rubin anticipates our current situation, suggesting that "long-term, stable lesbian and gay male couples" are moving up the hierarchy; they are less stigmatized and are beginning to be "accorded moral complexity" in a way that other sexual minorities are not (282). Still, she insists on the costs of sexual marginality even for these more privileged figures. She writes, "The system of sexual oppression cuts across other modes of social inequality, sorting out individuals and groups according to its own intrinsic dynamics. It is not reducible to, or understandable in terms of, class, race, ethnicity, or gender. Wealth, white skin, male gender, and ethnic privileges can mitigate the effects of sexual stratification. A rich, white male pervert will generally be less affected than a poor, black, female pervert. But even the most privileged are not immune to sexual oppression" (293). While ongoing critiques of the circulation of racial, economic, gender, and national privilege in gay and lesbian communities are crucial, Rubin's words act as an important reminder that queer studies today should continue to hold the repression of sexuality in focus. As she writes, "A radical theory of sex must identify, describe, explain, and denounce erotic injustice and sexual oppression" (275); Rubin reminds us of the urgency of denouncing sexual oppression, no matter who is the target of this oppression.

Benign Sexual Variation

Throughout her career, Rubin has insisted on the value of empirical research. In her interview with Butler, in particular, Rubin emphasizes the lack of respect for empirical work in the academy, particularly in comparison with work that is considered theoretical, or conceptually rich. She argues that "empirical research and descriptive work are often treated as some kind of low-status, even stigmatized, activity. . . . There is a disturbing trend to treat with condescension or contempt any work that bothers to wrestle with data" (91–92). Rubin offers a critique of a knee-jerk idealism, suggesting the difficulty and the rewards of thoughtful and rigorous empirical research. This emphasis on the importance of data takes on a particular urgency in the context of sexuality studies; Rubin argues that theories of sexual perversion (she focuses in particular on theories of sadomasochism) completely disregard the existence and experience of individuals and communities who engage in such practices or identify themselves with them. In his contribution to this volume, Epstein insists on the significance of

Rubin's anthropological training and emphasizes the importance of fieldwork and ethnography to her sense of sexual politics and ethics.

The ethical significance of the description of existing practices — instead of theory or prescription about what best practices might be — surfaces in "Thinking Sex" in Rubin's discussion of sexology. While a lot of scholarly writing about sexology has tended to focus on the pathologizing force of this body of work, Rubin emphasizes its descriptive richness. Approvingly referring to Havelock Ellis's *Studies in the Psychology of Sex* as "resplendent with detail," Rubin argues that "sexology and sex research provide . . . a welcome posture of calm, and a well developed ability to treat sexual variety as something that exists rather than as something to be exterminated" (284). It was this emphasis on description that allowed Rubin to keep her cool and keep thinking — as Duggan argues — during the height of the conflicts in feminism. It also allowed her, for instance in the prescient and even-handed essay "Of Catamites and Kings," to anticipate and defuse other conflicts, including the border war between butches and female-to-male transsexuals.[15] As an ethical injunction forged in the context of the sex wars and an attempted clean sweep of "antifeminist" sex practices and gender embodiments, Rubin's call for description, data collection, and nonjudgmental taxonomy is something that we should keep in mind. She has given us a model of how to think in the middle of a crisis and how to avoid solving conceptual problems by militating against other people's existence.

A Happy Foot Soldier in the Fight Against Forgetting

In "Blood under the Bridge" Rubin borrows the phrase "the fight against forgetting" from Jonathan Ned Katz to talk about the importance of remembering and crediting the scholars and activists who came before us. Rubin has been fighting this battle for a long time, and her work of archiving and tracing genealogies has been as crucial as her conceptual, empirical, and historical research. Rubin's investment in this fight is legible in "Thinking Sex" — in her careful and generous list of acknowledgments, in her discussion of the contributions of late-nineteenth- and twentieth-century sexology, and in her crediting of "social construction theory" not only to Foucault but also to Allan Bérubé, John D'Emilio, Jeffrey Weeks, and Judith Walkowitz. Since the publication of "Thinking Sex," Rubin has worked even harder to reconstruct forgotten lineages for sexuality studies, including tracing the importance of figures like Mary McIntosh, Kenneth Plummer, and John H. Gagnon and William Simon.[16] "Blood under the Bridge" continues and extends this project of reconstruction and remembering.

In the context of Rubin's lifelong habit of "paying it backward," my attempt to identify "Thinking Sex" as a point of origin for sexuality studies did not fly at the conference. In the welcome statement published in the conference program, I wrote that "Thinking Sex" might "be said to have inaugurated the contemporary field of sexuality studies," and I reiterated this claim in my opening comments before Rubin's keynote. It was not the kind of thing that Rubin could allow. She has insisted that the history of the discipline is marked by amnesia and neglect; by emphasizing this point, she demonstrates not only her commitment to the archive but also her remarkable intellectual humility. So while, out of respect, I must withdraw this earlier statement, it still seems to me that "Thinking Sex" must be understood as a point of articulation for the emergence of sexuality studies. That is to say, the conceptual elegance and forcefulness of Rubin's call for a distinct focus on sexuality crystallized an intellectual and political moment, and so made sexuality studies in the form that we recognize it possible. "Thinking Sex" reminds us to keep pushing backward, to join in the fight against forgetting, and to remember the many shoulders on which we — all of us — now stand.

This last point brings me to a final reason why it is important to revisit "Thinking Sex" now. It is clear from reading the essays and testimonials in this volume how important Gayle Rubin is as a model of intellectual, scholarly, and activist practice for so many of us in the field. With her searching curiosity, political passion, and intellectual humility and generosity, Rubin exemplifies the kind of engaged scholar many of us would like to be. Across the last several decades of her career, Rubin has moved between activist and academic contexts, writing for academic journals as well as community magazines and newsletters; in these contexts, she has put herself on the line again and again. Rubin has shown us how to honor commitments both to the accumulated wisdom and ethical practice of scholarship and to the experience of oppressed and outcast people. Thinking about Rubin's personal example challenges us to reflect on our scholarly practice — about how we honor our debts to the past and to the various communities we answer to.

In my opening comments on the night of Rubin's talk, I discussed my regret over not having been at the Barnard conference (I was eleven at the time, living in Kentucky). I was excited about being in the presence of both Gayle Rubin and Carole Vance, and, somewhat carried away by the moment, I described my feelings with a term I had recently learned from Ann Cvetkovich: F.O.M.S., or Fear of Missing Something. When Rubin took the stage, she expressed surprise at my fascination and said she wished there were a term that could express her feelings about that time — maybe F.O.H.B.T., or Fear of Having Been There. Encountering each other — with some disbelief on both sides, I think — across this divide made me realize that there is a reason why that period is called the sex *wars*. In response to my request to write about "Thinking Sex," Rubin had written an essay called "*Blood* under the Bridge." The violence of the moment, transformed into a kind of retrospective glamour in my eyes, reemerged as violence. Part of what "Rethinking Sex" taught me was to recognize the pain and losses of this period, which I had encountered to that point mainly through the mode of hero worship, archival fetishism, and lesbian, feminist, and queer nostalgia. I was already used to thinking of my own erotic and gender dispositions—particularly my identification with butch/femme—as a way to embody histories of stigma, violence, and trauma.[17] But I tended to think of the history that I had incorporated as farther in the past—in 1950s bars, for instance—whereas the sex wars were for me a period of glory and revolt, a proximate and enabling past. But like other kinds of wars, sex wars leave wounds that never completely heal.

It may be the case that the traumatic temporality of the sex wars keeps that time alive for younger generations of feminists and queers. There is no doubt, though, that many people took a lot of risks and incurred a lot of damage—to their careers, their reputations, and their sense of personal safety—in building the contemporary field of gender and sexuality studies. In honoring "Thinking Sex" and the contributions of Rubin and others during the sex wars, we thank them for the work they did in building the world we now live in. This world is a lot different from and better than any world I could have imagined when I was growing up, or even when I was reading those dirty lesbian novels in Paris or poring over records of the Barnard conference in the library. I look to Rubin's writing to imagine what this world might look like ten, twenty, thirty years from now. In this sense, the first words of "Thinking Sex" still sound as urgent to me as ever: "The time has come to think about sex." The time has come; it is coming; it will come again.

Notes

1. Gayle Rubin and Judith Butler, "Interview: Sexual Traffic," *differences* 6, nos. 2–3 (1994): 83.

2. Gayle Rubin, "Thinking Sex: Notes for a Radical Theory of the Politics of Sexuality," in *Pleasure and Danger: Exploring Female Sexuality*, ed. Carole S. Vance (Boston: Routledge and Kegan Paul, 1984), 267–319 and Rubin, "The Traffic in Women: On the 'Political Economy' of Sex," in *Toward an Anthropology of Women*, ed. Rayna Reiter (New York: Monthly Review Press, 1975), 157–210.

3. Many people contributed to planning, organizing, and realizing "Rethinking Sex." I would like to thank members of the organizing committee: Erin Cross, Demie Kurz,

Shannon Lundeen, Luz Marin, Melanie Micir, Wally Pansing, Poulomi Saha, and Bob Schoenberg. We also had a great deal of support from across the University of Pennsylvania, especially from the Office of the Provost; the School of Arts and Sciences; the Alice Paul Center for Research on Women, Gender, and Sexuality; the Women's Studies Program; the Lesbian Gay Bisexual Transgender Center; and the English Department. I would also like to thank the Mellon Foundation and Dr. William J. Zachs and the Zachs-Adam Family Fund for their generous funding of the conference. A full list of sponsors (as well as conference speakers and the program) can be found at www.sas.upenn.edu/wstudies/rethinkingsex/.

4.   Although "Rethinking Sex" was the first conference that I know of to commemorate "Thinking Sex," it is not the first conference to celebrate the anniversary of one of Rubin's essays. In 2005 the University of Michigan Institute for Research on Women and Gender organized a conference called "The Traffic in Women: Thirty Years Later."

5.   Gayle S. Rubin, "Thinking Sex: Notes for a Radical Theory of the Politics of Sexuality," in *The Lesbian and Gay Studies Reader*, ed. Henry Abelove, Michèle Aina Barale, and David M. Halperin (New York: Routledge, 1993): 3–44. By "original context," I mean both the specific publication context of *Pleasure and Danger* as well as the general context of debates in feminism in the late 1970s and early 1980s.

6.   Although the historical links between feminism and queer studies remain underexplored, several critics have attempted to map the connections. Annamarie Jagose provides a helpful account that focuses on controversies over the reception of "Thinking Sex" in her essay "Feminism's Queer Theory": "Before there was queer theory — that is, before queer theory became the most recognizable name for anti-identitarian, anti-normative critique — feminist scholarship had already initiated a radically antifoundationalist interrogation of the category of woman" ("Feminism's Queer Theory," *Feminism and Psychology* 19, no. 2: 160). See also Jagose, *Queer Theory: An Introduction* (New York: New York University Press, 1996), esp. chaps. 5, 6, 7; Lisa Duggan and Nan D. Hunter, *Sex Wars: Sexual Dissent and Political Culture* (New York: Routledge, 1995), especially the introduction, where Duggan discusses queer's "girl-history" (14); and Heather Love, "Feminist Criticism and Queer Theory," in *A History of Feminist Literary Criticism*, ed. Gill Plain and Susan Sellers (Cambridge: Cambridge University Press, 2007), 301–21.

7.   This special issue represents only a fraction of the work presented at the conference. Over three days, thirty invited speakers and several local scholars addressed such topics as neoliberalism and sexual politics; transgender lives; queer diasporas; health and the management of bodies and populations; pedagogy and the institutionalization of gender and sexuality studies; sexual practice, pleasure, and community; new imaginaries of kinship and sociality; globalization and its effects; histories of HIV; the politics of emotion; and the queer afterlife of conflicts in feminism. Rather than

try to represent everything that happened at the conference — as if such a thing were possible — this issue focuses on Rubin's scholarship, her activism, and her legacy as a way to map out an interdisciplinary, empirical, and feminist genealogy for queer studies.

8. Rubin, "Thinking Sex," 293.

9. See Rubin's account of the genesis of the essay in "Sexual Traffic": "'Thinking Sex' had its roots back in 1977–78," (71).

10. "Blood under the Bridge," 19.

11. For an account of the importance of social science in this genealogy, see Gayle Rubin, "Studying Sexual Subcultures: Excavating the Ethnography of Gay Communities in Urban North America," in *Out in Theory: The Emergence of Lesbian and Gay Anthropology*, ed. Ellen Lewin and William L. Leap (Urbana: University of Illinois Press, 2002), 17–68.

12. A list of the essay's multiple publications would include Vance, *Pleasure and Danger* (1984), Abelove et al., *The Lesbian and Gay Studies Reader* (1993), *American Feminist Thought At Century's End: A Reader*, ed. Linda S. Kauffman (Cambridge, MA: Blackwell, 1993); *Social Perspectives in Lesbian and Gay Studies: A Reader*, ed. Peter M. Nardi and Beth E. Schneider (London: Routledge, 1998); *Sexualities: Critical Concepts in Sociology*, ed. Ken Plummer (London: Routledge, 2002); and *Queer Cultures*, ed. Deborah Carlin, assoc. ed. Jennifer DiGrazia (Upper Saddle River, NJ: Pearson/Prentice Hall, 2004). The essay has also been widely excerpted and translated. In recognition of the essay's broad influence, we have decided to leave an inconsistency in the citations in this volume; different essays cite different publications that include "Thinking Sex," and these citations leave a trace of the different ways that readers encounter Rubin's work.

13. The significance of Rubin's essay as a point of origin for sexuality studies — and as a departure from feminism — has been the subject of debate among several recent scholars. Judith Butler draws attention to the imbrication of gender and sexuality in "Thinking Sex" but that the essay has been instrumentalized as an origin point for a form of "lesbian and gay studies" that excludes gender from its purview. Butler, "Against Proper Objects," *differences* 6, nos. 2–3 (Summer 1994): 1–26. For a significant counterargument, as well as an insightful account of recent debates, see Jagose's "Feminism's Queer Theory" (esp. 166–68), in which she argues persuasively that the form of lesbian and gay studies circulating in the early 1990s (and visible in *The Lesbian and Gay Studies Reader*) is more expansive and inclusive than Butler allows.

14. Cathy J. Cohen, "Punks, Bulldaggers, and Welfare Queens: The Radical Potential of Queer Politics?" *GLQ* 3 (1997): 437–65.

15. Gayle Rubin, "Of Catamites and Kings: Reflections on Butch, Gender, and Boundaries," in *The Persistent Desire: A Femme-Butch Reader*, ed. Joan Nestle (Boston: Alyson, 1992), 466–82.

16. For other accounts of Rubin's characteristic generosity and long memory, see the contributions by Stryker, Henderson, and Duggan in this volume.

17. For a reading of butch/femme in relation to histories of violence—as well as a redefinition of trauma in everyday feminist and queer contexts—see Ann Cvetkovich, *An Archive of Feelings: Trauma, Sexuality, and Lesbian Public Culture* (Durham: Duke University Press, 2003).

BLOOD UNDER THE BRIDGE: REFLECTIONS ON "THINKING SEX"

Gayle Rubin

To the incomparable Eve Sedgwick, whose absence at the conference,
and in our lives, has been so acutely felt and sadly noted.

The Fight against Forgetting

$\mathcal{T}$wenty-five years after its publication, I have been asked to reflect on my essay "Thinking Sex." A quarter of a century is a long time. One indicator of time's passage is the technology of textual production. I bought my first computer a year after "Thinking Sex" went to the publisher. "Thinking Sex" was written the old-fashioned way: on a typewriter. It was edited when "cut and paste" still meant slicing up paper with real scissors and reassembling the pieces with actual glue. Reading back through the reams of material generated by the controversies of the early feminist sex wars, I was continually reminded that almost all of the innumerable flyers, leaflets, articles, broadsides, and letters to the editor were done without computers. In the early 1980s there was an Internet, but it was still mostly the preserve of military personnel, scientists, and computer programmers. Most communication was still by way of landline telephones and snail mail.

Another indicator of change is the status of the essay itself. Although the paper resulted from the intersection of several different intellectual agendas and political concerns, its initial reception was filtered through the acrimonious controversies of the feminist sex wars. These conflicts have at times obscured the essay's intellectual concerns and scholarly contributions. As a result, many of the

GLQ 17:1
DOI 10.1215/10642684-2010-015
© 2010 by Duke University Press

early responses to "Thinking Sex" fluctuated between patronizing condescension and hostile indignation.[1] As these conflicts within feminism have cooled, the essay's academic aspects have become more visible and salient. Its reception has shifted from the scholarly to the scandalous and back again.

"Thinking Sex" was first published in Carole Vance's 1984 book *Pleasure and Danger*, the anthology of papers from the 1982 Barnard Sex Conference, where I had given a version of "Thinking Sex" as a workshop.[2] The Barnard conference has become extremely famous, in large part because it was the occasion of one of the most volcanic battles in the feminist sex wars. What actually happened at Barnard has been widely misunderstood. In her opening remarks at the "Rethinking Sex" conference, Heather Love commented that she, who was not in attendance at Barnard, had a fear of having missed something. I, on the other hand, nurse the horror of having been there. The attack on the Barnard conference was a particularly repellent episode in what was unfortunately a repetitive pattern of conduct. Some antipornography advocates preferred to resort to ad feminem attacks and character assassination rather than to debate substantive issues. They attempted to excommunicate from the feminist movement anyone who disagreed with them, and they aggressively sabotaged events that did not adhere to the antiporn party line. Their conduct left a bitter legacy for feminism. Like many others involved in the sex wars, I was thoroughly traumatized by the breakdown of feminist civility and the venomous treatment to which dissenters from the antiporn orthodoxy were routinely subjected.[3]

I had been working on the ideas presented at my Barnard workshop for several years prior to the conference. I had lectured on these subjects at the University of California, Berkeley; the University of California, Los Angeles; the University of California, Santa Cruz; and the New York Institute for the Humanities. In all of these venues, audience responses were unremarkable, and the discussions that ensued were typical of academic events: spirited and engaged, at times argumentative, yet always polite.

Once I had been identified as a public enemy by early feminist antipornography activists, however, my appearances became occasions for protests against my speaking, not just on pornography but on any topic at all. The protest against my participation at the Barnard conference generated the most press of any of these attempts at silencing and intimidation, but it was neither the first such occurrence nor the last. The opposition began a few years before the Barnard conference and continued for more than a decade after. There were some early and, in comparison with later events, relatively mild episodes in the Bay Area in the late 1970s. For example, around 1979, I was scheduled to make a presentation about

Michel Foucault on a panel for an informal Marxist–feminist discussion group in Berkeley. Several antiporn members of the group felt I should not be allowed to speak. After a campaign to have me removed from the panel failed, those opposing my participation boycotted the discussion. In another incident, a local group of gay and lesbian leftists imploded over having invited me to participate on a panel discussion of political differences and similarities between lesbians and gay men. These kinds of situations proliferated and became increasingly vitriolic. Nor was I the only target. The list of ostensibly unacceptable feminists expanded over time, and eventually included, among many others, Dorothy Allison, Pat Califia, Lisa Duggan, Dierdre English, Amber Hollibaugh, Nan Hunter, Joan Nestle, Cindy Patton, Carole Vance, and Ellen Willis.

Revisiting those days is at best bittersweet. Nonetheless, this is an occasion to situate my essay in the context in which it was produced and to remember the historical conditions that shaped it. Jonathan Ned Katz, one of the founders of the modern field of gay, lesbian, bisexual, and transgender history, ends his e-mails with the slogan "Fight Against Forgetting."[4] While these memories can be painful, I am happy to be a foot soldier in the fight against forgetting.

Texts are produced in particular historical, social, and cultural circumstances, and are part of discursive conglomerates that shift over time. As texts are read in new contexts, the conversations and issues that formed them are often forgotten or unknown. Various parts of "Thinking Sex" were conceived throughout the late 1970s and early 1980s, and were shaped by three main developments. The first was the paradigm shifts then taking place in the study of sexuality. The paper attempted to synthesize an analytic framework that had emerged in gay history, feminist history, and the history of sexuality in the late 1970s. These theoretical interests informed an ethnographic research project on urban gay men, gay neighborhood formation, and the political economies of sexual location. The second development consisted of the feminist sex wars, in which I was deeply involved, and of which the events of the Barnard conference were a part. The third was the lurking menace of the socially conservative Right, which was gaining increased influence over policy, public discourse, state bureaucracies, and the legal regulation of sexuality in the United States.

Shifting Paradigms of Sex

With all due respect to the organizers of the "Rethinking Sex" conference, I do not believe that my essay "inaugurated the field of contemporary sexuality studies."[5] My own work was a product of a broader set of intellectual transformations in the study of gender and sexuality that were well under way in the 1970s. My work resulted from many of the same developments that influenced writers and scholars such as Allan Bérubé, George Chauncey, Madeline Davis, John D'Emilio, Martin Duberman, Jeffrey Escoffier, Estelle Freedman, Eric Garber, Jonathan Ned Katz, Liz Kennedy, Joan Nestle, Esther Newton, Jim Steakley, Martha Vicinus, and Jeffrey Weeks, just to name a handful of people working on what would become gay and lesbian studies. This burst of scholarly activity was produced largely by social movements — feminism and gay liberation — taking place both inside and outside the academy. The early 1970s were the heady days of the first Berkshire Conference on the History of Women, the conferences of the Gay Academic Union, and the founding of journals such as *Feminist Studies* and *Signs*. By the mid-1970s, the cross-pollination of concepts and data from anthropology, sociology, and history had resulted in a new theoretical formation. By 1977 Weeks drew from his training in both sociology and history to articulate a framework for gay history that would come to be labeled "the social construction of sex."[6]

Social construction was little more than the application of ordinary social science tools to sexuality and gender. What seemed so radical was in many respects a conventional set of approaches to an unconventional and highly stigmatized set of subject areas. As Vance has often observed in conversation, what is most odd is not that social constructionist theories of sexuality were developed, but how long it took. By showing that same-sex eroticisms and cross-gender behavior were historically and culturally specific, social construction cleared away obsolete assumptions, generated new research programs, and legitimized new topics. Despite initial controversy and some persistent arguments, the major assumptions of social construction now form the familiar ground on which most queer scholarship takes place. It is easy to forget what the field was like before that paradigm shift, when, among other things, much of gay history was the search for glorious ancestors, and male homosexuality and lesbianism were understood to be stable and largely unchanging phenomena. The accumulation of data within the old paradigm was incredibly valuable, however, and provided the foundation for social construction to emerge. "Thinking Sex" was part of the intellectual ferment reshaping the study of sexuality in the late 1970s.[7] Generated by the excitement of my initial encounters with the social constructionist framework, the essay was an attempt to work out some of its implications, especially with respect to my own ethnographic research on urban sexual populations and locations.

I have previously complained in print about the amnesia that obscures the early strata of homophile and gay liberation scholarship.[8] I do want to note, at least in passing, that the neglect of this body of work stemmed in part from the paucity of institutional support for it. Some who did this work were not affiliated with any university.[9] Those affiliated with universities were, to put it mildly, not well rewarded. Many were graduate students whose advisers told them bluntly that they were committing academic suicide, and these warnings were not unrealistic. Many others who did this early work of queer scholarship endured systematic unemployment or underemployment in the academy. These kinds of subjects, and the scholars who studied them, were generally treated as disreputable within their disciplines, and such research was not deemed appropriate for publication in the prestigious academic journals. Some of the most important work in gay history, such as D'Emilio's study of the homophile movement, Steakley's revelations of the Nazi persecution of homosexuals, and Bérubé's early research on gay San Francisco, was published not in academic journals but in programs for gay pride celebrations; in the *Body Politic*, a Canadian gay liberation newspaper; and in *Gay Community News*, the gay liberation newspaper from Boston.[10] One of Bérubé's first essays on gay men and lesbians in World War II was published in *Mother Jones*.[11] These were great periodicals, but they did not count toward tenure. There was a sea change in the 1990s, when doing various kinds of queer and sexuality scholarship (especially for junior scholars in some fields) was no longer a career killer. This change occurred earlier in the humanities and more slowly in the social sciences, where LGBTQ studies are still struggling to establish a durable institutional presence.

While academia did not nurture the early gay and sexuality scholarship, there was nevertheless a dense intellectual and social network that did. When we did not have departments, we had study groups where community-based and university-affiliated researchers could share their discoveries. Two such informal groups were extremely important to me. One was an intensely educational and stimulating "feminism and the history of sex" study group with participants such as Nancy Chodorow, Ellen DuBois, Barbara Epstein, Michelle Rosaldo, Mary Ryan, Judith Stacey, Kaye Trimberger, and Martha Vicinus. The second was the San Francisco Lesbian and Gay History Project, founded around 1978–79 by Bérubé, Escoffier, and Garber. The membership was fluid, but Freedman, Hollibaugh, and I were active long-term participants, and D'Emilio and Bert Hansen were frequent visitors.[12]

Bérubé's research provided an anchor. He discovered archival data on women who passed as men in early San Francisco.[13] He found documentation on the surveillance of gay bars in California conducted by the Alcoholic Beverage Commission, as well as the court cases that established the legal rights for homosexuals to drink in public.[14] I remember the first time he spoke of a shoebox of letters written by gay men during World War II; these letters started the project that resulted in his pathbreaking book *Coming Out Under Fire*.[15] I first heard Garber speak of his work on African American gay men and lesbians in Harlem in the early twentieth century at a meeting of the History Project.[16]

I cannot say enough about the intellectual excitement and impact of the History Project. Nevertheless, it was not insulated from the early phases of the sex wars. In 1979, after Bérubé presented his slide show on passing women, several additional lesbians joined the group. Some of these individuals entered with ideological commitments that led them to try to expel me, both because of my research, which was on the gay male leather and S/M population, and because of my involvement in the then nascent lesbian S/M community. In the end, I was able to stay, and those who were most opposed to my presence left the History Project. I maintained my membership, but it was, in Erving Goffman's terms, "spoiled."[17] I was sufficiently radioactive that for many years after I was not asked to share my research at any of our public presentations.

Speaking Bitterness: The Feminist Sex Wars

The name "Barnard Sex Conference" is actually shorthand for "The Scholar and the Feminist IX: Towards a Politics of Sexuality," the ninth iteration of "The Scholar and the Feminist" conference held annually at Barnard College since 1974. The Barnard Sex Conference's concept paper was titled "Towards a Politics of Sexuality." The planning committee for the conference included Barnard faculty, graduate students from Columbia University, and New York feminist intellectuals and activists, who responded to an open letter calling for participation. The invitation letter, written by Vance, the conference's academic coordinator, was sent to Barnard College faculty, all members of previous Scholar and Feminist planning committees, and academics and activists who worked on sexuality.[18] The planning committee met every two weeks for eight months, functioning as a study group on sexuality. Minutes of the meetings of the planning committee and comments by each member of the planning group were included in a seventy-two-page booklet, *Diary of a Conference* (see GLQ Archive, this issue).

Like the conference itself, the *Diary* was innovative, ambitious, and fresh. It was to be distributed to attendees, and since it was intended to serve as the conference program, it included the schedule of events and the list of speakers. However, it was much more than a program. It was designed to be an archival document, not only of the planning process but also of the day itself. There were even blank pages so attendees could take notes. Each workshop was given a page containing a description of the workshop, a list of the presenters, and often a suggested bibliography. The workshop pages featured faux postcards that were used to list the presenters' credentials. The speakers were asked to send in some kind of graphic to be used as the image on the front of the postcard. The image could reference the workshop topic, but, in the spirit of a diary, it could also be something personal or even merely something each speaker found meaningful, interesting, visually compelling, or amusing.

Plenary speakers for the opening and closing sessions included DuBois, Alice Echols, Linda Gordon, Hollibaugh, Hortense Spillers, and the poets hattie gossett, Cherrie Moraga, and Sharon Olds. The eighteen afternoon workshops featured diverse topics and presenters. Workshop leaders included Allison, Meryl Altman, Dale Bernstein, Mary Calderone, Arlene Carmen, Muriel Dimen, Oliva Espin, Elsa First, Roberta Galler, Faye Ginsburg, Bette Gordon, Diane Harriford, Susan Hill, Shirley Kaplan, Barbara Kruger, Maire Kurrik, Kate Millett, Carole Munter, Nestle, Newton, Mirtha Quintanales, Pat Robinson, Kaja Silverman, Sharon Thompson, Shirley Walton, and Paula Webster. Topics addressed in the workshops included Jacques Lacan, abortion rights, gay and lesbian rights, pornography, teen romance, popular sex advice literature, creativity and theater, artistic vision, butch/femme roles in both gay and straight relationships, class, race, psychotherapy, politically correct and incorrect sex, body image, disability, the sexuality of infancy and childhood, prostitution, and psychoanalysis. My workshop was "Concepts for a Radical Politics of Sex" (figs. 1 and 2).

The conference's reputation, however, bears almost no relationship to the substance of the event. A small number of antipornography activists from New York were outraged by the conference, or what they imagined it to be. As recounted in Vance's detailed epilogue to *Pleasure and Danger*, these antagonists staged a noisy protest outside the conference, distributed leaflets denouncing it as antifeminist, and thoroughly spooked the Barnard administration.[19] As Vance noted, the leaflet was "a masterpiece of misinformation" that served "as a template for subsequent reaction to the conference."[20] She observed, "The leaflet, along with the rumors and distorted newspaper reporting it inspired, depicted a phantom conference, restricted to but a few issues which matched the anti-pornographers' tunnel vision concerns about sexuality. . . . That such diversity of thought and experience should be reduced to pornography, S/M, and butch/femme — the anti-pornographers' counterpart to the New Right's unholy trinity of sex, drugs, and rock 'n' roll — is an example of the effective use of symbols to instigate a sex panic."[21]

Ironically, the conference's major theme, reflected in workshops, the concept paper, and the resulting anthology, was that sexuality is for women both a

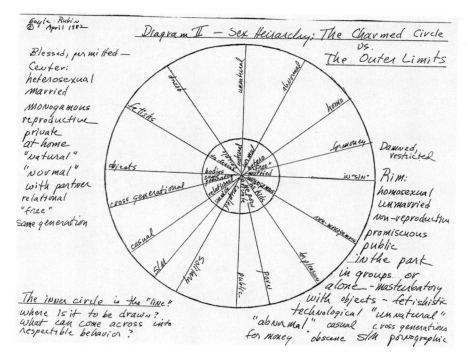

Figure 1. Sex Heirarchy: The Struggle over Where to Draw the Line. Distributed as handout at Rubin's workshop at the Barnard Conference, 1982. Courtesy of Gayle Rubin

means of pleasure and a source of danger. To be sure, there was no deference at Barnard to the specific claims of antipornography feminism. There was a workshop on pornography. As noted in the description recorded in the *Diary*, "This workshop will situate pornography within the context of a number of other discourses which construct sexual difference and the female subject in similar ways, most notably advertising and dominant cinema. We will also argue that pornography cannot be isolated from a larger critique of the existing symbolic order, or from such seemingly diverse structures as the family or the church."[22] Such nuance was anathema to the leadership of the antiporn movement, whose ideology situates pornography as the major engine of female subordination and the single most pernicious institution of male supremacy.

One of the architects of the leaflet and protest against the Barnard conference was Dorchen Leidholdt from New York's Women Against Pornography (WAP). Her response is captured by Susan Brownmiller: "'Then,' Dorchen recalls with a shudder, 'came the Barnard conference.'"[23] Brownmiller's description typifies the antiporn account of the conference:: "The ninth annual 'The Scholar and the Feminist' conference at Barnard College on Saturday, April 24, 1982, pro-

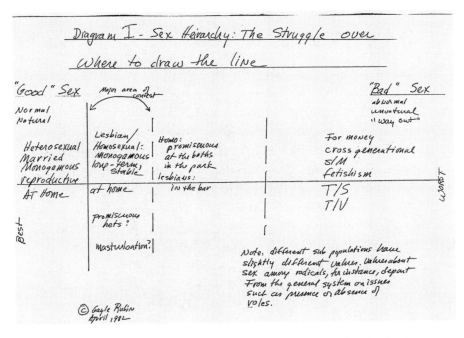

Figure 2. Sex Heirarchy: The Charmed Circle vs. the Outer Limits. Distributed as handout at Rubin's workshop at the Barnard Conference, 1982. Courtesy of Gayle Rubin

claimed 'Towards a Politics of Sexuality' as its groundbreaking theme. Months of planning by Carole Vance, a Columbia anthropologist, and a team of advisers of her choosing had gone into the day's proceedings, intended to produce a joyful exploration of 'politically incorrect' sexual behavior, to counter the 'fascist' and 'moralistic' tendencies of WAP. The bizarre result was a somewhat nervous, somewhat giddy, occasionally tearful exposition of the pleasures of s/m. . . . Not every speaker at Barnard that day addressed s/m or butch-femme roles. A few invitees read academic papers" (314–15).

In actuality, none of the eighteen workshops specifically focused on S/M and only one on butch/femme. Although these topics certainly did come up during various discussions—not surprising after attendees had been handed leaflets specifically denouncing them—they were hardly the dominant focus. With three workshops, psychotherapy and psychoanalysis got far more attention than S/M, and abortion rights were more heavily emphasized than butch/femme. The common denominator of the workshops was, in fact, people reading academic papers. The account of the conference promulgated by antipornography crusaders had a few grains of reality swirling in a noxious brew of hyperbole and misinformation. Vance did not assemble a group of "advisers of her choosing." She had issued an open call to which interested parties had responded. All of this was documented in the *Diary*. But no one saw the *Diary* on the day of the conference, because the *Diary* had been confiscated by the panicked Barnard administration.[24]

Instead, the some eight hundred attendees arriving at the Barnard College gates were confronted by a small group of protesters who wore T-shirts emblazoned with "For a Feminist Sexuality" on the front and "Against S/M" on the back.[25] They were handing out leaflets that accused the conference organizers of endorsing "the backlash against radical feminism" and of having "thrown their support to the very sexual institutions and values that oppress all women."[26] The leaflet singled out several participants for special condemnation because of their allegedly "un-feminist" sexual behaviors or political opinions. These included Allison and two unnamed proponents of "butch femme roles," presumably Nestle, Hollibaugh, or Moraga. The leaflet complained about the participation of Brett Harvey because of her involvement with No More Nice Girls, a reproductive rights group characterized as "a group of women writers who publish in the *Village Voice* and who contend that pornography is liberating."[27] The leaflet's rationale for the objection to No More Nice Girls was that one of its founders was Willis, who did write for the *Voice* and who was one of the first feminists publicly to take issue with the antipornography analysis.[28] My participation was attacked because of my association with Samois, a lesbian S/M group from San Francisco. Califia, also a member of Samois, was denounced in the leaflet despite having no role at all in the conference (Califia did attend). The leaflet claimed I was there "representing" Samois, which I was not. Leidholdt would later claim in *off our backs* that "we weren't protesting the exclusion of WAP but of the whole sexual violence part of the movement. It's particularly dangerous when you're including someone like Gayle Rubin."[29]

There were actually two contradictory versions of the WAP complaint: the first was that the Barnard conference was a blatant celebration of S/M. The second was that the perverted agenda was all the more insidious because it was a hidden one. Leidholdt told a reporter from *off our backs* that "the bias was so hidden at the Barnard conference," and she complained that "nowhere in the program were workshop leaders' affiliations with Samois or LSM (New York's Lesbian Sex Mafia) given."[30] This complaint bears some scrutiny. Of the almost forty speakers and workshop leaders, only two were members of either organization. But in any case, of what relevance were such memberships? Should all participants in academic events list all of their recreational, social, and political associations? I was a graduate student at the University of Michigan speaking at an academic conference, so I listed my academic affiliation, as was appropriate. Evidently, I should have had the decency to wear a black leather triangle or perhaps a scarlet letter.

Whether people supported or opposed the conference's aims, the exaggerated and inaccurate characterizations promulgated by the leaflet and subsequent press coverage remain to this day the conference's dominant legend. While there were arguments over the conference's legitimacy, these rarely challenged the accuracy of the phantom conference narratives. For example, a decade after Barnard, Leidholdt still proclaimed that "along with waging a no holds barred attack on radical feminists and our politics, conference speakers, organizers, and workshop leaders promoted and defended the sexuality of dominance and submission. An at times thinly disguised, at times overt defense of sadomasochism was an underlying theme."[31] Even Jane Gerhard's largely sympathetic account of the conference describes it as composed of "sessions on sexual practice, S/M, butch/femme roles, pornography, children's sexuality, and sexual therapies."[32] While they differ in their evaluations, Leidholdt's and Gerhard's descriptions substantially agree on the conference's ostensible emphasis and fail to mention the majority of topics discussed.

There are many reasons for the persistence of the conference's image as a venue to celebrate kinky sex. But one was surely the confiscation of the *Diary*. As Vance noted, "The unavailability of the *Diary* to registrants on that day made the conference's purpose more vulnerable to distortion. Leaflets were handed out before any papers or presentations were made, and registrants' perceptions of what occurred were colored by the leaflet's inflammatory and sensational charges."[33] By the time the *Diary* was finally republished and provided to participants several weeks later, the outlandish claims and febrile descriptions of the antiporn contingent's narrative had taken root.

As Vance recounts, in the week preceding the conference, "antipornography feminists made telephone calls to Barnard College officials and trustees, as well as prominent local feminists, complaining that the conference was promoting anti-feminist views and had been taken over by 'sexual perverts.' Lunatic as these claims were, they had a galvanizing effect on the representatives of a sexually conservative women's college. . . . Within days, Ellen V. Futter, President of Barnard, interrogated the staff of the women's center, scrutinized the program, and—concerned about the possible reactions of funders to sexual topics and images—confiscated all copies of the conference booklet."[34]

Jane Gould, the director of the Barnard Women's Center, recounts being summoned to the president's office just prior to the conference. Gould later learned that "the president's office had been inundated with calls from Women Against Pornography attacking the conference, calling it pornography, and announcing their intention to picket on the day of the conference. One of the calls informed the president that the conference planning had been dominated by a California lesbian group called Samois, which supported sadomasochism."[35] I should note that no one from Samois was part of the planning group: no one seems to have considered the logistical implausibility of a San Francisco group participating in meetings in New York every two weeks for eight months. But these myths persevere. Gerhard even lists me as a conference planner, which I was not. That she does so demonstrates the triumph of the narrative over the facts.[36]

When Gould entered the president's office, she found "Futter, the director of public relations, and the college lawyer . . . all with copies of the *Diary*. President Futter's expression said it all. She plunged right in, saying that she regarded the publication as a piece of pornography and that she was not going to tolerate its distribution to the conference participants and to the public. . . . She insisted that it must be destroyed, shredded immediately."[37] Vance notes that while the Barnard administration confiscated all fifteen hundred copies two days before the conference, she and members of the planning committee were not informed of the confiscation until less than twenty-four hours before the conference.[38] Barnard administrators directed Vance to say that the *Diary* was "delayed at the printers." She ignored this demand and informed participants that the president of Barnard College had confiscated and censored the *Diary*. After considerable pressure and legal threats, Barnard College agreed to pay to reprint the *Diary*, removing two lines of type with the names of Barnard College and the conference funder, the Helena B. Rubinstein Foundation, and to distribute the reprinted document to conference participants.[39]

The *Diary* was finally reprinted and mailed out to attendees in June. In August Andrea Dworkin sent out copies of the *Diary* with a cover letter stating:

> This is a copy of the so-called Diary put together by the planners of the recent conference on sexuality at Barnard College. . . . *Please read this Diary from beginning to end. Please do not skip any parts of it.* Please look at the pictures. Please read it right away: however busy you are please do not put off reading this. This Diary shows how the S&M and pro-pornography activists . . . are being intellectually and politically justified and supported. It shows too the conceptual framework for distorting and significantly undermining radical feminist theory, activism, and efficacy. There is no feminist standard, I believe, by which this material and these arguments taken as a whole are not perniciously anti-woman and anti-feminist. It is doubtful, in my view, that the feminist movement can maintain its political integrity and moral authority with this kind of attack on its fundamental and essential premises from within.[40]

The news coverage of the conference further enshrined the vision of the phantom conference. The periodical *off our backs* was the closest thing to a newspaper of record of the feminist movement. It was therefore extremely distressing that its coverage so closely mirrored the WAP accounts. There was an avalanche of letters to the editor from those of us with a different perspective: from me, Frances Doughty, Barbara Grier, Hollibaugh, Nestle, Newton, Vance, Walton, and Willis. There is a letter from Samois. There is even a letter from Cleveland Women Against Violence Against Women in which the organization distanced itself from the protest leaflet.[41] But while the articles from *off our backs* are readily available online, the letters are not. A digitized version of *off our backs* is available through Proquest, but the letters have not been included in the digital archives. The incomplete digitization of *off our backs* ensures that the one-sided and distorted picture of the events remains canonical. To get a sense of the full range of the discussion in *off our backs*, it is necessary to consult crumbling newsprint. As yet, there has been no comprehensive history of the feminist sex wars, and one challenge is that so many of the primary documents are not easily accessible.[42]

The West Coast Sex Wars:
Women Against Violence in Pornography and Media and Samois

Tracking the actual events of the Barnard conference demonstrates the absurdity of the claims that the conference was characterized by a single-minded devotion to S/M, butch/femme, and an uncritical promotion of pornography. The ease with which such distortions were treated as credible and their remarkable persistence call for both analytic attention and historical contextualization. Why were some feminists protesting a feminist conference, and why were they wearing T-shirts emblazoned with the slogan "Against S/M"? Why was Samois, then a small and obscure San Francisco lesbian S/M group, supposed to be involved in, much less responsible for, a conference three thousand miles away? Part of the explanation lies in events that took place prior to the Barnard Sex Conference and far from New York. Many people, particularly those from the East Coast, think that the Barnard conference initiated the feminist sex wars. But there were earlier episodes, and one important battle front had already opened in the San Francisco Bay Area in 1978. The controversies that engulfed the Barnard conference are more intelligible with some knowledge of this prehistory.

The West Coast battles took place between Women Against Violence in Pornography and Media (WAVPM), the first feminist antipornography organization, and Samois, the first lesbian S/M organization, both active in the San Francisco Bay Area in the late 1970s. Their skirmishes generated many of the patterns and themes that characterized the early phases of the sex wars. "Pornography," a genre of media, and "sadomasochism," a sexual preference and practice, are different kinds of things. Yet the terms were construed as opposites and used to articulate a range of political differences. The conflict between WAVPM and Samois helped establish "pornography" and "sadomasochism" as critical positions, ideological frameworks, and antithetical worldviews that were then deployed throughout the sex wars.

WAVPM was founded in the San Francisco Bay Area in 1976 and held the first national feminist conference on pornography in 1978.[43] New York's WAP was established in 1979, shortly after the WAVPM conference. It is not widely understood how much the feminist antipornography movement was also, from its inception, a war against S/M imagery and practice. Diana Russell, one of the founders of WAVPM, articulated these fusions (and confusions) in a 1977 article in the feminist journal *Chrysalis*. Russell rarely gets the credit she clearly deserves for her contributions to the antiporn movement, which is often attributed instead to Catharine MacKinnon and Dworkin.[44] Yet Russell provided the early movement with most of its intellectual leadership, analytic language, and ideological coherence.

In the *Chrysalis* article, she asserts that pornography is "degrading" to women by nature, that it is inherently misogynist, and that it is vicious, antiwoman propaganda. Moreover, she used S/M porn to represent all that she found repugnant in pornography: "Before disagreeing with this statement, go see some of it! You might try a batch of movies regularly shown at the San Francisco Kearny Cinema (or its equivalent in other cities). The titles are self-explanatory: 'Lesson in Pain,' 'Corporal Punishment,' 'Slave Girl,' 'Golden Pain,' 'Club Brute Force,' and 'Water Power.'" [45] At the time of this writing, San Francisco had probably twenty or so porn film theaters, of which only two, the Kearny and the North Beach, showed films with bondage or S/M themes. Yet these two theaters are repeatedly singled out in San Francisco antiporn literature. Similarly, there were probably hundreds or thousands of porn movies shown annually, but the titles of the small number of kinky films are used as if these represented pornographic films as a whole. S/M materials in Russell's essay were used to persuade readers of the truth of the indictment against pornography, and their mere existence was taken both as representative of all porn and to confirm that porn is intrinsically foul.

Russell continues:

> Pornography is not made to educate but to sell, and for the most part, what
> sells in a sexist society is a bunch of lies about sex and women. Women are

portrayed as enjoying being raped, spanked, or beaten, tied up, mutilated, and enslaved, or they accept it as their lot as women to be victims in such experiences. In the less sadistic films, women are portrayed as turned on and sexually satisfied by doing anything and everything that men want or order them to do. . . . Some pornography I saw recently doesn't even include sex: Women are kidnapped, beaten, tied up, then hung upside down like pieces of meat. And that's the end of the movie. Domination and torture are what it is about.[46]

Several features of what would become recognizable as antipornography rhetoric are apparent in this passage. One common tactic is lists that mix some things that are clearly horrible, such as rape, with some other things that might be pleasurable, such as being spanked. Disgust mobilized by the front-loaded images of horror are then directed at things that might ordinarily be more difficult to get people upset about, for example, a woman finding pleasure in heterosexual intercourse.[47]

Describing a different film, Russell exclaims:

In another movie I saw, boiling candle wax was dripped onto a bound woman's breasts. Had she consented beforehand? Even if she had, this is a violent act—one which was followed by her acting the willing and adoring lover of her torturer. So, even where models have consented to participate, they don't necessarily know what they're in for, and often they are in no position to maintain control.[48]

Russell assumes that no one could enjoy hot candle-wax dripping on bound breasts; that such experiences could not be part of legitimate lovemaking; and that the act is intrinsically violent. One implication is that any woman who might actually enjoy such a practice must have something wrong with her. Russell's analysis betrays a limited concept of human sexual variation and an assumption that S/M is intrinsically degrading and repulsive. Such premises allow her to make the more explicit claim that the models could have agreed to participate in such films only because they were uninformed, duped, or coerced. In other words, the image's content, and Russell's own revulsion, substitute for evidence that anyone was actually tricked, abused, or coerced in the making of the film. As I have pointed out elsewhere, there is confusion between the image's content and the conditions of its production; if such criteria were consistently applied, we would have to assume that all of the actors blown up, murdered, shot, burned, drowned, or otherwise killed in movies were actual fatalities.[49]

Russell's arguments, assumptions, language, and rhetorical tactics were incorporated into the early WAVPM literature. For example, each issue of WAVPM's newsletter, *Newspage*, contained a statement, "Who Are We?" In the September 1977 issue, it reads:

> Women Against Violence in Pornography and Media is a core group of approximately 35 Bay Area women who are meeting because we share a common concern about the alarming increase of violent crimes against women. Media, including pornography, is our primary focus. We believe there is a relationship between what we see and hear in the media, and how we think and consequently act. *We want to put an end to all portrayals of women being bound, raped, tortured, mutilated, abused, or degraded in any way for sexual or erotic stimulation.*[50]

This statement mirrors the language and analysis of Russell's essay. Like Russell, WAVPM was blaming pornography, and especially S/M imagery, for violence against women. Both Russell and WAVPM precluded the possibility of any legitimate S/M erotica, whose elimination was plainly stated as an explicit political goal of the organization. The mechanics of its abolition were left unspecified.

In a later *Newspage*, WAVPM published a list of frequently asked questions and their answers. Although the group's stated purpose was "to educate women and men about the hatred of women expressed in pornography and other media-violence to women," the entire document focuses on pornography. In WAVPM literature, other forms of "media-violence" quickly became a subsidiary theme and an occasional afterthought, unless their objectionable aspects could be blamed on pornography.

> Q: What kinds of images are you talking about when you say you are opposed to "violence in pornography and media"?
>
> A: We are talking about books and magazines which depict women being bound, beaten, and abused. We are protesting the message of these images — that beating and raping women, urinating and defecating on women, is erotic and pleasurable for men; and that women desire this kind of treatment, or at least expect it. We are talking about record-album photos, fashion and men's magazine lay-outs, department-store window displays and billboards, in which women are shown bound, gagged, beaten, whipped, and chained.
>
> Q: But not all pornography is violent. So you object to pornography in which there is no violence.

A: *Yes.* Not all pornography is violent, but even the most banal pornography objectifies women's bodies.[51]

While WAVPM's critique was ostensibly directed against pornography, assumptions about sadomasochism in word, deed, and representation were integral to its analysis. WAVPM swept all S/M erotica up into its category of images that should not exist, and its program demanded the elimination of all S/M imagery or at least its banishment from public visibility. When WAVPM began to stage public protests in the spring of 1977, its focus was on S/M as much as porn, or rather on this confused composite target made up of porn, S/M, violence against women, and female subordination.

It was not surprising that WAVPM's rhetoric, program, and targets of protest alarmed local S/M activists, particularly the feminist ones. Samois formed in 1978. S/M activism had been inaugurated in 1971 with the formation of the Eulenspiegel Society in New York, which was followed by San Francisco's Society of Janus in 1974. Eulenspiegel and Janus were initially mixed-gender and mixed-orientation groups, but by the late 1970s they were predominantly heterosexual. Ferment over S/M had begun to appear in the lesbian feminist press in the mid-1970s. There were attempts to form lesbian S/M organizations at least as early as 1975, but Samois was the first ongoing lesbian S/M organization. The group articulated an ideological defense of S/M as a legitimate eroticism, even for feminists. Samois never claimed that S/M was particularly feminist, only that there was no intrinsic contradiction between feminist politics and S/M practice. Nor did Samois claim that S/M was an inherently liberatory practice, only that it was not inherently oppressive.[52]

Since Samois was a lesbian group, many of whose members, including me, had already been active in the women's movement, it was attuned to developments in feminism in a way that the more heterosexually oriented Eulenspiegel and Janus were not. Several of us quickly perceived that WAVPM's program was as much anti-S/M as antipornography. We naively assumed that the members of WAVPM were uneducated about S/M and would welcome dialogue and discussion. As it turned out, WAVPM had no interest in discussing issues with any feminist who disagreed with them, much less with people who engaged without apparent guilt in forms of sexuality they felt exemplified the worst manifestations of patriarchy.[53]

Shortly after Samois was formed, we started sending letters to WAVPM asking to meet to discuss their position on S/M. These requests were consistently rebuffed. However, the tensions between the two groups escalated in April 1980, when flyers suddenly appeared around the Bay Area announcing a WAVPM fund-raiser: a forum on sadomasochism in the lesbian community. Since WAVPM had refused efforts to discuss their position on S/M, Samois objected to the forum and responded with a leaflet. One of WAVPM's favorite slogans was that "pornography was a lie about women." The Samois leaflet was titled "This Forum Is a Lie about S/M." The leaflet expressed three objections to the forum:

> 1. WAVPM, without taking an "official" position on S/M has nonetheless promoted a false image of S/M sexuality and helped to create a climate that is oppressive and dangerous to S/M-identified people. WAVPM's most obvious error is the equation of consensual S/M with violence. . . .
> 2. Panelists have made . . . public statements that equate S/M with self destruction, male supremacy, fascism, misogyny, or mental illness. The anti-S/M arguments you will hear at this forum are as biased and big-oted as homophobic attacks on lesbians and gay men or right-wing attacks on independent feminist women. These arguments are based on biological determinism, conventional morality, and psychiatric notions of sexual per-version. We protest the promulgation of negative stereotypes of S/M.
> 3. Consensual S/M is not anti-feminist or anti-woman. S/M people are a stigmatized sexual minority, and as such are subjected to street harassment, job and housing discrimination, violence, and other forms of persecution.

All of the speakers at the forum denounced S/M. Eventually, many of their talks became articles in the anthology *Against Sadomasochism: A Radical Feminist Analysis*.[54] After the forum, WAVPM evidently had an internal debate on whether to take an official position on S/M. When the organization declined, several disgruntled members decided to edit the anti-S/M anthology.

One of the biggest successes of the feminist antipornography movement has been to intensify a shift in the locus of legal and social concern about sexual imagery away from genital proximity and toward kinkiness. The movement helped transform popular conceptions of "hard core," and legal definitions have shifted as well. The distinction between hard- and soft-core porn once had mainly to do with whether there was genital exposure and contact. Increasingly, "hard core" refers to something the viewer finds repugnant or considers "way out there," and all too often consists of depictions of kinky or S/M sexuality.[55]

S/M continued to be a potent flashpoint throughout the feminist sex wars, in part because the antipornography argument depended on its indictment of S/M, its contention that pornography overwhelmingly featured S/M content, and its use of S/M imagery as an effective tool of persuasion. WAVPM pioneered a characteristic fusion of anti-S/M and antiporn propositions that shaped subsequent feminist antiporn ideology and activity. Opposition to S/M has always been a major subtext of the feminist antiporn movement: indispensable to its analytic coherence, the source of its most rhetorically potent examples, and a primary target of its prescriptions for social change. Samois challenged the fundamental credibility of both the logical structure and empirical claims of WAVPM's case against porn. Thus the disputes between Samois and WAVPM prefigured much of the subsequent struggle in feminism over sexual practice and sexual representation. They help explain why S/M (engaged in by a relatively small proportion of the population, feminist or otherwise) was such a flashpoint, and why the name of Samois such a significant talisman.

By the time of the Barnard conference, the specific confrontation between WAVPM and Samois had been generalized. S/M had become a code for any feminist opposition to the antipornography creed. Since antiporn feminists seemed unable to accept that there might be any rational basis for disagreement, S/M also functioned as an explanation for behavior they apparently considered both inexplicable and despicable. Given the stigma of S/M, it was also a convenient slur with which to try to discredit any opposition. Feminists who did not go along with the antiporn program were accused of being tools of the patriarchy, dupes of the pornographers, sadomasochists and other sex perverts, leftists, Marxists, bourgeois academics, liberals, libertarians, heterosexuals, lesbians, and antifeminists. Some of these characterizations (such as academics, heterosexuals, lesbians, liberals, leftists, and the occasional sadomasochist) were of course true, although it was not clear how they invalidated our arguments and empirical claims. Some characterizations were erroneous, some were debatable, and many were completely idiotic. All were deployed to impugn our right to speak on the issues and to excommunicate us from the ranks of legitimate feminists. Feminists who opposed antiporn dogma were often called sadomasochists or supporters of sadomasochism, whatever their actual sexual preferences.[56] All of this history came into play not only at Barnard but also well beyond.

Barnard Redux

The Barnard Sex Conference, it turned out, was the opening act for a series of similar conflicts. As Vance perceptively noted in the Barnard aftermath, "Some feminists decried these tactics, but the fact that the people who had deployed them were not totally discredited guaranteed that they would be repeated. The principle was established: Zealotry and unprincipled behavior were acceptable in the service of 'protecting' women."[57] In 1986 they were indeed repeated when the Five College Women's Studies Project held a conference called "Feminism, Sexuality, and Power" at Mount Holyoke. I had been invited to give the keynote, on new theories of sexuality. The organizers experienced something quite different from what they had planned, as Margaret Hunt reported in *Gay Community News*:

> More than a hundred feminist activists met at Mt. Holyoke College for a symposium intended . . . to explore the variety of ideas about the ways that sexual practices are affected by history, culture and politics. . . . the conference organizers had in mind a quite broad based approach to sexuality and power. They planned a program which included a substantial amount of material on the ways class and race interacted with gender in the organization of sexuality and they took care to represent a variety of erotic lifestyles to avoid the prevalent Western bias of much scholarship on sexuality. What they got was a pitched battle over the question of lesbian S/M, an issue which so dominated the conference as to make all other matters fade into the polished neo-gothic Mt. Holyoke woodwork.[58]

After this debacle, Meryl Fingrudt, one of the organizers, lamented:

> Radical feminism, as it was presented at our conference, has a very narrow range of vision. . . . it was at the level of intellectual and personal freedoms that these radical feminists threw me into despair. The speakers refused to be moved off the issues of pornography and S/M and they were downright nasty to their sisters. . . . They refused to debate or sit on the same panel with anyone who held another point of view. . . . Above all, it was unnerving to see, with each successive presentation, incredibly narrow and specific lines drawn around sexual practices that were permissible if one wanted to be a real feminist. . . . any inquiry that proposes to raise questions about the content of these categories or even argue that these are dangerously limiting is labeled non-feminist, anti-feminist, or fascistic.[59]

The Five Colleges conference ended up feeling like Barnard, Act II.[60]

Act III was played out in Australia, in 1993, when several American scholars whose work dealt with sexuality and LGBT studies were invited to the Humanities Research Centre (HRC) at the Australian National University (ANU). Among the visiting fellows from the United States were Henry Abelove, D'Emilio, Duggan, David Halperin, Patton, Vance, Vicinus, and me. Several Australian radical feminists, including Sheila Jeffreys, Denise Thompson, and Renate Klein, sent a letter to the university's vice chancellor to protest our presence and attack the HRC for having invited us. "Some of the women invited," said the letter, "hold what can only be described as anti-feminist positions. . . . In particular we want to protest in the strongest possible terms against the HRC's bias in inviting Gayle Rubin, Cindy Patton and Carol [*sic*] Vance to be conference participants. . . . The work of these women from the US displays a zeal in defence of male supremacist meanings and values that amounts to an outright anti-feminism."[61] A few days later, the *Sydney Star Observer* ran an article with the headline "ANU denies conferences showcase anti-feminism." Thompson is quoted in the article as saying, "Not only do these women from the US lack any ability to think through questions of sex and power, they are also anti-feminist." Thompson also blasted the ANU for "importing tenth-rate yanks."[62] The HRC and ANU politely but firmly stood by their invitations and continued with their plans. Some of us among the visiting fellows took to calling ourselves the Tenth-Rate Yanks. It would have been a great name for a band.

Over the years, there have been plenty of mini-Barnards. Many of those who were involved in the attacks on Barnard, the Five Colleges conference, and the HRC are still actively working in pursuit of the same, or closely related, agendas. They continue to dismiss anyone who disagrees with them as antifeminists, sado-masochists, and supporters of patriarchal violence.[63] We might hear less about them these days because so many of them have left the women's movement as their arena of action to work in the federal government and international nongovernmental organizations where they influence decisions with great public impact. Most now describe their target as "sex trafficking," to which they are bringing the same agenda they brought to pornography and which they hope to codify in international law and policy.[64] For example, Dorchen Leidholdt helped found the Coalition Against Trafficking in Women (CATW) and has served as its codirector. Laura Lederer served as senior advisor on trafficking in persons to the undersecretary of state during the Bush administration.

Rethinking "Thinking Sex"

Once I write a paper, I rarely reread it. But the "Rethinking Sex" conference seemed a good time to reacquaint myself with "Thinking Sex." I am often asked what I might have written differently. There is a part of me that always wants to go back and do yet another edit on any article that has left my hands, but I could never fix this piece. Any serious revision would require another article, one set in these different times. Yet there are certainly some things I would have done differently, had I known then what I know now. My remarks about transsexuality, sex work, and the sexuality of the young were far too sketchy for such complex topics. Nor is it possible here to redress those lacunae fully; a few brief comments will have to suffice.

Every theory has what Max Weber famously called "inconvenient facts," examples or data that stress the capabilities of any given intellectual scheme.[65] Both sex work and transsexuality are in a sense such "inconvenient facts," in that they reveal the limitations of the theoretical models and conceptual distinctions developed in "Thinking Sex." The essay had useful things to say about each, and I tried to note the ways in which each did not fit the argument's framework, although I was more explicit about prostitution than about transsexuality.[66] Nonetheless, both phenomena exceed the parameters the essay was so careful to construct.

Susan Stryker has gently taken "Thinking Sex" to task for having "clearly categorized transgender practices as sexual or erotic acts rather than expressions of gender identity or sense of self." She further notes that "Thinking Sex" contributed to an analytic framework that transgender theories had to overcome: "As the transgender movement began to regather force in the early 1990s, it posed a challenge to the new queer theory similar to the one posed by sexuality to feminism — it asked whether the framework of queer sexuality could adequately account for transgender phenomena, or whether a new frame of analysis was required. These are the questions that led, in the years ahead, to the development of the new interdisciplinary academic field of transgender studies."[67]

Of course, Stryker is completely correct in her critique of the treatment of transsexuality in "Thinking Sex" and in her observation that "transgender phenomena are not intrinsically sexual (having more to do, more often than not, with regulatory schema of bodily integrity, visual coherence, and bureaucratic intelligibility than with wanton ways of fucking)."[68] The contrast between transgender studies now and the cruder tools available in the early 1980s illuminates some of the very positive changes that have occurred in the interim.

Since transgender studies did not yet exist when I was writing "Thinking Sex," I had limited resources with which to respond to the nasty vein of antitranssexual sentiment that had developed within feminism in the 1970s and was articulated most comprehensively by Janice Raymond.[69] Although I wanted to undermine the foundations on which such antitrans screeds were built, there were many alternative strategies I might have used. One approach would have been to ground my argument in feminism's own core critiques of gender roles and anatomical determinism, although that would have unduly complicated other agendas of the essay.

I should reiterate that antifeminism was not one of my objectives. While the essay has sometimes been interpreted as a rejection of feminism, I saw it as completely within the best traditions of feminist discourse, particularly the constant self-critical striving toward more analytic clarity and descriptive precision about inequality and injustice. Unfortunately, as time erodes the details of context, such conversations, internal to feminism, are often seen as more oppositional than they were ever intended to be.[70]

Then there are the children. I clearly underestimated the size of the impending tsunami about the sexuality of the young. When I finished writing "Thinking Sex" in 1983, the outlines of the panics over children were clear, but their scale and duration were not.[71] The panics that seemed episodic in 1983 now are a permanent feature of our social and political landscape. When the history of the last quarter of a century is finally written, one of the distinguishing features of this period will be the extent to which legitimate concerns for the sexual welfare of the young have been vehicles for political mobilizations and policies with consequences well beyond their explicit aims, some quite damaging to the young people they are supposed to help. The rhetoric of child protection has anchored many conservative agendas with respect to intensifying women's subordinate status, reinforcing hierarchical family structures, curtailing gay citizenship, opposing comprehensive sex education, limiting the availability of contraception, and restricting abortion, especially for young women and girls.

Laws and policies that are supposed to protect children have been used to deprive young people of age-appropriate and eagerly desired sexual information and services. Laws intended to protect children and young people, such as very broadly drawn child pornography statutes, have been used to prosecute them (such as the cases where minors have been charged with breaking the law by texting nude images of themselves). Almost anything, from promoting abstinence to banning gay marriage and adoption, can be and has been framed as promoting children's safety and welfare.[72] A critical evaluation of the details, impact, and scope of child protection laws and policies is long overdue; yet people who try to engage in such analysis are often attacked and accused of supporting child abuse.

In the early 1980s one could still have a thoughtful discussion about the sexuality of the young. It has become increasingly perilous to address the many complex questions about children, sex, and minors that need to be thoroughly discussed and carefully vetted: these include what kind of sexual information, services, and behavior are appropriate for the young, and at what ages; what constitutes sexual abuse and how can it be prevented and minimized; how should young people learn about sex; what are the appropriate roles of adults in the sexual lives and learning of children; what kinds of representations of sexuality should be available to minors, and at what ages; should sexually active minors be treated in punitive ways, and where is the line between protection and punishment; in what ways do the policies, legal apparatus, and structures of fear that have been built over the last several decades enhance or damage the experience of growing up; what is pedophilia, and what is child molestation; who abuses children; what is child pornography; and for what offenses is someone labeled a "sex offender"? I do not have answers to all of these questions, but I think it is tragic that discussion of most of these questions has been reduced to a collection of crude sound bites, stereotypes, and scare tactics that have been cynically manipulated into stampeding the public and politicians into many ill-considered changes that have not promoted safety or sound policies for minors.

One example is California's 1994 initiative, Three Strikes and You're Out. This law was passed in the emotional wake of a horrible crime: the abduction, rape, and murder of a young girl. But the law was an example of bait and switch: rather than protect young people from serial rapists, the primary effect of the law has been to incarcerate tens of thousands of Californians, many on relatively minor charges, including drug use and possession. Three Strikes has contributed to the out-of-control expansion of a vast prison gulag and diverted critical resources from other needs, including one of the most important for children: primary, secondary, and higher education.[73]

The fear of sexual abduction, rape, and murder of children by strangers has substantially reshaped many areas of society. It is a major concern of parents, and haunts the young. Yet it is relatively rare. According to *Newsweek*, more children drown in swimming pools each year than are abducted by strangers.[74] By a large margin, the leading cause of fatalities among teenagers is automobile accidents.[75] Yet most people are not terrified of cars, and few parents are as afraid of swimming pools as they are of "sex offenders," ostensibly lurking behind every bush and lamppost. Despite the facts that most sex abuse is perpetrated at home and by family members, most murdered children are killed by their parents, and most kidnapped children are abducted by noncustodial parents, the family is depicted as a place of safety threatened by dangerous strangers. The ever-growing apparatus of regulation and control adopted to address these issues is directed primarily toward such strangers. "Child protection" is a bit like the defense budget, the intelligence bureaucracy, and the endless wars on terror: there are genuine issues and real problems, but much of the response consists of uncontrolled institutional expansion, escalating expenditure of resources, poorly defined targets, and few effective ways to measure success.

In her statement about her Barnard workshop on the sexuality of infancy and childhood, Kate Millett observed: "There is, in short, a great deal of sexual politics frustrating the sexual expression of children and the young. You and I will live to see this discussed, almost for the first time in history. Considering we were all children once, and if we are very good, we're children still — we all have a stake in this. The emancipation of children is our emancipation in retrospect, and that of the future as well."[76] Millett's comments (and some of mine in "Thinking Sex") now seem hopelessly naive and unrealistically optimistic. But she was right to point out that all of us who have reached adulthood are former children. Much of my concern in these areas is a result of having grown up in the 1950s, when it was hazardous to be a sexually active female teenager.

Like most other girls, I had plenty of experience with both "pleasures and dangers." I had to contend with my share of unwanted sex, but I also encountered many barriers to sex I wanted. Contraception was unavailable, abortion was illegal, and the stigmatization of sexually active young women was ferocious. Sex education in school consisted of a film about menstruation, enhanced by surreptitious reading of disreputable novels like *The Catcher in the Rye* and gleaning sexual terms from the rare unabridged copies of *Webster's* dictionary. Getting pregnant was ruinous: when I was in high school, girls who got pregnant were summarily expelled. They lost their chance at further education and became social nonpersons, at least in the universe visible to those of us who remained in school. Second-wave feminism was in part a reaction to this punitive regime. Social conservatives, on the other hand, seek to reconstitute such a system, or something worse. They often justify their program as necessary to protect a sentimentalized notion of childhood innocence.

Writing "Thinking Sex," I dimly saw the outlines of the shape of things to come, but badly miscalculated their reach, persistence, and consequences. My comments on sex and children were made in a different context, in which I assumed (wrongly, as it turned out) that no one would imagine that I supported the rape of prepubescents. Even now, as I write this, I am aware that whatever I say will be interpreted in the worst possible way by some antipornography advocate or right-winger, and misconstructions are inevitable. Children are not, in fact, a major area of my interest or expertise. But why should even an exploration of such issues need to be done so gingerly, and feel so dangerous? That it does is an indication of something deeply wrong.

Issues of urban space have remained major and enduring areas of my research interest. The parts of "Thinking Sex" that are most germane to my current work are those that grew out of my ethnographic project on gay men in San

Francisco, and I am even more focused now than I was then on topics such as geographies of sexual location, and the formation and dissipation of gay neighborhoods. While the term *gentrification* had been coined in the 1960s, the study of gentrification was just becoming a coherent field in the late 1970s and early 1980s, and there were only a handful of studies on the relationship of gay neighborhoods and populations to that emerging literature.[77] I was not yet conversant with the early gentrification literature when I wrote "Thinking Sex." My field research had made it clear, however, that the location of gay populations and institutions was enmeshed in conflicts over land use and that homosexuals were convenient scapegoats for the crisis in affordable housing in San Francisco.[78]

It was even more obvious that large redevelopment projects threatened existing gay enclaves and that sexual stigma was a readily exploitable resource for making land available for capital-intensive development. In 1984 I commented that areas such as Times Square in New York and San Francisco's Tenderloin, North Beach, and South of Market were on the verge of being "made safe for convention centers, international hotels, corporate headquarters, and housing for the rich."[79] There is now a sizable literature on the transformation of Times Square, including Samuel Delany's elegiac *Times Square Red, Times Square Blue*.[80] In San Francisco, the Tenderloin and North Beach have not yet been conquered, but South of Market, the location of my research, has been substantially rebuilt and socially reconstructed. Blocks that once housed maritime union halls and where gay men congregated are now the sites of luxury condominium towers. Moreover, the other gay neighborhoods of San Francisco from the 1960s and 1970s are either gone or shrinking. On rereading "Thinking Sex," I was surprised to see my observation that the gay neighborhoods that we could take for granted in the early 1980s might prove temporary.[81] The attrition of urban gay concentrations in the early twenty-first century has become a serious challenge for gay social life and political aspirations, and its potential consequences have not yet been fully articulated.

One aspect of the essay of which I am most proud is its "protoqueerness." I wanted to move the discussion of sexual politics beyond single issues and single constituencies, from women and lesbians and gay men to analyses that could incorporate and address with more intricacy the cross-identifications and multiple subject positions that most of us occupy. I continue to believe that our best political hopes for the future lie in finding common ground and building coalitions based on mutual respect and appreciation of differences and that the best intellectual work is able to accommodate complexity, treasure nuance, and resist the temptations of dogma and oversimplification.

Notes

Thanks to Bob Schoenberg and Ann Matter, and to the many departments and units at the University of Pennsylvania that supported the conference "Rethinking Sex." Thanks to Steven Epstein, Sharon Holland, and Susan Stryker for their gracious and generous comments. Thanks especially to Heather Love, for having brought us all together, and for honoring my work. Thanks to Melanie Micir and Poulomi Saha for taking such good care of the logistics. For help on this essay, I am immensely grateful to Heather Love, Carole Vance, Claire Potter, Andrew McBride, and Valerie Traub.

1. See, e.g., B. Ruby Rich, "Is There Anything New under the Covers?" *In These Times*, February 20–26, 1985, 19. In "Review: Feminism and Sexuality in the 1980s," *Feminist Studies* 12 (1986): 525–61, Rich dismissed me without engaging at all with "Thinking Sex" in an essay covering several books, including *Pleasure and Danger*. In *Sex, Power, and Pleasure* (Toronto: Women's Press, 1985), 17–18, 150–55, Mariana Valverde managed to dismiss "Thinking Sex" while using conceptual language (such as the "Domino Theory") almost identical to mine, but without attribution. See also Elizabeth Wilson, "The Context of 'Between Pleasure and Danger': The Barnard Conference on Sexuality," *Feminist Review*, no. 13 (1983): 35–41, although Wilson's comments were based on the lecture rather than the published version. A welcome exception was Michèle Aina Barale's thoughtful and engaged comments in "Review: Body Politic/Body Pleasured: Feminism's Theories of Sexuality, a Review Essay," *Frontiers: A Journal of Women's Studies* 9 (1986): 80–89. Exemplary of the hostile reviews was Pauline B. Bart, "Review: Their Pleasure and Our Danger," *Contemporary Sociology* 15 (1986): 832–35. See also Sheila Jeffreys, *Anticlimax: A Feminist Perspective on the Sexual Revolution* (London: Women's Press, 1990), 274; and Bat-Ami Bar On, "The Feminist Sexuality Debates and the Transformation of the Political," in *Adventures in Lesbian Philosophy*, ed. Claudia Card (Bloomington: Indiana University Press, 1994), 51–63.

2. Gayle Rubin, "Thinking Sex: Notes for a Radical Theory of the Politics of Sexuality," in *Pleasure and Danger: Exploring Female Sexuality*, ed. Carole S. Vance (Boston: Routledge and Kegan Paul, 1984), 267–319.

3. See Robin Morgan, *The Anatomy of Freedom: Feminism, Physics, and Global Politics* (Garden City, NY: Anchor Books/Doubleday, 1984); 115, and Ellen Willis, "Who Is a Feminist? A Letter to Robin Morgan," *Village Voice*, Literary Supplement, December 1982, 16–17.

4. The historian Jonathan Ned Katz coined this slogan, which now graces the Web site www.outhistory.org, a community-created, nonprofit site on lesbian, gay, bisexual, transgender, queer, and heterosexual history.

5. "Welcome Statement," "Rethinking Sex" conference brochure, www.sas.upenn.edu/wstudies/rethinkingsex/.

6.   Jeffrey Weeks, *Coming Out: Homosexual Politics in Britain, from the Nineteenth Century to the Present* (London: Longman, 1977). See also Bert Hansen, "The Historical Construction of Homosexuality," *Radical History Review* 20 (Spring–Summer 1979): 66–75; Robert Padgug, "Sexual Matters: On Conceptualizing Sexuality in History," *Radical History Review* 20 (Spring–Summer 1979): 3–23.

7.   This paradigm shift happened across a broad swath of researchers more or less simultaneously. In addition to my own essay, see Judith Walkowitz and Daniel J. Walkowitz, "'We Are Not Beasts of the Field': Prostitution and the Poor in Plymouth and Southampton under the Contagious Diseases Act," *Feminist Studies* 1, nos. 3–4 (1973): 73–106; Michel Foucault, *The History of Sexuality, Vol. 1, An Introduction* trans. Robert Hurley (New York: Pantheon, 1978); Padgug, "Sexual Matters: On Conceptualizing Sexuality in History"; Hansen, "The Historical Construction of Homosexuality"; Judith Walkowitz, *Prostitution and Victorian Society: Women, Class, and the State* (Cambridge: Cambridge University Press, 1980); Carole S. Vance, "Social Construction Theory: Problems in the History of Sexuality," *Homosexuality, Which Homosexuality?*, ed. Dennis Altman et al. (London: GMP Publishers, 1989), 13–34; Vance, "Anthropology Discovers Sexuality: A Theoretical Comment," *Social Science and Medicine* 33 (1991): 875–84; Steven Epstein, "A Queer Encounter: Sociology and the Study of Sexuality," in *Queer Theory/Sociology*, ed. by Steven Seidman (Cambridge: Blackwell, 1996), 145–67; and Gayle Rubin, "Studying Sexual Subcultures: The Ethnography of Gay Communities in Urban North America," in *Out in Theory: The Emergence of Lesbian and Gay Anthropology*, ed. Ellen Lewin and William L. Leap (Urbana: University of Illinois Press, 2002).

8.   Gayle Rubin and Judith Butler, "Interview: Sexual Traffic," *differences* 6, nos. 2–3 (1994): 62–99.

9.   Two key independent scholars were Jonathan Ned Katz and Allan Bérubé. See Jonathan Ned Katz, *Gay American History: Lesbians and Gay Men in the U.S.A.* (New York: Thomas Crowell, 1976); Katz, *Gay/Lesbian Almanac: A New Documentary* (New York: Harper and Row, 1983); Allan Bérubé, *Coming Out Under Fire: The History of Gay Men and Women in World War Two* (New York: Free Press, 1990).

10.   John D'Emilio, "Dreams Deferred: Part 1," *Body Politic* 48 (1978): 19; D'Emilio, "Dreams Deferred: Part 2: Public Actions, Private Fears," *Body Politic* 49 (1979): 24–29; Jim Steakley, "The Gay Movement in Germany Part One: 1860–1910," *Body Politic* 9 (1973): 12–17; Steakley, "The Gay Movement in Germany Part Two: 1910–1933," *Body Politic* 10 (1973): 14–19; Steakley, "Homosexuals and the Third Reich," *Body Politic* 11 (1974): 1–3; Allan Bérubé, "The First Stonewall," *San Francisco Lesbian and Gay Freedom Day Program* (1983), 27; Bérubé, "Behind the Spectre of San Francisco," *Body Politic* 72 (1981): 25–27; and Bérubé, "Lesbian Masquerade," *Gay Community News*, November 17, 1979. For more on *Gay Community News*, see Amy Hoffman's wonderful memoir, *An Army of Ex-Lovers: My Life at the Gay Community News* (Amherst: University of Massachusetts Press, 2007).

11. Allan Bérubé, "Coming Out Under Fire," *Mother Jones*, February–March (1983), 45.

12. See John D'Emilio, "Allan Bérubé's Gift to History," *Gay and Lesbian Review Worldwide* 15, no. 3 (2008): 10–13.

13. Bérubé, "Lesbian Masquerade."

14. Bérubé, "First Stonewall."

15. Bérubé, *Coming Out Under Fire*.

16. See Eric Garber, "A Spectacle in Color: The Lesbian and Gay Subculture of Jazz Age Harlem," in *Hidden from History: Reclaiming the Gay and Lesbian Past*, ed. Martin B. Duberman, Martha Vicinus, and George Chauncey Jr. (New York: New American Library, 1991), 318–31; and Garber, "Gladys Bentley: The Bulldagger Who Sang the Blues," *OUTLook: National Lesbian and Gay Quarterly* 1 (Spring 1998): 52–61.

17. Erving Goffman, *Stigma: Notes on the Management of Spoiled Identity* (New York: Simon and Schuster, 1963).

18. Carole S. Vance, "Invitation Letter" (September 1981), in *Diary of a Conference on Sexuality*, ed. Hannah Alderfer, Beth Jaker, Marybeth Nelson (New York: Faculty Press, 1982), 1.

19. Carole S. Vance, Epilogue to *Pleasure and Danger: Exploring Female Sexuality*, ed. Carole S. Vance (Boston: Routledge and Kegan Paul, 1984), 434.

20. Carole S. Vance, "More Danger, More Pleasure: A Decade after the Barnard Sexuality Conference," in *Pleasure and Danger: Exploring Female Sexuality*, 2nd ed., ed. Carole Vance (London: Pandora, 1992), xxii.

21. Vance, Epilogue, 434. In the epilogue, Vance introduced the terminology of "sex panic" rather than that of "moral panic," which was used by Cohen, then Weeks, and me. See Stanley Cohen, *Folk Devils and Moral Panics: The Creation of the Mods and Rockers* (Oxford: Marin Roberton, 1980); Jeffrey Weeks, *Sex, Politics, and Society: The Regulation of Sexuality since 1800* (London: Longman, 1981): 14–15; and Rubin, "Thinking Sex," 297–98.

22. Vance, *Diary*, 47.

23. Cited in Susan Brownmiller, *In Our Time: Memoir of a Revolution* (New York: Dial, 1999), 314.

24. See the *Diary*; Vance, Epilogue; and Vance, "More Danger, More Pleasure."

25. Vance, Epilogue, 433–34.

26. Coalition for a Feminist Sexuality and Against Sadomasochism, "We Protest." Leaflet distributed at Barnard Sex Conference, April 1981. From the author's collection.

27. Carole S. Vance, "Letter to the Editor," *Feminist Studies* 9 (1983): 589–91; and Ellen Willis, "Letter to the Editor," *Feminist Studies* 9 (1983): 592–94.

28. Ellen Willis, "Feminism, Moralism, and Pornography," in *Beginning to See the Light: Pieces of a Decade* (New York: Alfred A. Knopf, 1981): 219–27.

29. Tacie Dejanikus, "Charges of Exclusion and McCarthyism at Barnard Conference," *off our backs* 12, no. 6 (1982): 5.

30. Dejanikus, "Charges of Exclusion and McCarthyism," 5.

31. Dorchen Leidholdt, "Back to Barnard," *off our backs* 23 (Oct. 1993): 30.

32. Jane F. Gerhard, *Desiring Revolution: Second-Wave Feminism and the Rewriting of American Sexual Thought, 1920 to 1982* (New York: Columbia University Press, 2001), 188.

33. Vance, Epilogue, 434.

34. Vance, "More Danger, More Pleasure," xxi.

35. Jane Gould, *Juggling: A Memoir of Work, Family, and Feminism* (New York: Feminist Press at the City University of New York, 1997), 200.

36. Gerhard, *Desiring Revolution*, 184. The actual members of the planning committee were listed in the *Diary* and also in *Pleasure and Danger* (1984), xvii.

37. Gould, *Juggling*, 200.

38. Vance, Epilogue, 431–32.

39. Vance, personal communication, June 2010.

40. Andrea Dworkin, memo, circulated but unpublished, August 1981, author's personal collection, emphasis in the original.

41. Letters to the Editor, *off our backs* 12, no. 7 (1982): Rubin, 24, Hollibaugh, 25, Walton, 25, Newton, 25, Doughty, 26; 12, no. 8 (1982): Ellen Willis, 32, Joan Nestle, 32, Barbara Greer, 33; 12, no. 10 (1982): Samois, 26, Cleveland WAVAM, 26.

42. But see Feminist Anti-Censorship Taskforce et al., eds., *Caught Looking: Feminism, Pornography, and Censorship* (East Haven, CT: Long River Books, 1992); *Heresies: The Sex Issue* 12 (1981); and Lisa Duggan and Nan D. Hunter, *Sex Wars: Sexual Dissent and Political Culture* (New York: Routledge, 1995) for a useful chronology and incisive commentary.

43. See Laura Lederer, *Take Back the Night: Women on Pornography* (New York: William Morrow, 1980). This is the most representative collection of essays from the early feminist antiporn movement.

44. MacKinnon mentioned pornography in passing in her 1982 and 1983 *Signs* articles, but did not become a prominent figure in the antiporn movement until the 1983 Minneapolis ordinance. Catharine MacKinnon, "Feminism, Marxism, Method, and the State: An Agenda for Theory," *Signs* 7.3 (Spring 1982): 515–44; and MacKinnon, "Feminism, Marxism, Method, and the State: Toward Feminist Jurisprudence," *Signs* 8.4 (Summer 1983): 635–58. See also Gayle Rubin, "Misguided, Dangerous, and Wrong: An Analysis of Anti-Pornography Politics," in *Bad Girls and Dirty Pictures: The Challenge to Reclaim Feminism*, ed. Alison Assiter and Avedon Carol (Boulder, CO: Pluto, 1993), 18–40.

45. Diana E. H. Russell and Susan Griffin, "On Pornography: Two Feminists' Perspectives," *Chrysalis* 4 (1977): 11.

46. Russell and Griffin, "On Pornography," 12. Russell appears to be unaware that the relative lack of explicit sex in some S/M films often resulted from attempts to avoid prosecution. The threshold of explicitness for bringing obscenity charges was often lower for S/M materials.

47. Carole Vance has a particularly lucid analysis of the rhetorical tactics involved in such sexual "laundry lists" in an essay on the 1989 imbroglio over the National Endowment for the Arts (NEA). (Carole Vance, "Misunderstanding Obscenity," *Art in America* 78, [May 1990]: 49–55). In addition, one must be careful to understand how potentially loaded terms are used in antiporn literature, and how their meanings can slip. One example, found in the Russell passage cited here, is mutilation. We generally think of mutilation as deliberate and terrible injury causing permanent physical damage, but mutilation is often used in antiporn texts to refer to practices of body modification such as genital piercing, nipple rings, or even tattoos. In this context, one person's idea of mutilation is another's idea of personal adornment.

48. Russell and Griffin, "On Pornography," 13.

49. See, for instance, Rubin, "Misguided, Dangerous, and Wrong."

50. WAVPM, "Who Are We?" *Newspage*, September 1977.

51. *Newspage*, November 1977, my emphasis.

52. Samois, ed., *What Color Is Your Handkerchief? A Lesbian S/M Sexuality Reader* (Berkeley, CA: Samois, 1979) and the organization's carefully worded statement of purpose printed on the last page of *Coming to Power: Writings and Graphics on Lesbian S/M* (Boston: Alyson, 1982). See also Gayle Rubin, "Samois," in *Encyclopedia of Lesbian, Gay, Bisexual, and Transgender History in America*, ed. Marc Stein (New York: Scribner, 2004), 67–69; and Rubin, "The Leather Menace," in *Coming to Power*, 194–229.

53. Pat Califia, "History of Samois," in *Coming to Power*, 243–81.

54. Robin Linden et al., *Against Sadomasochism: A Radical Feminist Analysis* (East Palo Alto, CA: Frog in the Well, 1982).

55. Linda Williams traces "a major change taking place in American obscenity law and the prosecution of sex crimes as they have moved away from the notion of explicit sex and toward the targeting of scapegoatable 'deviants' . . . in the definition of obscenity, explicitness has given way to the deviant sexuality of the 'other,' defined in relation to a presumed heterosexual, non-sadomasochistic norm that excludes both fellatio and cunnilingus." (Williams, "Second Thoughts on *Hard Core*: American Obscenity Law and the Scapegoating of Deviance," in *Dirty Looks: Women, Pornography, and Power*, ed. Pamela Church Gibson and Roma Gibson [London: British Film Institute, 1993], 47, 49).

56. Dorchen Leidholdt and Janice G. Raymond, *The Sexual Liberals and the Attack on Feminism* (New York: Pergamon, 1989). See also Dorchen Leidholdt, "A Small Group," *off our backs* 15, no. 10 (1985): 26; Nan Hunter, "Sex-Baiting and Dangerous Bedfellows," *off our backs* 15, no. 7 (1985): 33; Hunter, "Modern McCarthyism," *off our backs* 15, no. 11 (1985): 26; and Lisa Duggan, "The Binds That Divide," *off our backs* 15, no. 11 (1985): 26.

57. Vance, "More Danger, More Pleasure," xxi.

58. Margaret Hunt, "Discord in the Happy Valley: Report of a Conference on Feminism, Sexuality, and Power," *Gay Community News* 14, no. 21 (1986).

59. Meryl Fingrudt, ". . . An Organizer," *off our backs* 17, no. 3 (1987): 24.

60. It was at this conference that I first met Eve Sedgwick. Eve's paper was called "Spanking and Poetry: Starting with the Fundamentals." Eve too was attacked in some of the press coverage for ostensibly participating in the S/M conspiracy.

61. Multiple authors, "A Protest at the Emphasis of the Humanities Research Centre's 1993 Conferences," Australian National University, 9 March 1993, p. 1. See Sheila Jeffreys's account in *The Lesbian Heresy: A Feminist Perspective on the Lesbian Sexual Revolution* (Melbourne: Spinifex, 1993), 95–97.

62. Barbara Farrelly, "ANU denies conferences showcase anti-feminism," *Sydney Observer*, March 19, 1993.

63. Leidholdt and Raymond, *Sexual Liberals and the Attack on Feminism*.

64. CATW campaigns against decriminalizing prostitution, supports the Mann Act, and supports the federalization of antiprostitution enforcement. See action.web.ca/home/catw/readingroom.shtml?x=113289; www.catwinternational.org/bioDorchenLeidholdt .php; action.web.ca/home/catw/readingroom.shtml?x=113289. Jeffreys is also currently involved in feminist antitrafficking and antiprostitution activism. See Vance, this issue, and Rubin, "The Trouble with Trafficking: Afterthoughts on the Traffic in Women," in *Deviations: Essays in Sex, Gender, and Politics* (Durham, NC: Duke University Press, forthcoming).

65. H. H. Gerth and C. Wright Mills, *From Max Weber: Essays in Sociology* (New York: Oxford University Press, 1958), 147.

66. For my comments on prostitution, see Rubin, "Thinking Sex," 286–87.

67. Susan Stryker, *Transgender History* (Berkeley, CA: Seal, 2008), 130–31.

68. Susan Stryker, "Thoughts on Transgender Feminism and the Barnard Conference on Women," *Communication Review* 11 (2008): 218.

69. Janice Raymond, *The Transsexual Empire: The Making of the She-Male* (New York: Teachers College Press, 1979). See also Penny House and Liza Cowan, "Can Men Be Women? Some Lesbians Think So! Transsexuals in the Women's Movement," *Dyke, a Quarterly* 5 (1977): 29–35. For responses to Raymond, see Sandy Stone, "The 'Empire' Strikes Back: A Posttranssexual Manifesto," in *Body Guards: The Cultural Politics of Gender Ambiguity*, ed. Kristina Straub and Julia Epstein (New York: Routledge, 1991), 280–304; and Carol Riddell, *Divided Sisterhood: A Critical Review of Janice Raymond's "The Transsexual Empire"* (Liverpool, UK: News from Nowhere, 1980). Raymond has also moved into antiprostitution activism and was the co–executive director of the Coalition Against Trafficking in Women (CATW) from 1994 to 2007.

70. In addition, the politics of the sex wars led some critics to claim that I had rejected feminism in attempts to discredit me and to bolster their argument that those who

disagreed with the antipornography analysis were not feminists. See, for example, Jeffreys, *The Lesbian Heresy*, 128; and *Anti-Climax*, 274. For a contrasting assessment, see Annamarie Jagose's careful and detailed discussion of the relationship of queer theory to feminism, in which she correctly notes that the gulf between queer theory and feminism has been exaggerated and comments that "Thinking Sex" was "a resolutely feminist intervention." Jagose, "Feminism's Queer Theory," *Feminism & Psychology* 19, no. 2 (2009): 165.

71. Joel Best, *Threatened Children: Rhetoric and Concern about Child-Victims* (Chicago: University of Chicago Press, 1990), 23–24. See also Paula Fass, *Kidnapped: Child Abduction in America* (New York: Oxford University Press, 1997); and Steven Mintz, *Huck's Raft: A History of American Childhood* (Cambridge: Harvard University Press, 2004), 335–71.

72. See Ann Burlein, *Lift High the Cross: Where White Supremacy and the Christian Right Converge* (Durham, NC: Duke University Press, 2002); Janice Irvine, *Talk about Sex: The Battles over Sex Education in the United States* (Berkeley: University of California Press, 2002); and Judith Levine, *Harmful to Minors: The Perils of Protecting Children from Sex* (Minneapolis: University of Minnesota Press, 2002).

73. See *The Legacy* (dir. Michael J. Moore; 2006); Ruth Wilson Gilmore, *Golden Gulag: Prisons, Surplus, Crisis, and Opposition in Globalizing California* (Berkeley: University of California Press, 2007); and Joe Domanick, *Cruel Justice: Three Strikes and the Politics of Crime in America's Golden State* (Berkeley: University of California Press, 2004).

74. "What Should You Really Be Afraid Of?" *Newsweek*, May 24–31, 2010, 64.

75. Anna Quindlen, "Driving to the Funeral," *Newsweek*, June 11, 2007, 80.

76. Vance, *Diary*, 59.

77. Manuel Castells, *The City and the Grassroots* (Berkeley: University of California Press, 1983), 138–72; and Manuel Castells and Karen Murphy, "Organization of San Francisco's Gay Community," in Norman. I. Fainstein and Susan S. Fainstein, eds., *Urban Policy Under Capitalism* (Beverly Hills, CA: Sage Publications, 1982), 237–59.

78. For the escalating costs of housing in the early 1980s, see Susan S. Fainstein, Norman I. Fainstein, and P. Jefferson Armistead, "San Francisco: Urban Transformation and the Local State," in *Restructuring the City: The Political Economy of Urban Redevelopment*, Revised Edition, ed. Susan S. Fainstein, Norman I. Fainstein, Richard Child Hill, Dennis R. Judd and Michael Peter Smith (New York: Longman, 1986 [1983]), 202–44.

79. Rubin, *Thinking Sex*, 296–97.

80. Samuel R. Delany, *Times Square Red, Times Square Blue* (New York: New York University Press, 1999). Also on the development of Times Square, see Marilyn Adler Papayanis, "Sex and the Revanchist City: Zoning Out Pornography in New York,"

Environment and Planning D: Space and Society 18 (2000): 341–53; and Bart Eeck-
hout, "The Disneyfication of Times Square: Back to the Future?" in *Critical Perspectives on Urban Redevelopment*, ed. Kevin Fox Gotham (Oxford: Elsevier Science,
2001), 379–428.

81. Rubin, "Thinking Sex," 296.

DIARY OF A CONFERENCE ON SEXUALITY, 1982

The following images and text are taken from *Diary of a Conference on Sexuality*, the program designed by Hannah Alderfer, Beth Jaker, and Marybeth Nelson and published in conjunction with the ninth "Scholar and the Feminist" conference, "Towards a Politics of Sexuality," held at Barnard College on April 24, 1982. Better known as the Barnard Sex Conference, the conference was a key event in the feminist sex wars of the 1980s. Organized by Carole Vance to explore the politics of sexuality, the conference was picketed by antipornography groups. While these protesters focused their objections on issues of pornography, S/M, and butch/femme, the conference addressed a much wider array of questions about women's experiences of sexuality, some of which are represented here.

No ordinary conference program, the *Diary* included Vance's invitation to presenters, a coauthored "Concept Paper" that described the conference's aims and guiding questions, a list of speakers and schedule of events, as well as minutes from planning meetings, bibliographies of suggested reading, and a page devoted to each workshop. The *Diary* was, as Gayle Rubin writes in her article in this volume, "intended to be something of an archival document." Each speaker created a page in the *Diary* to represent her workshop; many of these included a "postcard" featuring some image that she found meaningful personally or in the context of the workshop. These images added to the visual impact of the program, which was designed by Alderfer, Jaker, and Nelson. With its striking images, its combination of politics, scholarship, and personal reflection, and its moments of insight, polemic, and humor, the *Diary* remains a compelling record of feminist collaboration.

In the days leading up to the conference, members of antipornography groups contacted the Barnard administration and issued a warning about what

GLQ 17:1
DOI 10.1215/10642684-2010-016
© 2010 by Duke University Press

they saw as the "antifeminist" nature of the proceedings. In response, Barnard administrators confiscated 1,500 copies of the *Diary* two days before the conference. (For a full account of these events, see Rubin's essay in this volume and Vance's epilogue in *Pleasure and Danger: Exploring Female Sexuality* [1984], the collection that emerged out of the Barnard conference.) Despite subsequent reprinting, the *Diary* remains exceedingly rare. (A complete online version of the *Diary* will be available soon at diaryofaconference.com.) In this *GLQ* Archive, we have reproduced the cover of the *Diary*, Vance's invitation to participants, the table of contents, meeting minutes, the "Concept Paper," pages for several of the workshops, and personals from conference participants.

For the cover of this special issue, the artist and scholar Aristea Fotopoulou was commissioned to recreate a photograph from the *Diary*. The original image, which accompanied Vance's Concept Paper, shows a naked woman lying suspended between two beds (see page 62 in this issue). While Fotopoulou's visual homage captures the sensuality as well as the vulnerability of the original, the slight variations of bodily morphology and mise-en-scène between the two images snag the attention, shuttling the viewer between different feminist temporalities and their various articulations of pleasure and danger.

—Heather Love

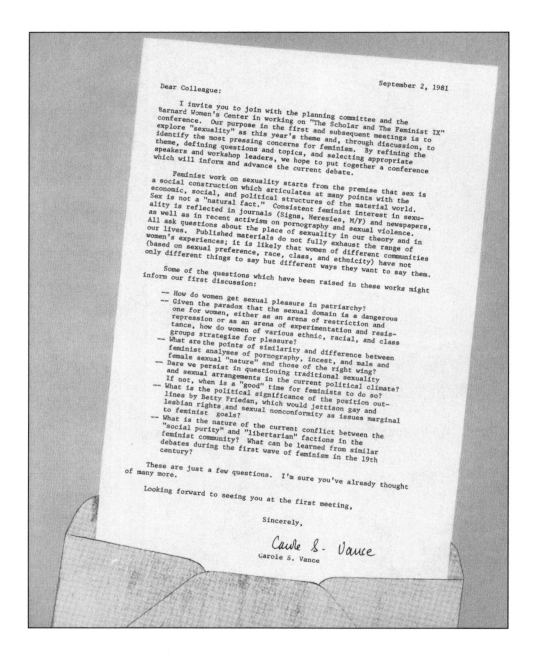

September 2, 1981

Dear Colleague:

I invite you to join with the planning committee and the Barnard Women's Center in working on "The Scholar and The Feminist IX" conference. Our purpose in the first and subsequent meetings is to explore "sexuality" as this year's theme and, through discussion, to identify the most pressing concerns for feminism. By refining the theme, defining questions and topics, and selecting appropriate speakers and workshop leaders, we hope to put together a conference which will inform and advance the current debate.

Feminist work on sexuality starts from the premise that sex is a social construction which articulates at many points with the economic, social, and political structures of the material world. Sex is not a "natural fact." Consistent feminist interest in sexuality is reflected in journals (Signs, Heresies, M/F) and newspapers, as well as in recent activism on pornography and sexual violence. All ask questions about the place of sexuality in our theory and in our lives. Published materials do not fully exhaust the range of women's experiences; it is likely that women of different communities (based on sexual preference, race, class, and ethnicity) have not only different things to say but different ways they want to say them.

Some of the questions which have been raised in these works might inform our first discussion:

-- How do women get sexual pleasure in patriarchy?
-- Given the paradox that the sexual domain is a dangerous one for women, either as an arena of restriction and repression or as an arena of experimentation and resistance, how do women of various ethnic, racial, and class groups strategize for pleasure?
-- What are the points of similarity and difference between feminist analyses of pornography, incest, and male and female sexual "nature" and those of the right wing?
-- Dare we persist in questioning traditional sexuality and sexual arrangements in the current political climate? If not, when is a "good" time for feminists to do so?
-- What is the political significance of the position outlines by Betty Friedan, which would jettison gay and lesbian rights and sexual nonconformity as issues marginal to feminist goals?
-- What is the nature of the current conflict between the "social purity" and "libertarian" factions in the feminist community? What can be learned from similar debates during the first wave of feminism in the 19th century?

These are just a few questions. I'm sure you've already thought of many more.

Looking forward to seeing you at the first meeting,

Sincerely,

Carole S. Vance

Carole S. Vance

Diary of a Conference on Sexuality

DEAR DIARY,   TUES. OCT. 20

"What does sexuality mean?" is still a question. How do we define it?
How can we put put on a conference, if we haven't defined it? Have we approached it too narrowly, treating it as a thing apart from the whole of women's
lives?

Some have said that in our discussions there has been too much attention to
experience and the personal, while others claim there has been too little. Is
it possible we use these terms to mean different things? Let's clarify first,
rather than assuming the other possibility that we are arrayed along a continuum of valuing/not valuing personal and experiential data, and our sense of too
much/too little is simply a function of where we stand on that continuum.

Sexuality is an intersection of many levels of experience, political and
personal. We come to this material trained in a particular discipline, with
its own methods and concepts, aimed at one of a number of possible levels of
analysis or domains. It is unlikely that any one of us succeeded in integrating all these disciplines. It may be unrealistic to look for the magic speakers
to perform the integration of personal/social. It is more realistic to think
that the planning committee can move toward an integration by thrashing it out
in discussions. The vision of the conference is to move beyond the "equal representation" of different disciplines toward the presentation of an integrated
way to recognize the simultaneous significance of all the factors (levels of
analysis). We're unlikely to achieve it, but it's important to try.

A brief report was given by a few members who attended the discussion at
the Lesbian Herstory Archives on "Censorship, Pornography, Feminism, and Sexuality" on October 16, 1981. The meeting was attended by a wide variety of
women: women concerned about violence and pornography, lesbians involved in
S/M, feminist pornographers and others. Some comments: is it possible that the
meaning of S/M can only be understood when the question of the "right" to practice it has been seen as a separate question? The concentration on "rights" (to
practice or to be considered a legitimate lesbian feminist) makes it difficult to
think about other questions. What is the meaning of being a "sexual outlaw" as
some women identified themselves? What does it mean to organize your sexuality
around breaking taboos? The discussion raised important points about censorship,
not only by the state and other external bodies, but also by the self. What
about the role of the Right and Left, not only in the political scene at large,
but also in the feminist movement? A woman made a number of interesting comments about feminist pornography and the need to appropriate for ourselves
labels initially derisive. What has occurred in the lesbian community to create
an environment for S/M? Is one of its main attractions about crossing boundaries
of power and, perhaps symbolically, of gender? The meaning of sexual symbols,
taken in and out of their normal context, is interesting as well.

We have side-stepped the issue of women's aggression in sexuality. Do we
assume only men feel sexual aggression?

12

The sexual fringe groups have an interesting feature: they know what gives them pleasure and they are systematically going about getting it. That should give us pause. The appeal of indicating sexual desire via handkerchief color is its forthrightness and aura of automatic pleasure. Contrast this with the inability of some women to figure out what gives them sexual pleasure, let alone communicate this to others.

Despite their many points of disagreement, S/M and Women Against Pornography (WAP) are concerned with structure: S/M, in providing stylized and highly structured sexual interactions; WAP, in prescribing a politically acceptable framework for sex. S/M may gain ground in the lesbian feminist community, because a vacuum exists. Perhaps the bravado and excitement of coming out on S/M replaces the no longer attainable excitement of coming out as a lesbian in the feminist community 10 years ago. S/M may have great appeal, since it provides clear boundaries (the top, the bottom) with appropriate behaviors for each.

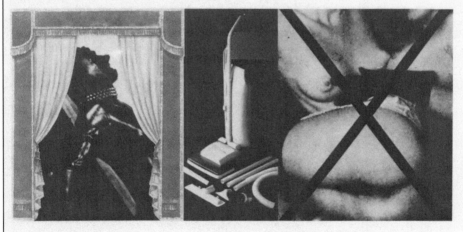

There is a vacuum about sexuality evident in feminists' theory and our lives. The feminist movement is in a political crisis, in part concerning sexuality. The Right has proposed a comprehensive theory of sexuality and the feminist response has been lacking.

13

We began discussing Rosalind Petchesky's article "Antiabortion, Antifeminism, and the Rise of the New Right." The article describes important features of the New Right: support for a return to the traditional family and opposition to social welfare under the banner of privatization of many aspects of life.

We discussed the attack on abortion as an attack on all women, regardless of sexual preference. At heart, feminism has tried to separate, or make possible the separation between, sexuality and reproduction. The Right wants to join these again, reducing women to reproductive animals. As such, it is an attack on women's autonomy and an eradication of our sexuality. Diminished access to or elimination of legal abortion also divides heterosexual and lesbian women, since heterosexuals are more easily placed into the breeding animal category, and divides women of different class groups, since some women will still have options regarding abortion while others do not.

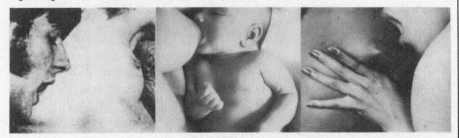

One important feature of the anti-abortion movement is its attack on teenagers'/daughters' access to abortion; its goal is to put daughters back under the control of the patriarchal father. In this context, teenagers are called "children." The concern about children's sexuality is reflected in the abortion issue, as well as in both Right and feminist commentaries on "childporn," which has become an issue out of proportion to its occurrence in the porn market and is a buzzword, designed to set everyone off. Yet we are also concerned about the abuse and exploitation of children in all realms, sexuality included. The Right's concern with preserving the presumed innocence of children returns in the abortion issue, as the fetus is presented as a child, i.e., an innocent deserving of protection. Feminists have not confronted the issue of childhood sexuality themselves.

Although the Right and feminists disagree in so many ways, a close examination of their material on sexuality shows both share the concern about male sexual violence.

14

A question related to childhood sexuality, heterosexuality, and age-discrep-
ant relations is: how do you view power relations? Some analysts view them as
overwhelming, destroying any possibility of choice or pleasure (i.e., "50 percent
of married women go to bed in fear each night"). Do we believe this? Does this
correspond to our experience? Your understanding of the effect of power imbalance would seem to determine your view of adult-child sex, heterosexuality, S/M.
In a situation of power imbalance, can the less powerful ever say "yes" or "no"?

Ironically, the Right campaign to protect the innocent confers enormous power
on the protector. The powerless innocent, safe in the bosom of the privatized
family, is completely at the mercy of the empowered protector.

The Right embodies an interesting inconsistency in regard to children:
they are at the same time innocents to be protected and little savages requiring careful socialization to suppress their anti-social drives.

Picking up on the theme of power relations, what about infants' and mothers'
reciprocal experience? How does that bear on sexuality? The mother is the slave
to the infant's demands; yet to the child, the mother is the child's master.

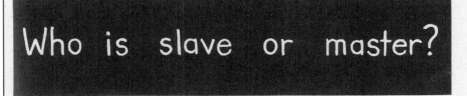

READINGS

Petchesky, Rosalind Pollack. "Antiabortion, Antifeminism, and the Rise of the New Right." *Feminist Studies* 7, No. 2 (Summer 1981), pp. 206-246.

15

"DEAR DIARY,"   (TUES. NOV. 10)

We continued last week's discussion on race and class. The chapters in
Common Differences suggest that sexuality has been a prominent feature in White
feminist analysis and action, whereas it has been relatively unimportant among
Black women. But what groups are we contrasting: White feminists and Black
women? Why not White feminists and Black feminists? Or White women and Black
women? To say it another way, what is the relationship of White feminist analysis to White women as a group; what is the relationship of Black feminist analysis to Black women as a group? Who speaks for whom? We have to acknowledge
the enormous diversity in both groups of women, based on age, cohort, class,
work experience, to name only a few factors. Is it perhaps misguided to talk
in terms of Black women's sexuality as if it is totally distinctive and unique?

Putting aside for the moment the question of similarity/difference between
Black and White women, how can the conference be structured in such a way as to
not feel exclusionary? But whom do we want to include? Who usually comes to
the conference? In fact, we're not drawing from the entire universe of women,
but from a subgroup. This is so for White women attending the conference, who
might be described as a mix of mostly middle class academic feminists, intellectuals, and employed activists. We're not trying to plan a conference for
all White women, so it is unrealistic to try to address concerns of all Black
women (or to think we could). It is more realistic to think in terms of the
Black women who do usually participate and represent similar categories.

Returning to the question of similarity and difference, what is the nature
of the difference we think exists? Examples follow: "the Black community is
more homophobic than the White community." Counterexample: argument, rejection. Other examples follow and meet the same fate. Purported differences rest
on slim evidence, frail evidence, and are easily disputed. Can we believe there
are no differences? How could racism, powerful in structuring social relations
and social experience, fail to have an impact on sexuality? Or is it the ex-
pectation that Black women's sexuality is different itself racist, derivative
of characterizations of Black women as "exotic," "closer to nature," "more
sensual." Yet some Black women themselves assert a difference, as in Common
Differences. Yes, but that is on one level: the level of how you present
yourself in regard to sexuality. An important theme for Black women has been
"I'm hipper than you, more knowledgable." Yet that public stance is different,
or may be different, from actual experience and inner feelings. We're really
talking about different levels of sexuality which are confusing and hard to
name but would include your actual experience, and the cultural images and projections about your (and your group's) experience. The discussion about the
differences between Black and White women regarding sexuality has occurred on
the level of presentation of self and public style, yet there are other levels
which have not been discussed at all. Do we even have the information about
what's going on for Black and White women at these other levels?

Consider the level, perhaps we could call it "political culture," that is:
how can an issue be talked about in your community-at-large? What are the
terms of discussion? Who sets the terms? How is sexuality perceived to relate
to other political issues? There appears to be a difference at this level between Black and White political culture, for example, the debate in the Black
Scholar about Michelle Wallace's book and the relationship between Black men
and women. It was a passionate and painful debate which touched on how far

26

YOU, HERE WITH ME?   YOU? HERE?
YOU?? HERE??

(I KNOW WHAT SHE THINKS... ANIMAL LIKE, HOT, CAN'T GET ENOUGH...)

(UH-HUH, I KNOW SHE THINKS I'M COLD AS ICE, A NYMPHO, DON'T FEEL SEX, TELL MY ANALYST ABOUT IT..)

dissension could go before endangering unity. The political culture in which sexuality could be discussed was different for White feminists, although they labored mightily to change the terms of the discussion previously used by the White Left. We also need to consider how the political culture of talking about sexuality changed historically for various groups: in the nineteenth century Black women from some groups had a stake in asserting their purity and respectability, rather than sexual knowledgability.

The gross manner in which we talk about Black and White differences is not satisfactory. It provides no specificity regarding class, age, and historical experience, factors which may be more significant than race. We need to deepen our analysis by talking about class and race in a more detailed and specific way that permits examination of both similarity and differences. This task appears closely tied up with specifying the levels of sexuality, neither staying at one level exclusively, nor moving from one level to another without knowing and indicating the transition. There are many analogies to gay/straight comparisons. Perhaps the overall question we need to ask is: how do women (of specific class, race, sexual preference, age groups) negotiate sexual pleasure? The answer to this question requires information about every level of sexuality before comparisons between different groups of women can be made.

Here are three suggested schemes to distinguish levels: 1) Private and public or; 2) What to do in bed/self-identity/lifestyle and community or; 3) Sexual behavior/inner experience, fantasy, psychological level/presentation of self, how you articulate your experience, public style/images and

27

representations available in the culture/political culture/ideology.
    Our frustration with levels appears instantly: the arrangement of each list
does not imply that the first item is the bedrock, necessarily, or that the
first item is causal in determining later levels. There is an interaction between the levels, obviously. We also know that levels of analysis are at best
heuristic devices to help us organize and think about experience and that each
list embodies ideological premises which may or may not be true. Does our
awareness of the arbitrariness of levels of analysis stop us from using them,
equivalent to stopping us dead in our tracks? No. Yet, in terms of an audience, it is difficult to communicate our understanding that any list of levels
is arbitrary and subject to questioning and revision at the very same time we
are using a level-of-analysis scheme.
    We tentatively agreed that any presentation about race and class must
address the question of similarity, not only the question of difference, and
that it must do so by differentiating between levels of analysis. Gay/straight
issues probably should be addressed in the same way. We should anticipate that
many groups, previously invisible, have organized around difference to assert
their visibility and have an ideological stake in defending difference. We are
thinking of the conference as a subversive undertaking, causing participants to
question some of their understandings and consider the complexity of the sexual situation. Perhaps in some ways it might be thought of as a teach-in, although it needn't be called that; this term, however, suggests that we all are
beginning at a very initial point in sexual theory. So rather than provide the
28

"TALK ISN'T CHEAP.   "PERHAPS WE'DE
DO YOU SUPPOSE   BETTER LOCK
WE'RE ALONE?"   THE DOOR..."

READY?

"answers," the conference should indicate that the answers don't exist and assert the importance of asking questions.

How can the theme of the conference be carried through the afternoon workshops? We want to avoid people choosing their pet topical workshop and coming out with the same ideas with which they went in. Perhaps this could best be done by working closely with workshop leaders and communicating to them the larger themes of the conference. Each topical workshop will be a window into the general themes of the conference. We briefly talked about ways of closing the conference and reviewed strategies of previous conferences.

READINGS

Davidoff, Lenore. "Class and Gender in Victorian England: The Diaries of Arthur J. Munby and Hannah Cullwick." *Feminist Studies* 5, No. 1 (Spring 1979), pp. 86-141.

Dougherty, Molly. *Becoming a Woman in Rural Black Culture.* New York: Holt, Rinehart and Winston, 1976, Part 3, pp. 71-110.

Gribbs, Joan and Sara Bennett (compilers). *Top-Ranking: A Collection of Articles on Racism and Classism in the Lesbian Community.* New York: Feb. 3rd Press, 1980.

Jaget, Claude, ed. *Prostitutes: Our Life.* Bristol: Falling Wall Press, 1980, pp. 95-113.

Joseph, Gloria and Jill Lewis. "Styling, Profiling, and Pretending: The Games Before the Fall."*Common Differences: Conflicts in Black and White Feminist Perspectives.* New York: Anchor, 1981, pp. 178-230.

Ladner, Joyce. *Tomorrow's Tomorrow.* New York: Anchor, 1971.

Rainwater, Lee. "Some Aspects of Lower Class Sexual Behavior." *Journal of Social Issues* 22, No. 2 (1966), pp. 96-108.

Robinson, Paul. "Kinsey." *The Modernization of Sex.* New York: Harper and Row, 1976, pp. 86-104.

29

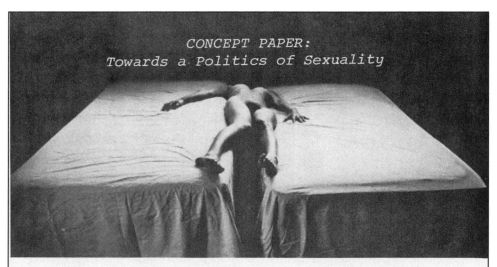

CONCEPT PAPER:
Towards a Politics of Sexuality

The ninth *The Scholar and the Feminist* conference will address women's
sexual pleasure, choice, and autonomy, acknowledging that sexuality is simultaneously a domain of restriction, repression, and danger as well as a domain of
exploration, pleasure, and agency. This dual focus is important, we think, for
to speak only of pleasure and gratification ignores the patriarchal structure
in which women act, yet to talk only of sexual violence and oppression ignores
women's experience with sexual agency and choice and unwittingly increases the
sexual terror and despair in which women live.

This moment is a critical one for feminists to reconsider our understanding
of sexuality and its political consequences. On the one hand, the feminist community has been engaged by intense discussion about sexuality. The debate has
moved from women's right to have sexual pleasure detached from reproduction to
sexual violence and victimization. Most recent issues include: the meaning and
effect of pornography; sexual safety versus sexual adventure; the significance
of sexual styles, for example, butch/femme; male and female sexual nature; and
politically correct and incorrect sexual positions. On the other hand, the
Right Wing attack on feminists' recent gains attempts to reinstate traditional
sexual arrangements and the inexorable link between reproduction and sexuality.
In doing so, the Right offers a comprehensive plan for sexual practice which
resonates in part with women's apprehension about immorality and sexual danger.
To respond convincingly, as feminists we cannot abandon our radical insights
into sexual theory and practice but must deepen and expand them, so that more
women are encouraged to identify and act in their sexual self-interest.

Behind feminist debates and the Right Wing's focus on sexuality, we think
are social and political changes wrought by capitalist transformations and the
women's movement during the 19th and 20th centuries, most notably the breakdown
in the traditional bargain women made, and were forced to make, with men: if
women were "good" (sexually circumspect), men would protect them; if they were
"bad," men would violate and punish them. As parties to this system, "good"
women had an interest in restraining male sexual impulse, a source of danger to

38

women, as well as their own sexuality which might incite men to act. Nineteenth
century feminists elaborated asexuality as an option for "good" women, using
female passionlessness and male sexual restraint to challenge male sexual pre-
rogatives and the characterization of women as intrinsically sexual. Recent
gains in the second wave of feminism call for increased sexual autonomy for women
and decreased male "protection," still within a patriarchal framework. Amid
this flux, women feel more visible and sexually vulnerable. The old bargain,
which opposed sexual safety and sexual freedom, is breaking down, but women's
fear of reprisal and punishment for sexual activity has not abated. For this
reason, the sexual problematic has commanded the attention of feminist theorists
in both centuries.

Feminist work on sexuality starts from the premise that sex is a social construction which articulates at many points with the economic, social, and political structures of the material world. Sex is not simply a "natural" fact. Although we can name specific physical actions (heterosexual or homosexual intercourse, masturbation) which occurred at various times and places, it is clear
that the social and personal meaning attached to these acts in terms of sexual
identity and sexual community has varied historically. In light of a wealth of
material, we restrict our analysis to 19th and 20th century America, while re-
taining the notion of historical and cultural construction of sexuality. Without denying the body, we note the body and its actions are understood according
to prevailing codes of meaning. Believing that biological sex is conditionable,
we return to the question "What do women want?"--a question we can entertain now
that it is *we* who are asking it.

Sexuality poses a challenge to feminist scholarship, since it is an intersection of the political, social, economic, historical, personal, and experiential, linking behavior and thought, fantasy and action. For the individual,
it is the intersection of past, current, and future experience in her own life.
That these domains intersect does not mean they are identical, as the danger of
developing a feminist sexual politics based on personal experience alone illustrates. We need sophisticated methodologies and analyses that permit the recognition of each discrete domain as well as their multiple intersections. Despite the many interrelationships of sexuality and gender, we do not believe
that sexuality is a sub-part of gender, a residual category, nor are theories of
gender fully adequate, at present, to account for sexuality.

Feminist work on sexuality confronts three problems: 1) multiple levels of
analysis, 2) limited data about women's experience, 3) overdeveloped theory, in
light of limited data.

1) We talk as if information about sexuality comes from a single source,
but in fact it comes from many sources: for example, sexual behavior and acts;
inner, psychological experience; the public presentation of our sexual selves;
sexual style; images and representations available in the culture; the place of
sexuality in the discourse of the political community to which we belong; sexual ideology. When we compare the sexual situation between and within groups of
women, it is important to remember that no conclusions can be drawn by comparing
only one layer of sexual information without considering the others.

Within feminism, we find it easier and more politically correct to talk
about sexual differences between women than sexual similarities. This is understandable, given our wish to acknowledge real diversity of experience and to insist on our visibility through difference from dominant groups, the same difference causing our long invisibility. We think it is important to simultaneously discuss women's similarities and differences, questioning whether the ac-

39

quisition of femininity and the conditions for its reproduction affect all women in a distinct way, cutting across sexual preference, sexual object, and specific behavior.

2) We base our theories on limited information about ourselves and, at best, a small number of other women. Given the complex grid of class, race, sexual preference, age, generation, and ethnicity, our personal experience can speak to but a small part of the sexual universe. Yet we wish to develop a framework inclusive of all women's experience. (Sexuality must not be a code word for heterosexuality, or women a code word for white women.) To do so we must make a renewed effort to talk with each other, agreeing to break the taboo that denies us access to information that lies beyond the boundaries of our lived sexual experience. Such is the only way to remedy our ignorance and avoid a sexual theory circumscribed by the boundaries of individual lives and idiosyncracies.

3) We find it easy to say publicly: "Women want...," "Women hate...," "Women are turned on by...," "Women are afraid of...," "Women like...." However, we find it excruciating to say publicly: "I want...," "I hate...," "I am turned on by...," "I am afraid of...," "I like...." Clearly, our hesitation to make the private and personal become public and potentially political has significant implications. Our theory, as it stands, is based on limited facts marshalled by overdeveloped preconceptions. It is also clear that any discussion of sexuality touches areas of unconscious conflict and fear. Feminists have been remiss in failing to address the power of unconscious sexual prohibitions and the appeal of primitive myths and metaphors about the Child, the Good Girl, the Man and the Family. Unarticulated, irrational reactions wreak havoc in our own movement and at the same time are cleverly used against us by the Right.

Sexuality is a bread and butter issue, not a luxury, not a frill. Women experience sexual pleasure and displeasure in their daily lives, even as women in different communities and different situations may articulate and organize around these experiences in different ways. Sexuality cannot wait until other, more "legitimate" issues are resolved. The division between socio-economic and sexual issues is false; we reaffirm their intimate connection in domesticity, reproductive politics, and the split between public and private, fantasy and action, male and female. We cannot postpone the consideration of sexual issues until after the "revolution." Such a tactic implies a belief in a natural, unfettered sexuality which will emerge after more basic issues of production and redistribution are resolved. Feminists who oppose the biologized woman or man cannot put their faith in a biologized sexuality.

We see the conference not as providing definitive answers, but as setting up a more useful framework within which feminist thought may proceed, an opportunity for participants to question some of their understandings and consider anew the complexity of the sexual situation. Our goal is to allow more information about the diversity of women's experiences to emerge. In morning papers and afternoon workshops, participants will consider the question: what is the status of sexual pleasure--in feminist theory and analysis and in the social world in which women live? and by so doing, inform and advance the current debate.

Much has been written about women giving and receiving pleasure; the conference is a step toward women taking pleasure and a contribution to envisioning a world which makes possible women's sexual autonomy and sexual choice.

January, 1982   Carole S. Vance
                                                             Academic Coordinator

40

OPENING SESSION 9:45—12:00

Moderator, Carole S. Vance

We've been wanting to write something together for a long time and are grateful to the conference for giving us the opportunity. It was both easier and harder to collaborate than we anticipated. Since we live in separate cities, we worked mostly by mail, taking turns redrafting the speech, which we did 5 1/2 times. The challenge of the topic was to balance the distanced and dialectical quality of historical analysis with our strong political and personal feelings about the issues and how feminism deals with them.

Linda Gordon and Ellen DuBois

It is every teacher's nightmare--an analogy on every writer's dream of death: Suppose I got up there and forgot everything, or worse, could think of nothing to say? What would happen?

In preparing my piece for "The Scholar and the Feminist IX" conference, I imagined just that, and every time I did I read another paragraph or stalked another book, or jumped up from whereever I sat or lay and scribbled another note. Fragments shored against a possible ruin is what it is! Truly, we strive as much in the name of a "good name" as we do for our ownselves. Here's hoping. When I read this again, in a different context, under other lights, my "twenty minutes," a perfect solitude before 10,000 others, in effect, will be over, or nearly. I won't know until then...

Hortense J. Spillers

I channeled my initial apprehensions about the conference into a quest for the perfect title to my talk. Music freak and DJ that I am, I conducted an unsuccessful mental search through my record collection hoping to locate that line which would say it all. As the deadline neared I dreamt up lots of titles and developed a special attachment to the following ones:

SAVING OURSELVES FOR THE REVOLUTION
WALKING AWAY FROM THE WILD SIDE
MOTHER KNOWS BEST?
THE WOMEN'S MOVEMENT GETS A HEADACHE

Alice Echols

42

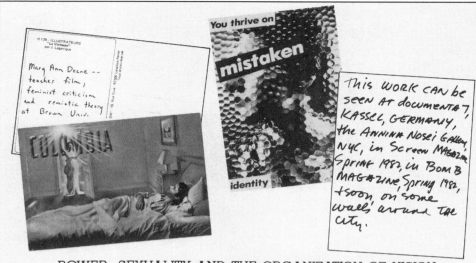

POWER, SEXUALITY AND THE ORGANIZATION OF VISION

A great deal of contemporary theory of film, representation, and processes of imaging has demonstrated how modes of looking are constructed along the lines of a sexual division. Classical systems of representation organize vision in sexual terms: the opposition male/female is aligned with those of subject of the gaze/object of the gaze and active/passive. Thus, the woman's relation to the camera and the scopic regime is quite different from that of the male. The cinema, for example, through its insistent inscription of scenarios of voyeurism, conceives of its spectator's viewing pleasure in terms of that of the Peeping Tom, behind the screen, reduplicating the spectator's position in relation to the woman as screen. Spectatorial desire is generally delineated as either voyeurism or fetishism, as precisely a pleasure in seeing what is prohibited in relation to the female body. This workshop will therefore explore both issues of the relation between the woman and the image and issues surrounding the possibility of female spectatorship. What happens when the woman appropriates the gaze? Can feminists use the visual in non-problematic ways or is the image so ideologically loaded that it can only be deconstructed?

Mary Ann Doane

Further, this workshop will investigate the dominant choreography of the image and consider the possibilities suggested by the removal of stereotype from the "natural." The preponderant definitions of sexual difference invade film, television, and the production of the art subculture. The notion of voyeurism and its attendant identifications structure the way in which we receive images. Perhaps we can begin to consider a practice which can interrupt the resonance of popular depictions with another definition of difference. My production, contextualized within the "art world," consists to some degree of replicating certain words and pictures and watching them stray from or coincide with the notions of fact and fiction. I am interested in the alternation between implicit and explicit, between inference and declaration. Thinking about assumption, disbelief and authority, I hope to strain the appearance of naturalism and to couple the ingratiation of wishful thinking with the criticality of "knowing better."

Barbara Kruger

SUGGESTED READINGS

de Lauretis, Teresa and Stephen Heath, eds. *The Cinematic Apparatus*. New York: St. Martin's Press, 1980.
Heath, Stephen. "Difference." *Screen*, Vol. 19, No. 3 (Autumn 1978), pp. 51–112.
Mayne, Judith. "The Woman at the Keyhole: Women's Cinema and Feminist Criticism." *New German Critique*, No. 23 (Spring/Summer 1981), pp. 27–43.
Mulvey, Laura. "Visual Pleasure and Narrative Cinema." *Screen*, Vol. 16, No. 3 (Autumn 1975), pp. 6–18.
44

DO WE WANT TO GET ON THE BUS?
OPTIONS FOR ORGANIZING AROUND REPRODUCTIVE RIGHTS

Noreen Connell was a member of New York Radical
Feminists (1971), went on to be a co-founder of
Women Office Workers (1975), became a president
of the N.Y. Chapter of N.O.W., and is now working
for Planned Parenthood of NYC. She will discuss
options avaiable in fighting the Right Wing
assault.

WE ARE EVERYWHERE

POLITICAL ORGANIZING AROUND SEXUAL ISSUES

The workshop will review and analyze efforts to organize for civil rights for lesbians and gay men in the United States. Factors leading to the Stonewall Rebellion (June 1969) in Greenwich Village which marked the beginning of the organized struggle for protection from discrimination will be examined. Post-Stonewall development of the lesbian/gay movement will be traced and compared to the development of other social change movements. Strategies for the future survival and growth of the lesbian/gay movement will be discussed.
Cheryl Adams

In less than five years the Right has utilized traditional patriarchal methods of political organizing to influence traditional patriarchal centers of political power, such as state legislatures and the U.S. Congress. The Right is now positioned not only to reverse the gains made by the feminist movement in the last decade, but to impose by force of law patriarchal values that have been eroded since the early sixties.

This has created a double dilemma for the feminist movement: (1) How can we fight back effectively and (2) Does being "effective" mean also utilizing traditional organizing methods directed at traditional centers of power?

The radical feminist movement has relied on education and consciousness raising as a means of organizing women to act in their sexual self-interest. Clearly this tactic is not sufficient to the current crisis. Consciousness raising and education must be viewed as only the first step in the process of political action.

In 1982 Congress may attempt to make abortion a capital crime. This gives little time, but extreme urgency, to the development of effective political action. This workshop leader will explore the options available.
Noreen Connell

"No More Nice Girls," a small pro-abortion action group, was formed early in 1981 by a group of New York feminists to draw attention to abortion rights as the cornerstone of women's sexual freedom. We've tried to dramatize the issue through a kind of street theatre, using strong, visual images to communicate our message. I will discuss the goals and tactics of "No More Nice Girls," describe our successes and failures, and talk about the importance of this kind of activism.
Brett Harvey

SUGGESTED READINGS

Abbott, Sidney and Barbara Love. *Sappho Was a Right-On Woman.* Stein and Day, 1973.
Booth, Heather. "Left with the Ballot Box." *Working Papers,* May/June 1981.
Ehrenreich, Barbara and Deirdre English. *Witches, Midwives and Nurses.* The Feminist Press, 1973.
Katz, Jonathan. *Gay American History.* Thomas Y. Crowell, Co., 1976.
Martin, Del and Phyllis Lyon. *Lesbian/Woman.* Bantam Books, 1972.
Stamm, Karen. "Strategies for Reproductive Rights." Newsletter of the Committee for Abortion Rights and Against Sterilization Abuse, March 1982.
Vida, Ginny, ed. *Our Right to Love.* Prentice-Hall, 1978.

46

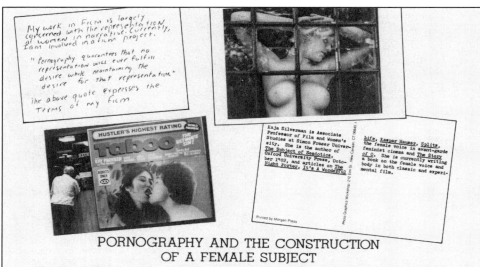

My work in Film is largely concerned with the representation of women in narrative. Currently, I am involved in a film project.

"Pornography guarantees that no representation will ever fulfill desire while maintaining the desire for that representation"

The above quote expresses the terms of my film

HUSTLER'S HIGHEST RATING

Taboo

Kaja Silverman is Associate Professor of Film and Women's Studies at Simon Fraser University. She is the author of The Subject of Semiotics, Oxford University Press, October 1982, and articles on The Night Porter, It's A Wonderful Life, Kaspar Hauser, Splits, the female voice in avant-garde feminist cinema and The Story of O. She is currently writing a book on the female voice and body in both classic and experimental film.

PORNOGRAPHY AND THE CONSTRUCTION OF A FEMALE SUBJECT

This workshop will situate pornography within the context of a number of other discourses which construct sexual difference and the female subject in similar ways, most notably advertising and dominant cinema. We will also argue that pornography cannot be isolated from a larger critique of the existing symbolic order, or from such seemingly diverse structures as the family or the church.

A number of current theories about pornography will be briefly summarized, and situated within the current debate about the female body. It will then be suggested that the pornographic discourse can best be read as a kind of allegory about how the female subject comes to maturity within a phallo-centric social order, and that its operations can help us to understand the operations of all of those other discourses which converge to produce what we currently call "woman."

We will propose that female subjectivity always begins with the zoning and inscription of the body; that "interiority" is an extension of that bodily organization; and that both of these operations—the mapping of the body and the articulation of a psychic economy—are the effect of discursive activities which often take quite concrete and material forms.

This workshop will suggest that there is a continuity from one dominant discourse to another, at least in so far as sexual difference is concerned. In other words, those discourses which make up the symbolic field overlap at the signifier "woman" so as to produce a stable and recognizable entity which seems both natural and eternal. That discursive matrix is determinative of the way in which women function not only sexually, but socially, economically and politically.

A brief theoretical investigation of these issues by Kaja Silverman will be followed by a screening of *Variety*, a super-8 film by Bette Gordon about a female ticket taker in a porno movie house. Gordon will expand upon the connection which her film establishes between pornography, advertising and Hollywood cinema either before or after the screening. The workshop will then be opened to a general discussion.

Bette Gordon and Kaja Silverman

SUGGESTED READINGS

Brown, Beverly. "A Feminist Interest in Pornography: Some Modest Proposals." *m/f*, No. 5/6 (1981), pp. 5–18.
Brown, Beverly and Parveen Adams. "The Feminine Body and Feminist Politics." *m/f*, No. 3 (1979), pp. 35–50.
Foucault, Michel. *The History of Sexuality*. Translated by Robert Hurley. New York: Pantheon Books, 1978.
Heath, Stephen. "Difference." *Screen*, Vol. 19, No. 3 (1978), pp. 51–112.
Pajaczkowska, Claire. "The Heterosexual Presumption: A Contribution to the Debate on Pornography." *Screen*, Vol. 2 (1981), pp. 79–94.
Siles, Peter. "Pornographic Space: The Other Place." *Film: Historical—Theoretical Speculations*, 1977 Film Studies Annual: Part 2. Pleasantville, New York: Docent Corporation.

47

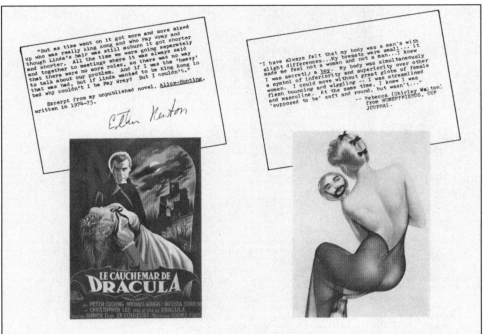

"But as time went on it got more and more mixed up who was really King Kong and who Fay Wray and though Linda's hair was still auburn it got shorter and shorter. All the time we were going separately and together to meetings where it was always said that there were no more roles, so there was no way to talk about our problem. And if I be King Kong in bed why couldn't I be Fay Wray? But I couldn't."

Excerpt from my unpublished novel, Alice-Hunting, written in 1974-75.

Esther Newton

"I have always felt that my body was a man's with slight differences...My breasts were small...it made me feel not a woman and not a man...I knew I was secretly a boy. My body was simultaneously a symbol of inferiority and superiority over other women. I could move without great globs of female flesh bouncing and wiggling -- I was streamlined and masculine. At the same time, I knew I was 'supposed to be' soft and round, but wasn't..."
-- Rebecca (Shirley Walton) from WOMENFRIENDS, OUR JOURNAL.

LE CAUCHEMAR DE DRACULA

with PETER CUSHING · MICHAEL GOUGH · MELISSA STRIBLING · CHRISTOPHER LEE dans le rôle de DRACULA
une HAMMER Film EN COULEURS - Réalisation TERENCE FISHER

BEYOND THE GAY/STRAIGHT SPLIT: DO SEXUAL "ROLES" (BUTCH/FEMME) TRANSCEND SEXUAL PREFERENCE?

Shirley Walton and Esther Newton have been friends for almost a quarter of a century. They began a joint journal in 1970 after each entered the Women's Movement. Published in 1976, *Womenfriends* is an exploration of similarities and differences between the two and how these affected the ongoing friendship. At the time, one was married and pregnant, while the other was just coming out publicly as a lesbian.

After years of living with the differences and remaining close friends, the two have just begun to discuss their sexuality more openly and specifically. The unspoken assumption was that Esther was "butch" while Shirley, because she is heterosexual, was "femme." But now it appears that each is most comfortable "initiating" and "orchestrating" sexual interactions. Does this mean that both are "butch?" If so, why does Esther play this out with women and Shirley with men? How and why do homo- and heterosexuality complicate, frustrate or facilitiate sexual desire and power?

The workshop will attempt to open up the Pandora's Box of sexual styles, attitudes and roles banished from the Feminist Movement as "politically incorrect." Esther and Shirley propose that these styles should be examined and lived. Discussion will be opened up to participants in and effort to develop a more precise language for our sexuality, using butch/femme as a starting point.

Shirley Walton and Esther Newton

SUGGESTED READINGS

Hollibaugh, Amber and Cherrie Moraga. "What We're Rollin Around in Bed With." *Heresies Sex Issue* #12 (1981).
"The Lesbian/Heterosexual Split." *Maenad*, Vol. 2, No. 2 (Winter 1982).
Nestle, Joan. "Butch-Fem Relationships." *Heresies Sex Issue* #12 (1981).
Walton, Shirley and Esther Newton. *Womenfriends*. New York: Friends Press, 1976.

THE SCARLET LETTER

THE DEFENSE OF
SEXUAL RESTRICTION BY ANTI-ABORTION ACTIVISTS

In the last ten years, the controversy over a woman's right to abortion has emerged as a critical issue dividing American women. The battle has made public the existence of competing ideologies regarding the control of female sexual activity. The debate also reveals that sexuality, generally consigned to the so-called "private sphere," cannot be separated from the position(s) women hold in the larger social order. What are the conditions that have made abortion so powerful and divisive as a rallying symbol in our culture at this historical moment? Who are the women fighting for sexual restriction and what interests are they defending?

In discussing these issues, I will be using research material I am collecting in a study of anti-abortion activists in a small city in the upper Midwest, Fargo, North Dakota, where the recent opening of an abortion clinic has catalyzed intense local activity on both sides of the debate. I undertook this research because I think that feminists cannot afford to write off "pro-life" women as villains or victims without first-hand knowledge of the circumstances that shape their worldview. The objective of my work and this workshop is to understand the consciousness and social and historical conditions which lead women in our society to defend the inevitability of motherhood as women's primary role.

As part of my presentation, I will be showing segments from a documentary on pro-life women that I am working on.   Faye Ginsburg

Having spent the last nine years setting up and managing abortion services in non-metropolitan areas of the United States (Fort Wayne, Indiana; Columbus, Georgia; and Fargo, North Dakota), I have not only had to study anti-abortion activists, but also listen to them and learn from them. Our clinics have run the course from emotional public hearings of 500 people or more in tiny city halls, to bomb threats and bomb evacuations, to marches on the facilities by angry mobs. Always I have marvelled at the intensity of the anti-abortion activists' commitment, and wondered why it was there. Is it a religious or moral value? Or is it even more deep-seated than that? I have concluded and will discuss that many anti-abortion activists view abortion with what I term a "scarlet-letter syndrome," a feeling so deep many press for guilt and punishment for sexual activity with an intensity that they exhibit in almost no other part of their lives.   Susan Hill

SUGGESTED READINGS

Eisenstein, Zillah. "Antifeminism in the Politics and Election of 1980." *Feminist Studies*, Vol. 7, No. 2 (Summer 1981), pp. 187–205.
Gordon, Linda. *Woman's Body, Woman's Right: A Social History of Birth Control in America*. New York: Penguin, 1977.
Harding, Susan. "Family Reform Movements: Recent Feminism and Its Opposition." *Feminist Studies*, Vol. 7, No. 1 (Spring 1981), pp. 57–75.
Mohr, James C. *Abortion in America*. New York: Oxford University Press, 1978.
Petchesky, Rosalind P. "Antiabortion, Antifeminism and the Rise of the New Right." *Feminist Studies*, Vol. 7, No. 2 (Summer 1981), pp. 206–246.

BEYOND POLITICS:
UNDERSTANDING THE SEXUALITY OF INFANCY AND CHILDHOOD

Today my chosen term is "education for sexuality," meaning education for being a sexual person. I use this rather than the archaic and meaningless term "sex education."

Human beings are distinct from all other mammals in: the capacity to stand upright, leaving the hands free (for carrying and other activities); the capacity to communicate with words including all the functions of the human mind; and the capacity for separation of sex-for-pleasure and sex-for-reproduction, which means that human sexuality is unique to humans as part of a bonding relationship.

Every infant begins with an unknowable number of possibilities for her/his own sexual evolution. From the moment of birth, the person cannot be prevented from becoming and being sexual throughout life. As the person develops, her/his sexuality at any given moment is the result of the cumulative congenital, environmental and interpersonal influences—and of the sexual experiences and sexual information which the person has experienced up to that moment.

By puberty, when the capacity to reproduce begins, the body, mind and sexuality of the child should all three *have been* developed in such a way that the child has full information about others as well as about himself or herself as sexual beings, knows that he or she is in charge of that self, and understands and accepts the nature and realities of sexual pleasure and how to manage it responsibly. All of this is necessary in order to ready the child to accept the responsibilities that should go with the inevitable and important relationships of intimacy that will be formed with other adolescents.   Mary S. Calderone

It is very difficult to imagine the sexual emancipation of children without coming to understand how necessary are the other relevant forms of emancipation: economic, legal and social. Not only their emancipation but ours—for the guilt and shame imposed upon children for sexuality has been imposed upon us, even as we impose it again, a new generation perpetuating the wrongs of the past. All that was imposed on us is with us still, the wounds of our childhoods a slow cancer eating us through life. There is no end to it unless we make one. Not until the nineteenth century was any outcry made even against the brutalization of children. It continues in every parent who strikes a child. Terror, bullying, pain and injustice are all things we learn before the age of reason, before reading and writing, decades before any hope of redress.

As it now stands children are forbidden sexual experience with themselves, each other or adults. Yet at the same time, they are treated as a sexual resource by adults. The conditions now, children having no rights or autonomy, nearly preclude any sexual relationships between children and adults which is not exploitative. The natural realm of expression of sexuality in children and youth is with each other, with peers and not with those who belong to a class which dominate them, and however well intentioned, can hardly refrain from abuse of one kind or another. There is, in short, a great deal of sexual politics frustrating the sexual expression of children and the young. You and I will live to see this discussed, almost for the first time in history. Considering that we were all children once, and if we are very good, we're children still—we all have a stake in this. The emancipation of children is our emancipation in retrospect, and that of the future as well.   Kate Millett

59

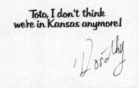
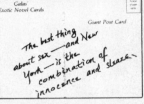

Toto, I don't think we're in Kansas anymore!

Dorothy

Galas' Exotic Novel Cards

Giant Post Card

The best thing about sex — and New York — is the combination of innocence and sleaze.

"Butch-fem was an erotic partnership, serving both as a conspicuous flag of rebellion and as an intimate exploration of women's sexuality."

Heresies Sex Issue 12

I came out in the powerful Lesbian subculture of the 1950's as a working class fem.

POLITICALLY CORRECT, POLITICALLY INCORRECT SEXUALITY

Dorothy Allison, currently a member of the editorial staff of *Conditions*, has interrupted her studies in anthropology at the Graduate Faculty of the New School For Social Research to concentrate on her writing. For the past three years she has been working on an ethnography of the female-dominant s/m subculture in New York City. Her work emphasizes both the political nature of commonly held concepts of gender and deviance, and the class bias which dominates sexual theory in both academic and feminist communities.

Dorothy Allison

Is the idea of "Politically Correct/Politically Incorrect Sexuality" valuable? Does it polarize or does it unify? Does it engender change, or does it doom us to repeat the subjective and historical past? Does it answer, or beg, the question of how the personal and the political are connected?

Feminism is a struggle for sexual liberation. I hope this workshop can, in confronting these questions, advance us along the road toward savoring the ambiguity at the heart of all sexual experience.

Muriel Dimen

"Society and the Bedroom: Third World Women's Perspectives on the Politics of Sexuality." Paper by Mirtha N. Quintanales.

A critique of current feminist debates regarding the nature of women's sexuality, women's sexual oppression and the meaning of women's sexual freedom.

Mirtha N. Quintanales

"The fem part of Butch-Fem sexuality—a dramatic monologue starting in the fifties and raising questions about the seventies. An exploration of fem lust, love and power."

Joan Nestle

SUGGESTED READINGS

Acker, Kathy. *Kathy Goes to Haiti.*
Allison, Dorothy. "Erotic Blasphemy." *The New York Native* #26 (December 7, 1981).
Buffalo Lesbian Oral History Project. Work of Avra Michelson, Liz Kennedy and Madeline Davis. Working papers at Lesbian Herstory Archives. Will appear as a book.
Colette. Anything.
Griffin, Susan. *Woman and Nature.*
Lorde, Audre. "Age, Race, Class and Sexuality: Women Re-defining Different." Lesbian-Feminist Clearinghouse, 1980.
Michelson, Avra. "Some Thoughts Towards Developing a Theory of Roles." Unpublished paper, 1979. At LHA.
Nestle, Joan. "Esther's Story." *Common Lives/Lesbian Lives* #1 (1981), pp. 3–9.
Nestle, Joan. "My Mother Liked to Fuck." *Womannews,* February 1982.
Moraga, Chérrie and Gloria Anzaldua, eds. *This Bridge Called My Back.* Massachusetts: Persephone Press, 1981.
Quintanales, Mirtha N. and Barbara Kerr. "On Difference and the Complexity of Desire." *Conditions* #8 (1982).
Smith, Barbara and Lorraine Bethel, eds. *Conditions* #5: Black Women's Issue, 1979.
Rubin, Gayle. "The Leather Menace: Comments on Politics and S/M." *Coming to Power.* San Francisco: SAMOIS, 1981.

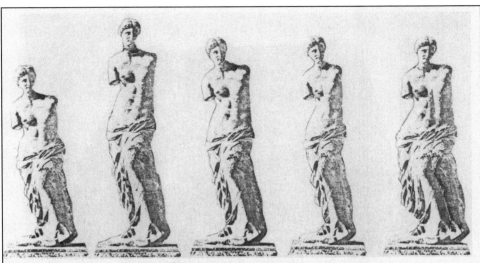

THE MYTH OF THE PERFECT BODY:
AGE, WEIGHT, AND DISABILITY

The myth of the perfect body oppresses all women. Through the perfection of our bodies we are expected to earn power, love and self-esteem. Since all of us obviously have "imperfect" bodies, we may regard ourselves and other women as damaged, worthless, contemptible and unlovable. As fat women, disabled women and aging women, we each face some unique stereotypes and sources of oppression, especially in the area of sexuality.

The body of a fat woman is frequently the object of ridicule, scorn and contempt. She is seldom seen as a suitable sexual partner. She, herself, may be unable to distinguish her sexuality from her shame. The fat woman is driven by the hope that if only she could lose weight and have the "perfect" body, then her self would be perfect and worthy of love.

The aging woman's body is sexually taboo. It sags, wrinkles, greys, aches and can no longer bear children. With her menopause, she is expected to lose her capacity for passion, fantasy and orgasm. Such oppressive myths lead to the sexual isolation of the aging woman. She is the woman we shall become. Our own fears of aging cause us to shun her.

The disabled woman's body is not "perfect" in either image, form or function. She is not regarded as a woman at all but as a helpless, dependent child. She is the sexless object—asexual, neutered, unbeautiful, and unable to find a lover. Even when idealized for surmounting obstacles, she receives a distancing admiration, rather than sexual desire, intimacy, or love. Anxiety, identification and dread may cause others to respond to the imperfections of a disabled woman's body with terror, avoidance, pity and/or guilt. We may wish her to remain invisible and to keep her sexuality a secret.

Women equate lack of "perfection" with lack of entitlement to sexual life. Society's standards of beauty are embedded in our initial interactions with parents, caretakers and health practitioners as they handle our bodies. In this way, external standards become internal realities. Too frequently our own bodies become our enemies.

Even in our attempts to create alternatives, we develop standards which oppress some of us. The feminist ideal of autonomy does not take into account the realistic needs for help that disabled, aging, and most women have.

This workshop will attempt to raise consciousness about what we have perceived and experienced to be the unacceptability of our female bodies. Together we must become able to live and love in our "imperfect" bodies.   Roberta Galler and Carol Munter

63

SEXUAL PURITY: MAINTAINING CLASS AND RACE BOUNDARIES

During much of the 19th century, "good" women were encouraged to maintain their sexual purity by denying their bodies. Today, "good" women can achieve some degree of sexual pleasure within prescribed limits. They are expected to choose partners similar to themselves: members of the same class and race. An improper choice suggests that a woman's sexuality must have taken on a sinister quality or that it has somehow gotten out of control. This aberrant sexuality accounts for a woman's failure to choose someone more suitable, more like herself. Women who pursue sexual pleasure with individuals beyond these boundaries—the Ph.D. with the auto repairman, the factory worker with the corporate executive, the Black with the White—risk disapproval and loss of status. Thus, it is likely that women who do cross these boundaries often keep it a secret; while other women hesitate, even if they feel it may lead to sexual pleasure.

The workshop will examine the meaning of these boundaries in women's lives and the impact of maintaining or crossing these boundaries on women's sexuality. This exploration would deepen and broaden our understanding of one of the many ways women are kept in their "place" and the effect it has on attaining sexual pleasure.   Diane Harriford

65

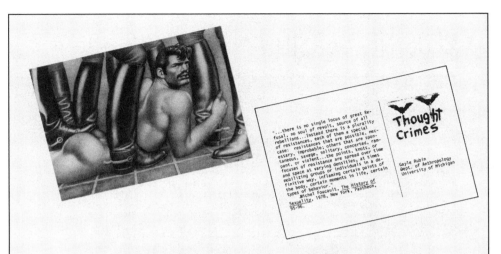

"...there is no single locus of great Refusal, no soul of revolt, source of all
rebellions...Instead there is a plurality
of resistances, each of them a special
case: resistances that are possible, necessary, improbable; others that are spon-
taneous, savage, solitary, concerted, ram-
pant, or violent ...the points, knots, or
focuses of resistance are spread over time
and space at varying densities, at times
mobilizing groups or individuals in a definitive way, inflaming certain points of
the body, certain moments in life, certain
types of behavior."
Michel Foucault, The History of
Sexuality, 1978, New York, Pantheon,
95-96.

Thought
Crimes

Gayle Rubin
Dept. of Anthropology
University of Michigan

CONCEPTS FOR A RADICAL POLITICS OF SEX

The social relations of sexuality have always been as political as the social relations of class, race, gender, and ethnicity. However, at certain periods of time, in certain societies, the organization of sexual behavior is more actively contested, and in arenas more visible and centrally located. Since 1977, in the United States and in much of the western capitalist world, sexuality has become the locus of intense, focused, and bitter political struggle. A generation of political activists, veterans of the 1960's and 1970's, have been taken by surprise by attempts to reimpose tighter standards of sexual morality.

There has been a lack of conceptual tools with which to record, analyze, and position the events of the many discrete battles in the new sex wars. Many radicals have assumed that the body of feminist theory contained the necessary concepts. But feminist analysis was developed to describe and criticize oppression based on gender. While sexual experience is affected by the social relations of gender, sexuality is nevertheless not the same thing as gender. Just as gender oppression cannot be understood by an analysis of class relations, no matter how exhaustive, sexual oppression cannot be conceptualized by way of an understanding of gender relations, no matter how complete.

We need to develop an analytical apparatus specifically engineered to see, describe, and criticize sexual oppression. This workshop will propose some elements of a radical political theory of sex. The agenda for building such a body of thought about sexuality would include the following items: (1) It is essential to learn, albeit critically, the existing body of knowledge about sexuality. Sexological work contains useful empirical information, as well as material from which some of the structures of erotic oppression can be inferred. (2) It is important to get rid of the idea of sex as an asocial or transhistorical biological entity. (3) The persistence of the western (and especially Anglo-American) idea of sex as a destructive force needs to be explored. (4) The idea that there is a single kind of "good" sex that is "best" for everyone needs to be criticized. (5) Above all, we need to understand that there is systematic and serious mistreatment of people based on sexual behavior. Oppression generated out of sexuality is just as real, unjust, and barbarous as are the oppressions of class, race, gender, and ethnicity.   Gayle Rubin

SUGGESTED READINGS

Califia, Pat. Sapphistry. Tallahassee, Florida: Naiad Press, 1980.
English, Deirdre, Amber Hollibaugh and Gayle Rubin. "Talking Sex." Socialist Review, July–August 1981, pp. 43–62.
Foucault, Michel. The History of Sexuality. New York: Pantheon, 1978.
Gagnon, John. Human Sexualities. Glenview, Illinois: Scott, Foresman and Co., 1977.
Samois. Coming To Power. San Francisco, California: Samois, 1981.
Walkowitz, Judith. Prostitution and Victorian Society. New York: Cambridge University Press, 1980.
Weeks, Jeffrey. Coming Out. New York: Quartet Books, 1977.
66

CLOSING SESSION   3:30—4:30

Dear Diary,

   They've asked me to speak at Barnard. My ghosts stand up and scream.
Somewhere i still harbor a belief that "The Politics of Sexuality" is a cover
i use to hide a continual obsession with sex. Wrap it in fancy words, hold it
in an upper class academy, give it a scholarly title but my desires have smells
and textures which are often at odds with feminist orthodoxy.

   I have to talk about passion in the future. But will there be a future
after Reagan? Will there be sexual difference after feminism? It's an iffy
race... Lesbian/old gay/a femme... Will our political theories hold a place
for women like me in the future? Maybe i'll be an odd piece of history/old
dinosaur bones that women in the future find facinating and bizarre.

   The conference gave me Esther. My desire today has a body, a pulse, a
start. That's how we all enter a dialogue with passion in the future.
Amber Hollibaugh

                    ✯ hattie gossett ✯

born:	central jersey factorytown
lives:	northern reaches of harlem
enjoys:	thinking conversating reading writing jazzing
	and acting out against all the bigdaddies
work herstory:	(partial) babysitter maid clerk annullee cleaning
	person waitress badgirl
n.b:	stay tuned to badgirls grapevine for news of forthcoming
	collection of writings by miz hattie

"i was born into this life the child of houseniggahs and i been struggling
trying to get home ever since."

But what of passion? I hunger
to ask women whose
desire I can almost taste
like milk on the edge of the lip
rich in a kind of deep
sweetness opening the circle
of her lips on the edge
of curling up on me
going sour. © *Cherrié Moraga, 1982.*

   Usually, when I'm selecting poems for a reading, I line a lot of possible
poems up in piles -- a small pile of mother poems, one of war poems, then poems
about the kids, city poems, father poems, and off to the side a big heaping
stack of love poems. Then I take one or two from each pile, to create the
appearance of balance: "O.K., a mother, a sex, a war, a sex, a father, a city,
a son, a sex." What a pleasure for me at Barnard today not to do that balancing
act, but to go directly to this most rich powerful mysterious and wonderful
subject. **Sharon Olds**
68

I have an oblique (perhaps slightly remote) take on the process set in motion by the planning meetings and that will soon culminate in the conference as an _event_. Looking back I find fragmentary but coherent recollections: of the initial struggle to find the words through which to speak (of) women's sexuality within the (mother) institution; the gaps to be bridged in language as a pre-condition to an intersection of discourses; the penultimate silence of the private in the face of an invitation (a summons?) to go public. _NKMiller_

9:50 A.M.   MONDAY, APRIL 12 — ON TWO HOURS SLEEP
DEAR DIARY,
     HERE'S HOPING YOU LOOK AS GOOD ON PAPER AS YOU DO NOW ON BOARDS. BEST OF LUCK ON YOUR JOURNEY THROUGH THE PRINTING PRESS! (PERSONALLY I THINK YOU CAN PULL IT OFF...)
                              LOVE MARYBETH

EXPLORED THE DREAM OF MY GIRLS AND

FOUND THE GIRL OF MY DREAMS.

                    Thanks to the Planning Committee,
                              Esther Newton

Dear Diary,
     Scholar and Feminist IX...meetings and meetings, planning for nine conferences, coordinating number one, still involved in the evolutionary process of scholar _and_ feminist conferences....Gradual, hesitant participation———efforts at linking, clear disagreement, not comprehending....What is sexuality anyhow?! Struggle to grasp complexity, to examine definitions, to remap thinking....Pensive, reflective, working to digest, working at understanding the explorations of others, celebrating silently the diversity, praising common bonding and ..... all leading to a day where we risk to explore openly a range of thinking about sexuality..... Excitement, challenge, exchange.

"We are thinking about the conference as a sub- versive undertaking" Nov. 10 '81

...further note from the Barnard Conf. Comm — but study group has been in B.R.d.

71

Fragments from my commonplace book--

"these pleasures which we lightly call physical"
Colette, The Ripening Seed.

"love, which, sexual or non-sexual, is hard work"
George Orwell, "Reflections on Gandhi."
--Quandra Prettyman Stadler

The Scholar and the Feminist IX planning committee met steadily from September 1981 to April 1982, during which time we reaffirmed that the most important sexual organ in humans is located between the ears.

Carole S. Vance

Dear Barbara,
    I just came back from a planning committee for the Barnard Conference. They are doing sexuality this year. You'll love it. It should be a very exciting event: a coming out party for feminists who have been appalled by the intellectual dishonesty and dreariness of the anti-pornography movement. I am the conservative on the committee. I mean, I understand the advanced position on porn, on s and m, but I can't understand the argument for pederasty! Ellen says its because I am a mother.
                                                        Love,
                                                        Judy

For me the planning committee meetings had a compelling, politically urgent quality, I hadn't experienced in a long time — maybe not since the early years of the women's liberation movement. I believe that as the sexuality debate goes, so goes feminism. The tendency of some feminists to regard women purely as sexual victims rather than sexual subjects, and to define the movement's goal as controlling male sexuality rather than demanding women's freedom to lead active sexual lives, reinforces women's oppression and plays into the hands of the new right. It is a dead end, a politics of despair. Feminism is a vision of active freedom, of fulfilled desires, or it is nothing. In these meetings we have been concerned with preserving and extending such a vision. Given the current social atmosphere, this is a radical act! *Ellen Willis*

Ode to an Herbivore

Orange and grave,
Trembling beneath
Chicory and queen's lace
I smile for
Your mild embrace.
My grassy top
Splits in the wind,
Flicking fragrance
To rabbits and
Flirting with
Herds of brown
Cows. Will I flower
At death?
Come then, gnaw me
Toward heaven.

Patsy Yaeger

THE TIME HAS COME TO THINK ABOUT GAYLE RUBIN

Susan Stryker

*M*ost readers of these pages are long familiar with Gayle Rubin's fierce intellect, passion, and astounding depth and range of knowledge. Those as yet unfamiliar with her work and influence should prepare for a memorable encounter with a woman branded by the conservative cultural critic David Horowitz as one of the "101 most dangerous academics in America."[1]

When Heather Love invited me to introduce Rubin's keynote address at "Rethinking Sex," a state-of-the-field conference on sexuality studies held at the University of Pennsylvania, March 4, 2009, in honor of Rubin's foundational contributions, I thought it would be prudent to refresh my memory of her two landmark articles: "The Traffic in Women" and "Thinking Sex," neither of which I had read recently.[2] In "The Traffic in Women," Rubin begins to develop her thoughts on the processes through which female humans are transformed into oppressed women by citing Karl Marx's observation that a cotton-spinning jenny is merely a machine for spinning cotton that "becomes *capital* only in certain relations. Torn from these relationships it is no more capital than gold is itself money or sugar is the price of sugar." Likewise, Rubin contends, substituting "woman" for "spinning jenny," a woman "only becomes a domestic, a wife, a chattel, a playboy bunny, a prostitute, or a human Dictaphone in certain relations. Torn from these relationships she is no more the helpmate of man than gold in itself is money . . . etc."[3] On turning my attention to "Thinking Sex," it struck me that there could be no more fitting words of tribute—no better way to demonstrate the extent to which Rubin's name has become synonymous with a certain kind of critically engaged, politically radical analysis of sexuality—than to imitate her own rhetorical strategy in "The Traffic in Women" by substituting her name, Gayle Rubin, for the words *sex* or *sexuality* in the opening paragraph of "Thinking Sex."

GLQ 17:1
DOI 10.1215/10642684-2010-017
© 2010 by Duke University Press

And so, if I may, here I present that first paragraph with its metonymic substitution, as I delivered it at "Rethinking Sex":

> The time has come to think about *Gayle Rubin*. To some, *Gayle Rubin* may seem to be an unimportant topic, a frivolous diversion from more critical problems of poverty, war, disease, racism, famine, or nuclear annihilation. But it is precisely at times such as these, when people live with the possibility of unthinkable destruction, that people are likely to become dangerously crazy about *Gayle Rubin*. Contemporary conflicts over *Gayle Rubin*'s values and erotic conduct have much in common with the religious disputes of earlier centuries. They acquire immense symbolic weight. Disputes over *Gayle Rubin*'s behavior often become the vehicles for displacing social anxieties and discharging their attendant emotional intensity. Consequently, *Gayle Rubin* should be treated with special respect in times of great social stress.[4]

It was my great honor that night to treat Gayle Rubin with the special respect she so richly deserves. I first met Gayle more than twenty years ago, in 1989, on the back patio at the Eagle, a gay leather bar in San Francisco, at an event she had helped organize — The Beat Jesse Helms Flog-A-Thon — which was a fund-raiser for the Democratic politician Harvey Gantt's sadly unsuccessful bid to unseat North Carolina's infamously racist and homophobic senior senator. I was a green little newcomer to the radical sexuality scene — a twenty-something grad student who, rather precariously, had one foot in the ivory tower at the University of California, Berkeley, and the other foot in the dungeons and drag bars of San Francisco. I was happy as a pig in a poke that night at the Eagle, wallowing in what was for me at the time a truly revelatory excess of politically progressive pervert power, when I found myself in an animated conversation with some leather dyke who seemed about ten years my senior, who had the charming remnants of a Carolinian accent, and who really seemed to know a lot about industrial and goth music. When it slowly dawned on me that I was talking to the Flog-A-Thon co-organizer, *the* Gayle Rubin, famous sex radical, founding figure of San Francisco's women's BDSM community, who had known Michel Foucault personally, I was more than a little starstruck.

Two decades later I'm still a little starstruck, and consider Gayle the most important role model for my own career, which, like Gayle's, has skirted the margins of academe before ultimately finding a place within it. I came out as transgender in 1991, just as I was finishing up my dissertation on the history of religion in antebellum New England. Actually, to be more precise, I came out as a lesbian-identified transsexual sadomasochist who was working on the history of the Mormons — and (surprise!) immediately felt the doors of academic employment quickly closing before me as I started my social transition from man to woman.

I know — what was I thinking? Honestly, I was thinking this: "If Gayle Rubin can produce a substantive body of critical and intellectual work, one that's explicitly grounded in her own bodily acts, desires, and identifications, and if she can do that while working on the edgy fringes of the academy where theory and practice meet, rather than producing safer and more palatable forms of disciplinary knowledge, if she can take precisely those ways of being in the world that marginalize her and instructively and productively dismantle them, and if she can do that and eventually land a job without apologizing for who she is and what she does — if Gayle can do all of that for kinky sex, then maybe, just maybe, I might be able to follow her example and do something similar for transgender people." That's what I set out to do in 1991, largely because Gayle's pioneering example made it seem possible to attempt such a thing.

I know that personally I owe Gayle Rubin a large measure of credit for whatever success I have had over the years in moving toward the goal of establishing transgender studies as a recognized academic specialization. Gayle has been a mentor and an inspiration, as I know she has been for so many other people. She first steered me toward the GLBT Historical Society in San Francisco, which was my intellectual home for many years, and where I found a community of independent scholars such as herself, Alan Bérubé, and Willie Walker. She invited me to join reading groups that helped shape my thinking. She wrote the letters of recommendation that eventually landed me postdoctoral positions and professorships, and she's shown me innumerable other kindnesses — so I was pleased to be able to express my gratitude in such a public forum as the 2009 conference in her honor at the University of Pennsylvania and am pleased to offer them again, here in the pages of *GLQ*.

But I would be remiss if I did not also acknowledge Rubin's formative intellectual influence in helping sharpen the critique transgender studies would make of existing scholarship, quite apart from her significance for me personally. At the 1982 Barnard Sex Conference, Rubin and the other "sex-positive" feminists ably demonstrated that *feminism* was too large a mantle to be claimed exclusively by any one faction of feminist thought. In arguing that consensual sadomasochism, pornography, and sex work could be framed as feminist practices, they forged the main lines of argument against a moralistic feminist orthodoxy that transgender scholars would continue to advance in the 1990s. Since trannies were lumped in with all the other perverts and outcasts from a good-girl feminism that considered trans folks to be either bad, sick, or wrong in our self-knowledges, it only behooved us to follow in the path of the powerful sisters who were talking back with such sass and eloquence in the face of feminist censure.

While it is certainly true that transgender scholarship in the early 1990s was necessarily on one side of the "sex wars" and not the other, just because we who were beginning to articulate that scholarship knew who our friends were didn't mean we always agreed with their assessment of us. Sex-positive, protoqueer feminism sometimes made the mistake of regarding transgender merely as an erotic practice rather than as something potentially more expansive, as an expression of self or a mode of embodiment that could not be reduced simply to sexuality any more than *woman* could. Rubin herself, for example, in charting what she called a "moral sex hierarchy" in her article "Thinking Sex," listed transsexuality and cross-dressing as examples of sexuality clearly labeled as "bad" within dominant discourse, without seeming to recognize that this was a reductive sexualization of entire genres of personhood.

One main goal of Rubin's article, of course, was to challenge the way that some schools of feminism established hierarchies that placed their own perspective above all others and claimed the power to judge and condemn everything else as morally suspect. She went on to note how early second-wave feminism floundered when it tried to apply the concept of class to the category woman and succeeded only when it developed an analytic specific to gender-based oppression. It followed, then, that feminism, as the study of gender, was likewise an insufficient frame of reference for nonnormative sexuality and that a new "sexuality studies" was called for that needn't abandon feminism any more than feminism needed to abandon political economy. Enacting those same discursive maneuvers to "rethink sex," transgender studies argued in turn that it addressed problematics of embodiment, identity, and desire not readily reducible to sexuality, problematics that eluded full capture by the concept of queerness. Rubin did not resist this miming of the movement of her thought; she was, rather, an enthusiastic participant in the conversations that reframed influential elements of her own earlier work.

For that generosity of mind and spirit, I am personally grateful, and I know the same is true for countless others in myriad ways. If I may be so bold as to use these pages on behalf of all of us whom Gayle Rubin has helped, in one way or another, I would like to express our collective gratitude. Rubin shaped the field of sexuality studies and planted seeds for future developments not only through her keen scholarship but also through the many scholars she's nurtured, encouraged, and cheered on. Simply put, she's a mensch—thank you, Gayle.

Notes

1. David Horowitz, *The Professors: The 101 Most Dangerous Academics in America* (Washington, DC: Regnery, 2006), 307–11.

2. Gayle Rubin, "The Traffic in Women: Notes on the 'Political Economy' of Sex," in *Towards an Anthropology of Women*, ed. Rayna R. Reiter (New York: Monthly Review Press, 1975), 157–210; Rubin, "Thinking Sex: Notes for a Radical Theory of the Politics of Sexuality," in *The Lesbian and Gay Studies Reader*, ed. Henry Abelove, Michèle Aina Barale, and David M. Halperin (New York: Routledge, 1993), 3–44.

3. Rubin, "Traffic in Women," 158. The quotation from Marx is from *Wage-Labor and Capital*, trans. J. L. Joynes (New York: International, 1971), 28.

4. Cf. Rubin, "Thinking Sex," 3–4.

THINKING SEX ETHNOGRAPHICALLY

Steven Epstein

$\mathcal{T}$he time has come to think about sex," Gayle Rubin wrote in 1984, at the outset of her famous essay dedicated to that endeavor.[1] While it is perhaps not surprising that such an injunction remains equally in order today, it is highly unusual for any particular essay to retain its intellectual and cultural salience over a quarter century. Such staying power is all the more rare for an essay written so conspicuously as an intervention *in the moment* and that is chock-full of topical references to the charged political context of the late 1970s and early 1980s — the Dade County "Save Our Children" campaign, the Family Protection Act, the Boston Public Library arrests, antiporn feminism, the emergent panic over the new epidemic of AIDS. One can point to exceptions, but most essays that engage so vigorously with the day's headlines suffer the curse of a shortened shelf life.

To be sure, there are several obvious reasons why "Thinking Sex" has proven so usefully anomalous in its longevity. Rubin's insistence that sexuality constitutes a relatively autonomous vector of oppression, one that intersects with, but is not reducible to, gender or any other axis of difference, continues to be a crucial interdisciplinary touchstone. "Thinking Sex" also retains its spark of freshness as a teaching tool. I think many can attest to the essay's sheer practical usefulness in getting undergraduates to analyze the meanings that adhere to sexuality in our society, the structures in place to enforce arbitrary boundaries, hierarchies, and exclusions, and the damage that such enforcement often does to individuals and to sexual communities. Rubin's persuasive rhetoric and clever turns of phrase — the "fallacy of misplaced scale" or the "hierarchical system of sexual value," with its "charmed circle" and its "outer limits" — lend themselves to effective classroom teaching, even if other really good phrases, like the "domino theory of sexual peril," now demand digressions to explain to students for whom

GLQ 17:1
DOI 10.1215/10642684-2010-018
© 2010 by Duke University Press

the Vietnam era is ancient history just what the domino theory originally entailed (278–82). If nothing else, "Thinking Sex" forces students to acknowledge their own latent biases and question the confidence with which individuals and institutions routinely "draw the line," dividing the universe of sexual practices into the "acceptable" and the "unacceptable."

One might further account for the continuing relevance of "Thinking Sex" by pointing to the enduring character of the threat to sexual openness that Rubin documented and analyzed, however much her examples reflected the time period in which she was writing. Of course, some things *have* changed in a quarter century. It is, for example, no longer the case that "a single act of consensual but illicit sex, such as placing one's lips upon the genitalia of an enthusiastic partner, is punished in many states with more severity than rape, battery, or murder" (288). Yet much of the persecution of sexual diversity that Rubin described is still very much present (as Rubin has reminded us in subsequent writing), as is the cultural logic by which "sex is presumed guilty until proven innocent" (278). At a moment of war and economic crisis, it may also be useful to recall Rubin's warning that it is especially in times of great social stress that sex is most likely to become the target of displaced social anxieties (267).

At a more subtle level, I would suggest that "Thinking Sex" became anointed as a classic because of how it took the insights of empirical studies of sexuality — particularly, historically informed ethnography — and drew out their intellectual and political implications in a way that facilitated an astonishingly interdisciplinary engagement. A perusal of Google Scholar, which lists more than one thousand books and articles that have cited the various reprintings of "Thinking Sex," convincingly establishes that the essay has become common intellectual property across the humanities and social sciences, from psychology to cultural studies to geography to philosophy to a perhaps thoroughly transdisciplinary queer studies. What uses have scholars made of this essay? It has been referenced in articles and books on topics ranging from hate crimes to daytime talk shows, lesbian teachers to queer ecofeminism, sex education to polyamory, sex addiction to gay/straight friendships. The sites of sexual conduct that Rubin's article has illuminated include masculinity in a Portuguese town, prostitution and pornography in Australia, heterosexism in Belfast, romance in *Seventeen* magazine, paraphilias in the *Diagnostic and Statistical Manual*, children's safety in cyberspace, difference from Virginia Woolf to Jeanette Winterson, social policy and mental illness in England, and Cuban and Puerto Rican gay masculinities in Miami (to name a few).

Thus "Thinking Sex" has become what the science studies scholars Susan

Leigh Star and James Griesemer call a "boundary object": something that bridges social worlds by virtue of being "both plastic enough to adapt to local needs and the constraints of the several parties employing [it], yet robust enough to maintain a common identity across sites."[2] Or perhaps it's Rubin herself who has become the boundary object, with many different kinds of readers finding different Gayle Rubins in these pages: the theorist, the activist, the polemicist, the sex radical, and so on. My point, however, is to emphasize yet another Rubin: the engaged and reflexive anthropologist caught up in empirical study of the lived realities of sexual experience and sexual community.

Rubin's anthropologist chops are not especially on display in "Thinking Sex." But I would argue that it matters that this essay was written by someone who has been committed to the close ethnographic study of how people live out their sexual desires and explore their sexual freedoms in real time. It has become commonplace to analyze sexuality as something produced and normatively regulated through discourse and representation, and certainly "Thinking Sex" offers important clues about how to pursue such an analysis. However, part of what Rubin has given social scientists (as well as ethnographically minded humanists) is a model of how to link discourse and representation to the domain of practice as enacted within the lived worlds of erotic communities that are marked by their own rituals, politics, institutions, and spatial configurations.

Schooled in the interactionist sociology of visionaries such as John Gagnon and William Simon, who, in the 1970s, sought to understand sexual interaction as meaningful, scripted behavior, and sensitive to the pioneering work of historians who depicted the radical otherness of sexualities past, Rubin became one of the first to (as she later described it) "contemplate doing ethnographic work on sexual communities in urban North America at a time when such projects were outside the accepted parameters of anthropological research."[3] Her study of San Francisco gay male leather culture, "with its singular concatenation of desires, experiences, and symbolisms," has called attention to the fine details of community organization and cultural and sexual rituals, the elaborate coding of urban space, the bitter politics of urban redevelopment, the histories of emergence and disappearance of subcultures, and the social pathways for the production of moral panic and sexual scapegoating.[4]

The historically minded, ethnographic sensibility that fuels Rubin's fieldwork also undergirds "Thinking Sex," surfacing explicitly from time to time as Rubin considers the history of erotic underworlds as well as the campaigns waged to wipe them out (270–71, 295–97). Her schooling in the empirical social sciences is likewise reflected in her commitment to describing how abstract representations of sexuality are grounded in the organization of concrete social institutions — most notably, the law, the constrictive and destructive functions of which are so well described in "Thinking Sex." Of course, the Gayle Rubin I am depicting here is no "truer" or more authentic than any of the other Rubins who have been laid claim to by other readers of "Thinking Sex." But this intellectual heritage and set of commitments is a crucial part of what has allowed her work to serve as such an enduring model of politically engaged and socially situated theory, analysis, and critique.

Notes

1.   Gayle S. Rubin, "Thinking Sex: Notes for a Radical Theory of the Politics of Sexuality," in *Pleasure and Danger: Exploring Female Sexuality*, ed. Carole S. Vance (Boston: Routledge and Kegan Paul, 1984), 267–319. Hereafter cited by page number.

2.   Susan Leigh Star and James R. Griesemer, "Institutional Ecology, 'Translations,' and Boundary Objects: Amateurs and Professionals in Berkeley's Museum of Vertebrate Zoology, 1907–39," *Social Studies of Science* 19 (1989): 393.

3.   Gayle S. Rubin, "Studying Sexual Subcultures: Excavating the Ethnography of Gay Communities in Urban North America," in *Out in Theory: The Emergence of Lesbian and Gay Anthropology*, ed. Ellen Lewin and William L. Leap (Urbana: University of Illinois Press, 2002), 53.

4.   Gayle S. Rubin, "Elegy for the Valley of Kings: AIDS and the Leather Community in San Francisco, 1981–1996," in *In Changing Times: Gay Men and Lesbians Encounter HIV/AIDS*, ed. Martin P. Levine, Peter M. Nardi, and John H. Gagnon (Chicago: University of Chicago Press, 1997), 104. Gayle S. Rubin, "The Miracle Mile: South of Market and Gay Male Leather, 1962–1997," in *Reclaiming San Francisco: History, Politics, Culture*, ed. James Brook, Chris Carlsson, and Nancy Joyce Peters (San Francisco: City Lights Books, 1998), 247–72; Rubin, "Sites, Settlements, and Urban Sex," in *Archaeologies of Sexuality*, ed. Robert A. Schmidt and Barbara L. Voss (New York: Routledge, 2000), 62–88.

THE "BEACHED WHALE"

Sharon P. Holland

Remember the past, but look to the future and above all treasure the
moment, for it will soon be gone.
—Gayle Rubin, "Blood under the Bridge"

$\mathcal{I}$n the middle of lifting belly, Gertrude Stein paused to consider (perhaps) the
making of Americans.[1] Lesbians, as a species of "queer," have been thinking sex
and writing sex for quite some time, so Gayle Rubin's 1984 piece should not have
surprised us very much—or at all.[2] But in many ways it did. If anything, Rubin's
piece was as much a new direction for sexuality studies as it was a response to
growing conservatism on the feminist left. Since Rubin's 1984 accounting is
already a historical approach, her essay notes the major shifts taking place in a
post–World War II era that made it increasingly possible for the state to think of
"family" in direct opposition to queer being. The historical trajectory for regulating sexuality outlined by Rubin is actually a utilization of the historical arc proposed by Michel Foucault in his groundbreaking work on sexuality. By giving sexuality a *history*—there used to be a time when we would say herstory and mean
it—Foucault created a narrative of its genesis in modernity, and that genealogy
has sustained queer studies work throughout the latter half of the twentieth century. These connections are important ones, but my question would be what other
historic events in the Americas would cause "sexuality" to ultimately matter to us?
The time has come to rethink our historical trajectory for sex(uality studies).

Imagine a world wherein some bodies are accessible to others 24/7—open
in a way that helped define, articulate, and defend the category of the human. In
this world, what would sexuality mean? What would be its practice? How would
we recognize it? My point here is a simple one: we understand bodies in sexuality through a regulatory regime that has the ability to punish some citizens for
nonconformity, to put it mildly, and to order sexual practice. But what becomes of

GLQ 17:1
DOI 10.1215/10642684-2010-019
© 2010 by Duke University Press

this body when stripped of its mooring to the "human"—what happens when this body is chattel—when it opens (itself?) up for fair use? And what would thinking about this body in one way for an extended period of time, say twelve generations or more, do for a people? Who would they become? And most importantly, what would their predilections be?

These are the questions about "the (queer) body" that have intrigued me for years. In this sense, the work here is very much in the spirit of Thomas Jefferson's little anecdotal section ("Manners") in *Notes on the State of Virginia*. I am very much of the opinion that the psychic life of being together in a certain way is learned as much as it is part of our cultural inheritance. When we say emotional baggage, let's mean it in a different way this time. Every time I read or teach canonical queer studies texts like Rubin or Foucault, I worry about these questions because I think that they have serious bearing on the shape, scope, and meaning of queer studies today. They shape what we say, how we say it, and who we see or center when we say "queer." As queer folk, we are constantly thinking about what being "hidden from history" might look like, and our writerly attempts are efforts to somehow alter the course of a future (something to "look forward to") without us.

These and other questions led me to return to think about one exchange during the question and answer period of Rubin's opening address at the "Rethinking Sex" conference. The exchange is rather brief, but interesting:

Audience Member: This is a historical question. Since I was too young to know about this stuff. . . . You gave a great recap of the feminist sex wars for those of us who weren't around. I am wondering if you can talk a bit about the relationship of the emergence of black feminism at the time to the feminist sex wars, because that's always been fuzzy to me. As all of this stuff at Barnard was going on, what was the relationship of Audre Lorde and Barbara Smith . . . were those movements in conversation with each other at all, or were they happening separately?

Gayle Rubin: I don't think it's a consistent relationship. There are other people who probably would know more about that than I. But certainly black feminism was emerging long before any of this happened, and the Combahee Collective document was printed in 1975 at least, maybe earlier, and the sex wars didn't really happen 'til later. And some black feminists were supporting the antiporn position and some were not. It's not a consistent relationship as far as I know. Certainly the antiporn people argued that pornography . . . one of their criticisms was they argued that pornography was inherently racist and particularly racist in various ways. That was a controversial claim, although there was certainly racism—there was plenty of racism in pornography, but whether it was more racist than say, the rest of society, was an arguable point.

I have a feeling that the gentleman who requested information about the presence of black feminism among us, so to speak, did not come away with a satisfying answer. In fact the entity called "black feminism"—a phrase coined during the era of identity politics—represents a particular politic that does not fit the present demands for sexuality studies' attention to global/transnational concerns or calls for a more "queer of color" critique. In other words, while the separate but equal call for our own self-determination led to an academic field called "black feminist criticism," contemporary calls for a realignment and subsequent sharing of theoretical grounding between a waning black feminism and a nascent queer studies seem to pull us in the other direction.

    At this point, what can an appeal to "history" do for us? The conference exchange that I reference above is grounded in a "historical question," and history takes us to a very familiar place—a story about a social movement for queer equality that had its discrete/discreet groups. Once black feminism can be cited in a discretionary vacuum, we no longer have the luxury of thinking about its issues as part of the effective terrain of queer studies—it will always be something that queer studies/sexuality studies refers to in order to have it perform its discretionary self. The connotation of the word *discretionary* is intended—something that can be "used as wanted." The work of identity politics backfires, as the discrete group becomes a free labor pool all over again; it pays attention to the racial (other) for the larger group, thus performing labor it not only *does not want to do* but also has believed it is experientially *incapable of doing*. A very odd situation, indeed, since one body is deemed more experientially fit to produce an inquiry that is, at its heart, intellectual rather than located in any one experience. I do not doubt that my parsing here will provoke scholars who have dedicated their intellectual endeavors to thinking through the relationship between the experiential and the intellectual. Feminist scholars from Joan Scott to Linda Alcoff have attempted to marshal "experience" for a postmodernist lexicon and had varying degrees of success with each endeavor. I am wholly sympathetic to that body of scholarship (black feminist critique, postpositive realist critique among others—both of them engaged in critical race theory) that tries to put experience *first*, that attempts to make experience matter to everyday discourse. What happens in the real market of academic ideas is that these attempts at discretion have been interpreted as discrete and therefore *unconnected*. What we get is a queer of color critique or a black feminist critique that constantly knocks on the back door of an over-whelmingly disinterested queer studies. And we also get queer studies following a historical trajectory that has failed to see itself as embedded in the messiness of sexual practices that predate the postwar period. To visualize this ordering, I turn to the collection of essays in which "Thinking Sex" is embedded to prove a worrisome point: that this structure of belonging in the emerging sexuality studies canon is still being replicated in our attention to the matter of black feminism. In *Pleasure and Danger*, Rubin's seminal piece is one among many and as such is not the only essay that attempts to chart a historical trajectory for the terrain of sexu-ality. In particular, "Interstices: A Small Drama of Words" is Hortense Spillers's failed attempt to rescue the black female body from a suspect feminist studies and deliver her into the arms of a fickle lover called sexuality studies. Untethered from history, black women, for Spillers, are "awaiting *their* verb" (74). Spillers is right to forecast an unforeseeable future for the black female body in sexuality studies. What does it really mean to await your "verb" — what does it mean to be "vestibu-lar" to culture? While Spillers's reclamation of the black female is for the culture at large, I don't think that when folks utter the words *black feminist/ism* they are thinking anything but *discretely*. Black females matter, but they do not matter to all of us. One could say that the difference between "Thinking Sex" and "Interstices" is one of critical disciplines and genres — Spillers works in a primarily psycho-analytic mode while Rubin opts for a grounding in new historicism. Consequently, it could be argued that the disciplinary boundary here is relatively nonporous. The regulation of the queer body nevertheless occurs against the backdrop of *some his-torical moment*, and it has been puzzling to me how queer scholars and theorists have treated the nearly three hundred years of chattel slavery in the Americas as a historical vacuum unworthy of sexuality's theorizing. To *whom* does this his-tory belong? How can the slavocracy's regulatory regime of sexual violence and pleasure, public and private, be missed? If we were to look at this more closely in the literature, this particular history's belonging is sutured to black being, and as such ontologizes black subjectivity — animates it to receive its object, and perhaps its *verb*. If these questions are necessarily disciplinarily bound, what becomes of sexuality studies' interdisciplinary mode?

But I digress. *Pleasure and Danger* is a text that, true to the 1980's for-mula for multicultural diversity, matches racialized bodies in their appropriate discursive universe — black folk talk about black things, Chicanas speak to the mestiza, and all is right with the emerging paradigm shift where white folks tend to speak for the discipline, disciplining in turn. Or do they? Perhaps by look-ing back through both essays it might be possible to trace when and where we

break out of this paradigm. In "Thinking Sex" when Rubin refers to "black" subjects, we enter a comparative neverland: the afterlife of her discursive intervention
or the thing that stretches queer life to its tragic limit. In one instance, Rubin
reiterates the fear of sexual backsliding in 1968 by recalling that antigay forces
feared the spread of information about sex would expose "white people (especially
white women) to the alleged 'lower' sexual standards of black people" (273). In
yet another, she hypothesizes that "the system of sexual oppression cuts across
other modes of social inequality . . . a rich, white male pervert will generally be
less affected than a poor, black, female pervert" (293). In each instance, the black
body stands as the thing against which the survival of whiteness must pit itself or
as the exemplar par excellence of social inequality. There is an implied history in
these examples, but no *historical record* proffered.

When the black subject does get a historical location, we learn what "gay"
really means. Rubin writes:

> The spectacular success of gay entrepreneurs in creating a variegated gay
> economy has altered the quality of life within the gay ghetto. . . . but it is
> important to recall what happened to similar miracles. The growth of the
> black population in New York in the early part of the twentieth century
> led to the Harlem Renaissance, but that period of creativity was doused
> by the Depression. The relative prosperity and cultural florescence of the
> gay ghetto may be equally fragile. Like blacks who fled the South for the
> metropolitan North, homosexuals may have merely traded rural problems
> for urban ones. (296)

Clearly a *history* of the Harlem Renaissance does not intersect with or stand in for
a gay *history*. History has a very discretionary boundary indeed. For the most part,
we have decided to drop the "like Black" (like "race") arguments on the queer
left, and Rubin cannot be faulted at all for thinking through a lens of difference
as if it were an *apartheid*; she and other "white" subjects had been through the
vanguard debates of the late 1970s that raged well into the end of the twentieth
century and had quickly learned the principle of damned if you do, damned if
you don't. I do not produce this critique to have us understand Rubin's contribution as backward or undertheorized—it is still one of the most important pieces
on sexuality in the interdisciplinary canon. What I am interested in is how the
early scholarship has helped frame the black female body as both exception and
rule, and in turn, how our understanding in the present tense does not do much
to override the rigidity of this patterned approach. In essence, I too have been

"*Re*-thinking Sex." Rubin speaks about "race" at several junctures, but it does not matter until it acquires a body we can believe in. Whiteness can have race all it wants, but we have to believe in this particular kind of embodiment *for it* in order for "race" theory to work.

In "Interstices," Spillers offers that "the relative absence of African American women/feminists, in and out of the academic community . . . is itself an example of the radically divergent historical situations that intersect with feminism" (74). It is not new to us that U.S. history is not one history but the histories of many peoples. When we treat these histories as intertwined, we find that the perceived historical record stands corrected. When we establish these histories as discrete entities, we run up against the problem of having our cake and eating it, too. This problem of discretion still nips at the edges of queer critique. How do we build a queer history whose margins do not automatically serve as border crossings? How can we get the whole to speak to its parts? As if in answer to this question, Spillers writes:

> *history* has divided the empire of women against itself. As a result, black American women project in their thinking about the female circumstance and their own discourse concerning it an apparently divergent view from feminist thinking on the issues. I am not comfortable with the "black-woman/feminist" opposition that this argument apparently cannot avoid.
>
> Feminist discourse can risk greater truth by examining *its profoundest symbolic assumptions*, by inquiring into the herstory of American women with a sharpened integrity of thought and feeling. (79, 80; emphasis mine)

My assessment of Rubin examines the *symbolic assumptions* that allow for a *dichotomized* racial scene to unfold. Spillers ends her essay with the following: "The goal is not an articulating of sexuality so much as it is a global restoration and dispersal of power. In such an act of restoration, sexuality becomes one of several active predicates. So much depends on it." One definition of a predicate is something affirmed or denied about something else — in fact Spillers' reliance upon the word *predicate* here is perfect, since its primary definition is, well, subject avoidant, while the service it can render seems endless. It can be everywhere and nowhere at once. Her wordplay reminds us that what is at stake is a slippery subject rather than a fixed one, but whiteness is fixed to the object so readily that what is "yellow, brown, black, and red" (96) hardly matters. I see Spillers's goal as two-fold here: to alert us about the wrong turn that sexuality studies is about to make and to avoid the problem of seeing such a term as remedied by a single substitution of "black" for white, and so on. The question at hand might be better handled if, as I have argued, we begin to think about the place of "history" in our theoretical trajectories.

Have we really reached an "integrity of thought and feeling" that is called for here? Can a history of the Americas during/under "slavery" ever be a queer history? I think the question is at least worth asking, if not contemplating.[3] Perhaps this is the appropriate moment to step out of the safety of history's closet once and for all.

Notes

My title is from Hortense Spillers's "Interstices: A Small Drama of Words," published at the same time as Rubin's "Thinking Sex: Notes for a Radical Theory of the Politics of Sexuality," in *Pleasure and Danger: Exploring Female Sexuality*, ed. Carole S. Vance (Boston: Routledge and Kegan Paul, 1984), 267–319. Both cited hereafter by page number. The epigraph is from the original version of Rubin's address to the "Rethinking Sex" conference at the University of Pennsylvania, March 4–6, 2009.

1. In *The Autobiography of Alice B. Toklas*, Stein informs us that *Tender Buttons* was conceived of while she was writing *The Making of Americans*, between 1907 and 1914. See Gertrude Stein, *The Autobiography of Alice B. Toklas* (New York: Vintage, 1990).

2. I am riffing off of Rubin's use of Foucault early in her essay. She writes: "The nineteenth-century homosexual became a personage, a past, a case history and a childhood, in addition to being a type of life, a life form, and a morphology, with an indiscrete anatomy and possibly a mysterious physiology. . . . the homosexual was now a *species*" ("Thinking Sex," 284).

3. My own work-in-progress on this question, "The Erotic Life of Racism," attempts to figure out this discretionary turn. "The Erotic Life of Racism" (under consideration at Duke University Press) bridges the gap between critical race and queer theory in order to fine tune understandings of queer theory's several and not very successful attempts to account for "race" in its short historical arc. Critical race theory is seen as attending to racism and racist practice, while queer theory is often viewed as dealing with the vicissitudes of autonomous desire. One of the major considerations of the text is the relegation of "black" experience to a certain kind of history, so that when black.female.queer becomes legible in queer theorizing, it is always in some familiar historical frame of reference. Moreover, the manuscript tries to argue that "the erotic"—a category that queer has harnessed for its exploration of a materialist and psychoanalytic autonomy of desire—does have its connection to racist practice.

THINKING SEX WITH AN ANDROGYNE

Joanne Meyerowitz

*M*ore than twenty-five years ago, when I first read Gayle Rubin's groundbreaking essay "Thinking Sex," it reshaped how I (and others) approached sexuality and gender. In a critical intervention, Rubin asked us to move beyond feminist theories of gender and treat sexuality as its own category of analysis. If feminism offered ways to analyze women's subjugation, if Marxism helped explain the oppression of the working class, then what body of literature, Rubin asked, might we turn to for understanding the subordination of various sexual dissidents? Feminism could address the social hierarchy of male over female, but it could not sufficiently account for the social hierarchies that placed heterosexual over homosexual, sadomasochist, fetishist, and so on. It was this insight that helped push many of us to separate gender and sexuality, and it also nudged us away from a homosexual-heterosexual binary. Rubin insisted on the multiplicity of "sexual dissidents" and in that way spelled out a central tenet of what was soon to be queer studies.[1]

About a dozen years later, in the course of historical research, I read the strange book *Autobiography of an Androgyne*, by the pseudonymous Earl Lind.[2] Published in 1918, the book, it seems, had little impact in its day. (In one of the few brief acknowledgments of the book's publication, in the *American Journal of Psychology*, the reviewer made the surprising admission that he or she had not even read the book.)[3] But Lind's *Autobiography* has come back to haunt us. In 1975, at the height of the gay liberation movement and at the start of its recuperative history project, Arno Press reprinted the book as part of its series Homosexuality: Lesbians and Gay Men in Society, History and Literature. And in 2008 it reappeared again, with an excellent introduction by Scott Herring, published by Rutgers University Press in its series Subterranean Lives: Chronicles of Alternative America. In its various incarnations—and in Lind's historical morph from

GLQ 17:1
DOI 10.1215/10642684-2010-020

androgyne to gay man to subterranean—the book serves as an open invitation to think sex, think gender, and complicate the categories of analysis we often take for granted today.

In the paragraphs that follow, I attempt to put Rubin's "Thinking Sex" in dialogue with Lind's book. Rooted in different historical moments, their works address distinct debates about the nature, politics, and ethics of sexual variance. Their analytic endeavors, like all analytic endeavors, bear the traces of the circuitous conversations, quirky encounters, and changing discourses in which they each engaged. Taken together, they remind us that our varied attempts to describe and explain gender and sexuality—to define them, knit them together, and tug them apart—have a complex history shaped and stamped by the particular contexts in which they evolved.

A Curious Text

In its 1918 first edition, *Autobiography of an Androgyne* had the trappings of a scientific tract. The publisher, the *Medico-Legal Journal*, announced on the copyright page that it intended the book solely for the professional class: its relatively small print run of one thousand copies would be "sold only, by mail order, to physicians, lawyers, legislators, psychologists, and sociologists." The book's introduction, written by the physician Albert W. Herzog, the journal's editor, duly mentioned Sigmund Freud, Richard von Krafft-Ebing, and a handful of other sexological experts, and promoted the book as "a psychological study, well worthy of a careful analysis."[4] Despite the cover of science, though, the book is not exactly a scholarly tome. It combines the conventions of early twentieth-century sexology with over-the-top confessional narrative, picaresque adventure, and sensational pornographic detail. The author, who calls himself Earl Lind, proclaims himself an "androgyne," "fairie," "effeminate man," and "invert," who has a female brain or mind in a mostly (but not entirely) male body. He (and I use the masculine pronoun because he claims to have lived his life primarily as a man and chose the pseudonym "Earl" for the authorial persona) explains his condition as innate, unfortunate, and pitiable but beyond his will to change, and then enlivens his story with extended accounts of his sexual exploits.

In his own telling, Lind spends most of his days living the seemingly uneventful life of a college-educated, native-born Protestant, middle-class white man, a deeply religious scholar with aspirations to missionary work, but he also leads a secret "double life," compelled by strong sexual longings—irresistible cravings to perform fellatio—that torment and distract him. In the late nineteenth century he becomes a flaneur, wandering at night through the poorer neighborhoods of New York City, dressed as a down-at-the-heels man, but with a distinctive fairy style — red bow tie, white gloves — and the assumed street names of Ralph Werther and Jennie June. This is a classic "slumming" narrative told by a class and ethnic outsider. In the story Lind pursues rough young men, mainly the native-born sons of Irish, Italian, and Jewish immigrants, and he also shows a special fondness for soldiers, sailors, and other men in uniform. And he goes into great detail about his sex life, resorting to Latin phrases when the English might seem vulgar or obscene. Over a dozen years, Lind claims to have engaged in around sixteen hundred sexual encounters — mostly fellatio — with around eight hundred different men. He regales the reader with stories of these encounters, and also with disturbing tales of brutal beatings, robberies, and gang rapes. Eventually Lind has himself castrated at age twenty-eight, partly, he says, because he thinks it will improve his health, partly because he finds his sexual behavior disturbing, and partly because he detests his facial hair, a sign of masculinity that he thinks castration will erase.

The book has something for almost everyone in contemporary queer studies. It works well, for example, with recent studies of affect, especially shame. Lind expresses self-loathing, humiliation, remorse, and melancholia, and uses the word *shame* repeatedly throughout the text. He conjoins the "feeling backward," though, with evident pride in his privileged class position, his religiosity and ethical standards, and also his ability to attract young men and satisfy them sexually.[5] And there is masochism. Lind frequently tells his sexual partners that he longs to be their slave, and when sexually abused, he revels in "the savagery and the beauty of my tormentors."[6] And there is armchair travel and social geography, with walking tours of lowbrow dives, sporting life, and daily doings in slums and barracks. And there is scholarship for those readers who prefer their historical texts to take the high road. Lind refers to sexual and gender variance found not only in the medical literature of his day but in zoology, anthropology, and history as well. And there is political activism. Lind calls directly for an end to prejudice against inverts and the laws that made it illegal for fairies to have sexual relations with men.

Given its ample appeal, it should come as no surprise that *Autobiography of an Androgyne* has cropped up in several recent works of scholarship. In the past twenty years, the book has made its way into a few histories, especially gay histories, as an example of New York homosexual life, early gay politics, the science of homosexuality, and the role of the fairy.[7] More recently it appears in a couple of studies (my own included) as a brief example of late nineteenth-century and early twentieth-century gender variance.[8] If one chooses to trace genealogies, this book fits easily into histories of sexuality and homosexuality, and it works nicely with histories of gender transgression, cross-gender identification, and transgender politics. *Autobiography of an Androgyne* has also played a part in a few works of recent literary criticism, for example, Anne Herrmann's *Queering the Moderns*, where it serves as an example of modernist auto-ethnography.[9]

Rethinking Gender

In her article "Thinking Sex," Gayle Rubin carefully and consciously grounded her work in a particular historical context, the early 1980s United States, with the rise of the New Right, the HIV/AIDS pandemic, and the feminist sex wars. At that moment, gender lay in the province of feminism, while sexuality, as Rubin requested, peeled off in a new direction. "Feminism," Rubin wrote, "is the theory of gender oppression" and not necessarily "the theory of sexual oppression."[10] But if in the late 1980s and 1990s we began to "think sex" in new ways, we began to "think gender" in new ways as well. More than twenty-five years later feminism is not the only theory of, or political approach to, gender oppression. Lind's *Autobiography of an Androgyne* is without a doubt antifeminist. In 1918, at the very height of the women's suffrage movement, Lind shows no interest in women's rights, status, or equality. *Au contraire.* "I have always felt," he writes, "that a woman should adore her husband so much as to delight in being treated as a slave, and to suffer gladly any abuse by her lord."[11] Men are strong, women are weak. Men dominate, women submit. Feminism can help us read these starkly essentialist constructions, but it cannot explain Lind's gender transgression or political stance.

In the past two decades, our studies of gender have construed it in ways that 1980s feminism did not. That is, at least from Judith Butler's *Gender Trouble* on, we have turned our attention to somewhat different frames of gender analysis and gender activism.[12] I refer here not just to gender performativity but also to transgender studies, which has changed how we construct gender studies as well as queer studies. The feminist version of gender generally uses masculinity and femininity to address what the historian Joan Scott called the "persistent inequalities between women and men."[13] For Scott and others, gender has worked to shore up those persistent inequalities and has also served as a model or metaphor that legitimated and naturalized other forms of social hierarchy. While feminism itself has changed substantially since the 1980s, it nonetheless remains, by definition (and for good political reasons), centrally concerned with social justice for women. A different version of gender, though, directs us more concertedly to the people who have transgressed the normative, including Lind. This version of gender studies overlaps with, borrows from, complements, and sometimes embraces feminism, but it does not center on justice for women or even on the binary language in which female is the inferior opposite of male. The hierarchy here is not male over female but one in which gender-normative people (feminine women and masculine men) are accorded privileges denied to gender transgressors. This version of gender studies focuses on the training and constraining of both masculinity and femininity more than on the subordination of women. This "New Gender Politics" has "complex relations to feminist and queer theory," but it is not identical to them.[14] As Lind's book attests, the more obvious activism here is not a protest against the subjugation of women but a call for the end to the policing of, brutality toward, and stigma associated with nonnormative gender performance.

In the context of the early 1980s, Rubin understandably found that feminism provides a theory of gender but not of sexuality. We might now say that feminism alone does not fully theorize gender either. Neither feminism nor gay liberation (especially in their 1970s and 1980s identity-based forms) provided sufficient theory for queer accounts of sexuality or of gender. All of this seems fairly obvious, I suspect, to most readers of *GLQ*, but it is worth mentioning nonetheless because it suggests how much the context in which we think and work has changed not only since 1918 but also since 1984.

Sex and Gender

When Rubin asked us to separate the study of sexuality from the study of gender, she knew and acknowledged that the two categories remained "related," even though they addressed, as she put it, "two distinct arenas of social practice."[15] *Autobiography of an Androgyne* illustrates the difficulties of drawing the boundaries between the two. As much as we might try to separate gender and sexuality analytically, the book reminds us that the arenas are not as distinct as we might imagine. A few historians have used the book (validly, I think) to illuminate the history of homosexuality; others of us have used it (again, validly) to illustrate the history of gender variance. Because the lines and branches of various histories cross and intersect, any given historical actor might well appear in more than one genealogy. But ultimately teasing out and emphasizing either the sex strand or the gender strand reduces the complexity of the person and the story in question. If we listen to Lind and the people around him in early twentieth-century New York, we can begin to discern the finer gradations of distinctions that melded gender and sexuality in that particular time and place. We can hear the language that was culturally available to explain the gender identification of a man-loving fairy who eventually chooses castration, and thereby avoid reducing a complicated historical story to the categories we use today. In *Autobiography of an Androgyne*, Lind recognizes the difference between what we now call gender and sexuality. (In the book, homologous terms include *mental sexuality* for gender identity and *sexual instinct* or *sensual practices* for sexuality.)[16] But Lind has no need to separate the categories. For Lind, the mixed-up biological sex of the "androgyne" explains both the feminine behavior and the longing for sex with men.

This is not simply an issue from the allegedly benighted essentialist past when both gender and sexuality could collapse into biological sex. I remember a few years back, when writing my book on transsexuality, I frequently tried to explain sexuality and gender to nonacademic friends and strangers. I would position gay and lesbian as issues of sexual identity, for example, and transsexual and transgender as issues of gender identity. At some point it dawned on me that the problem was not in the confused people whom I addressed. The problem was my own. I was trying too hard to separate analytically what was deeply intertwined, overlapping, and multiple. To give one overly simple contemporary example, a self-identified "dyke" today might be a self-identified "transman" tomorrow. The very same person might self-define at various times with a term associated with sexual identity and a term associated with gender identity. My own attempt to comb out the tangled categories of gender and sexuality had lost sight of the ways in which gender and sexuality remained inextricably knotted, not only conceptually but also in vernacular usage and everyday life.[17] Our recent attempts to pull gender and sexuality apart, and to highlight one or the other, can obscure the nuanced, hybrid, and local self-fashionings of contemporary queers in various parts of the world as well as of Lind (and other historical figures, including Radclyffe Hall and the many "inverts," "androgynes," "men-women," and "masquerades" of the early twentieth-century transatlantic world).[18] Our current scholarly versions of gender and sexuality are not the only possible ways to divide the conceptual turf or construct the conceptual categories.

Thinking Baby

The most puzzling piece of *Autobiography of an Androgyne* is not, I think, the interlinked gender and sexual transgression, the surprisingly graphic descriptions of sex, the self-revulsion and abjection, the ardent political plea, or the weirdly framed ethnic and class privilege. There is something else that troubles the categories that we routinely use today. In the book, Lind not only describes himself as feminine but also portrays himself as a baby. (The book's index actually has the terms *babying* and *babyishness* as major entries with multiple page numbers after each.) When promenading the streets as a fairy, Lind insists that he is not an adult but a baby or "baby-doll." His fairy persona includes a loud and proud infantilism. It partly reflects Lind's version of womanhood, in which the height of femininity is the "helpless cry-baby species of woman." Acting the baby also seems to be a way to try (not always successfully) to get young men to comfort, pet, and coddle a fairy. But acting the baby is also more. Lind describes sucking the phallus as akin to a baby sucking the breast. "All through my open career as a fairie," he writes, "I conducted myself with intimates in the same way as a baby of two years towards its mother." He casts his desire to perform fellatio as "the infant's nursing instinct . . . though with transferred object." This is a notion of pre-oedipal arrested development made literal, without any reference to Freud.[19]

What should we make of this, of the age crossing that was just as transgressive in its way as the gender crossing? Was the linking of femininity and babyhood common in the turn-of-the-twentieth-century United States? Was it one of the regular codes of fairy behavior? Or was it Lind's peculiar fantasy that was not necessarily shared by others? Does it suggest that Lind saw age as just as performative as some of us see gender? I don't have the answers, but I do know that the babyish behavior is a critical part of Lind's story that fails to appear in the histories that use his book for evidence. It is perhaps so confounding (or so queer) that it just gets swept to the side. And it reminds me that we need to listen to the whole story, to pay respect to the narratives of the past, and not just pluck out the conceptual categories that we traffic in today.

In short, our contemporary categories do not suffice for a document published ninety-two years ago. Feminism cannot fully explain the gender transgression and gender politics, and sexuality cannot wholly detach itself from gender. Moreover, neither queer studies nor transgender studies alone does justice to this particular source, and our usual roundup of categories — class, race, gender, sexuality — fails to capture the infantilism that suffuses the book.

Historical texts are useful in this way because they pry us out of the familiar and thereby position us, in a sense, to anachronize the present. Just as we might provincialize the United States by making the center of our focus somewhere outside it, so we might anachronize the present by centering our attention on a moment in the past. The past can show us that our own ways of seeing the world are contingent, curious, and changeable. In "Thinking Sex," Rubin knew that "critical tools" are "fashioned" in particular times and places to address "specific areas of social activity."[20] With that keen sense of history, we might imagine that in another ninety years some late twenty-first-century students will find our current deliberations on gender and sexuality as anachronistic and strange — and with any luck, as compelling — as Earl Lind's 1918 memoir seems to me today.

Notes

Many thanks to Heather Love for organizing the "Rethinking Sex" conference, at which I first presented a version of this essay, and for her helpful suggestions for revision.

1. Gayle Rubin, "Thinking Sex: Notes for a Radical Theory of the Politics of Sexuality," in *Pleasure and Danger: Exploring Female Sexuality*, ed. Carole S. Vance (Boston: Routledge and Kegan Paul, 1984), 267–319.
2. Earl Lind, *Autobiography of an Androgyne* (New York: Medico-Legal Journal, 1918).
3. Book note on *Autobiography of an Androgyne, American Journal of Psychology* 30, no. 2 (1919): 239. For another short review, see *American Journal of Surgery* 34, no. 4 (1920): 116.
4. Lind, *Autobiography*, copyright page, xiii.
5. On "feeling backward," see Heather Love, *Feeling Backward: Loss and the Politics of Queer History* (Cambridge, MA: Harvard University Press, 2007).
6. Lind, *Autobiography*, 135.
7. See, for example, Bert Hansen, "American Physicians' 'Discovery' of Homosexuals, 1800–1900: A New Diagnosis in a Changing Society," in *Framing Disease: Studies in Cultural History*, ed. Charles E. Rosenberg and Janet Lynne Golden (New Brunswick: Rutgers University Press, 1992), 110–13; George Chauncey, *Gay New York: Gender, Urban Culture, and the Makings of the Gay Male World, 1890–1940* (New York: Basic, 1994), 42–44, 51–55, 59–61; Jennifer Terry, *An American Obsession: Science, Medicine, and Homosexuality in Modern Society* (Chicago: University of Chicago Press, 1999), 113; Jonathan Ned Katz, *Love Stories: Sex between Men before Homosexuality* (Chicago: University of Chicago Press, 2001), chap. 21; and Henry L. Minton, *Departing from Deviance: A History of Homosexual Rights and Emancipatory Science in America* (Chicago: University of Chicago Press, 2002), 23–26. For earlier comments on *Autobiography of an Androgyne*, see Jonathan Katz, *Gay American History: Lesbians and Gay Men in the U.S.A.: A Documentary* (New York: Harper and Row, 1976), chap. 5.
8. See, for example, Joanne Meyerowitz, *How Sex Changed: A History of Transsexuality in the United States* (Cambridge, MA: Harvard University Press, 2002), 17; and Susan Stryker, *Transgender History* (Berkeley, CA: Seal, 2008), 41.
9. Anne Herrmann, *Queering the Moderns: Poses/Portraits/Performances* (New York: Palgrave Macmillan, 2000), chap. 7. See also Tracy Hargreaves, *Androgyny in Modern Literature* (New York: Palgrave Macmillan, 2005), 27–31.

10. Rubin, "Thinking Sex," 307.

11. Lind, *Autobiography*, 98.

12. Judith Butler, *Gender Trouble: Feminism and the Subversion of Identity* (New York: Routledge, 1990).

13. Joan Scott, "Gender: A Useful Category of Historical Analysis," *American Historical Review* 91, no. 5 (1986): 1066.

14. Judith Butler, *Undoing Gender* (New York: Routledge, 2004), 4.

15. Rubin, "Thinking Sex," 308.

16. Lind, *Autobiography*, 8, 30, 83.

17. On recent attempts to separate sexuality and gender, and on complex identities in the United States, see, for example, David Valentine, *Imagining Transgender: An Ethnography of a Category* (Durham, NC: Duke University Press, 2007).

18. On nuanced, hybrid, and local self-fashionings outside the United States, see, for example, Megan J. Sinnott, *Toms and Dees: Transgender Identity and Female Same-Sex Relationships in Thailand* (Honolulu: University of Hawai'i Press, 2004); Gayatri Reddy, *With Respect to Sex: Negotiating Hijra Identity in South India* (Chicago: University of Chicago Press, 2005). For recent commentary on Radclyffe Hall and sexual and gender identities in early twentieth-century Britain, see, for example, Laura Doan, *Fashioning Sapphism: The Origins of a Modern English Lesbian Culture* (New York: Columbia University Press, 2001); Alison Oram, *"Her Husband Was a Woman!" Women's Gender-Crossing in Modern British Popular Culture* (London: Routledge, 2007).

19. Lind, *Autobiography*, 9, 15, 29. In the book's introduction, Albert Herzog mentions Freud, but in the text itself, Lind does not.

20. Rubin, "Thinking Sex," 309.

DISABLING SEX

Notes for a Crip Theory of Sexuality

Robert McRuer

*T*he time has come to think about disability.

Of course, "Thinking Disability" was not, on the surface at least, what Gayle Rubin had in mind when she penned the famous opening lines of her 1984 essay "Thinking Sex: Notes for a Radical Theory of the Politics of Sexuality."[1] And, even as I perform a crip appropriation of those lines, I am aware that, for many, sex and disability at times seem not so much intersectional as incongruous: "What exactly *do* you do?" is about as frequent a question for disabled people, in relation to sex, as it historically has been for many queers. The motivation behind the question, however, has usually been different. Although stereotypes of the oversexed disabled person engaged in unspeakable acts do exist, disabled people are more commonly positioned as asexual — incapable of or uninterested in sex. Speaking to such expectations, the disability activist Anne Finger wrote more than a decade ago, in an assertion now well known in the disability rights movement, "Sexuality is often the source of our deepest oppression; it is also often the source of our deepest pain. It's easier to talk about and formulate strategies for changing discrimination in employment, education, and housing than it is to talk about our exclusion from sexuality and reproduction."[2]

But what if disability were sexy? And what if disabled people were understood to be both subjects and objects of a multiplicity of erotic desires and practices, both within and outside the parameters of heteronormative sexuality?[3] With such attitudes and questions in the background, I want to play with the title of this brief essay — "Disabling Sex" — stretching it to signify in a couple of different ways. I do that partly by linking "Thinking Sex" to another text from the same year that it has, without a doubt, never been linked to before. Deborah A. Stone's 1984 book *The Disabled State* is largely a history of varied welfare state policies (from Britain, Germany, and the United States).[4] It is chock-full of facts and statis-

GLQ 17:1
DOI 10.1215/10642684-2010-021
© 2010 by Duke University Press

tics. It mainly examines the push for restriction or expansion of various programs, and it is not particularly optimistic (given how consistently those programs collapse or fail). It is often very dry, even if, I argue, it contains some stunning arguments that the interdisciplinary field of disability studies, or any field, might still attend to. Hence one thing I am doing with my title, "Disabling Sex," is bringing the disabled state to bear on thinking sex. And this essay attempts to make the most of the potential incongruity — if it is not *entirely* unthinkable that a lover might say "what's that juicy opening line from Rubin's 'Thinking Sex?'" it is a bit harder to imagine "mmm, talk dirty to me, read me a few lines on the emergence of SSDI and worker's compensation from Stone's *Disabled State*."

Cripping Sex

Before staging a quick, promiscuous encounter between the two 1984 texts, however, I should emphasize that Rubin's famous article is, in fact, already saturated with disability in at least three ways. First, as Abby L. Wilkerson has suggested, Rubin's "charmed circle of sex" marks an able-bodied/disabled divide, even according to Rubin's own terms, since the location she identifies as "the outer limits" is where many crips end up.[5] Here, for instance, are some of Rubin's own terms: unnatural, nonprocreative, commercial, in groups, casual, cross-generational, with manufactured objects. Wilkerson goes on to consider "Hermaphrodites With Attitude . . . men with breasts, 'chicks with dicks,' anyone who is HIV-positive or schizophrenic or uses a wheelchair" and demonstrates that the project of thinking about particular bodies and practices populating the "outer limits" could be infinitely extended.[6] To add to Wilkerson's reflections on sexualized practices outside the charmed circle (and some of these are outer limits even for many inside disability communities): devoteeism; fetishizing of the accoutrements of deafness (or, for that matter, deaf wannabes); self-demand amputation; barebacking; hospital scenes (whether Bob Flanagan's very public ones or the ones staged by any ordinary person who wants to get off in a hospital gown during a hospital stay); potentially surveilled sex between people with cognitive disabilities in group homes; sex surrogacy (more about that later); or (to specify some of Rubin's "manufactured objects") sex involving crutches, oxygen masks, or prosthetic body parts. Recognizing his own new position outside the "charmed circle," one contributor to the Lammy Award—winning anthology *Queer Crips* takes pride and pleasure in his location there, noting that he was a pretty average straight guy until his accident, after which he begins using a chair, thinks in expansive ways about what he might do with his body, becomes gay, and is open to just about anything kinky.[7] Jump to the *center* of Rubin's charmed circle, conversely, and you have what Wilkerson calls "normate sex," which—following Erving Goffman—is probably only possible for one or two people; Goffman identifies this imagined normate as "a young, married, white, urban, northern, heterosexual Protestant father of college education, fully employed, of good complexion, weight and height, and a recent record in sports."[8]

Second, the "sex panics" Rubin details are invariably about disability somehow. The disturbance, disorder, and danger that Michel Foucault talks about in his lectures on the emergence of the abnormal individual are specifically positioned as threats to "public hygiene" and health, and certainly the "increasingly decomposed, ravaged, skeletal, and diaphanous physiognomy of the exhausted young masturbator" plays a key role in the story he has to tell, as masturbation is etiologically connected to everything from blindness to insanity.[9] And, of course, even as Rubin was writing in the mid-1980s, we were learning that "now, no one is safe" (to quote the famous *Life* magazine cover): queers, addicts, and sex workers out of control would infect everyone (and essentially kill them, but of course first comes significant disability).[10] Rubin was both aware of what was coming in relation to AIDS and savvy enough to link the coming panic to earlier historical moments that were likewise simultaneously about both panic over sex and horror at what might happen to the body. In her discussion of AIDS, she writes, "A century ago, attempts to control syphilis led to the passage of the Contagious Diseases Acts in England. The Acts were based on erroneous medical theories and did nothing to halt the spread of the disease. But they did make life miserable for the hundreds of women who were incarcerated, subjected to forcible vaginal examination, and stigmatized for life as prostitutes."[11]

Third, Rubin's "concept of benign sexual variation" only really works if we actually populate and extend it with bodies—bodies that are non-able-bodied, or rather bodies (and minds) that are simply off the grid of the historical able-bodied/disabled binary (normate sex may be founded on compulsory able-bodiedness, but that seems to me the first thing that goes out the window when we theorize and put into practice benign sexual variation). This point is implicit in what Rubin initially says about the concept—"variation is a fundamental property of all life, from the simplest biological organisms to the most complex human social formations"—and explicit in a range of queer bodily and sexual practices over the past few decades, from the ways that various lesbian feminist communities (including attendees at the 1982 Barnard conference that generated Rubin's essay) worked to value, include, or eroticize a range of nonnormative bodies (think, for instance, of Audre Lorde's imagined army of one-breasted women) to gay male attempts to have promiscuity in an epidemic, insisting that all of us are living with HIV and figuring out what kinds of pleasures might be shaped by taking that fact into account.[12] In these varied queer contexts, "disabling sex" signifies processes that are much more challenging, disruptive, resistant, and even, well, sexy.[13]

Around 1984

So what might any of this have to do with Stone's *Disabled State*? Rubin's project in "Thinking Sex" involved, at least partly, linking emergent forms of sexual hierarchization to the consolidation of industrial capitalism and paralleling resistance to that hierarchization to struggles around and against the bourgeois mode of production. Stone, as well, was concerned with how newly configured capitalist states were sorting bodies and behaviors into dominant and subordinated categories. At the same time that Rubin was insisting that "like the capitalist organization of labor and its distributions of rewards and powers, the modern sexual system has been the object of political struggle since it emerged and as it has evolved," Stone too was reflecting on distributions of rewards and powers and on how structures of inequality rigidified in and through that distribution.[14]

The trajectory of Stone's analysis, however, is slightly different from Rubin's. Stone is certainly concerned with the subordination of disabled people and with the injustices that attend the disabled state. Yet she approaches these questions through a textured consideration of how modern states have in effect *utilized* disability. Stone examines what she calls "the distributive dilemma" in modernity and places the social construction of disability at the absolute center of the political struggle to define a given society: in modernity, according to Stone, "we ask [disability] to resolve the issue of distributive justice."[15] A breathtaking pronouncement, really, and a task that Stone acknowledges disability is certainly not up to, not least given the contradictory (and unjust) capitalist context from which this demand emerges. Capitalism first establishes a system where we are "free" to sell our labor power and not particularly free to do anything else and *then* has to manage those subjects who cannot or will not participate in that compulsory organization of labor. Two distributive systems, one work-based and one need-based, of necessity arise, and Stone grapples with the wide range of issues generated by these conditions: first, the various rationales that emerge to locate people in one category or the other; second, the "validating devices" that emerge to accompany those rationales, determining "objectively" which system, work- or need-based, should be operative for a given person (the very fraught and incoherent notion of a "clinical concept of disability"—that is, a disabled state that can be observed and noted by authorities — is invented for this purpose); and, finally and perhaps most impossibly, the ideological maneuvering that kicks into gear — capitalist societies must somehow "maintain the dominance," Stone argues, of the primary, work-based distributive system, even if and as that system is really quite onerous to most people.[16] "Disability," as a putatively measurable social construction, is supposed to resolve all this.

Which is where one of Stone's other major contributions comes in, a contribution that is as simple and stunning as her pronouncement that disability is called on to resolve the question of distributive justice in modernity. Of necessity, given the state of affairs Stone describes, in *The Disabled State* (and the disabled state), disability emerges discursively as a *privileged* identity, which is why there is so much anxiety and suspicion around the disabled "category" and who gets to qualify for it. I find this 1984 insight incredible for many reasons, not least that twenty-five years later, if you surveyed the vast majority of disability studies 101 syllabi (including my own), stigma and exclusion would likely be the focus of a large portion of the introductory material. Like the deviants and perverts outside Rubin's charmed circle, disabled people are often positioned in disability studies as stigmatized (and of course Goffman himself links sexuality and disability, and his *Stigma* often shows up on one of the very first days of the imagined courses I just evoked — indeed, selections from *Stigma* are in fact the only pre-1970 readings included in *The Disability Studies Reader*).[17]

I am certainly not arguing against understanding disabled people as stigmatized in contemporary societies, and neither is Stone: the "privileging" that she theorizes is itself, after all, clearly a form of subordination and stigmatization dependent on what Paul K. Longmore terms "ceremonies of social degradation."[18] The privilege of belonging to the disabled category Stone describes is rooted in stigma because the need-based system has already been positioned ideologically by the modern state as inferior to the work-based system (or, put differently, has been invented by the modern state to vouchsafe the superiority of the work-based system). I am, however, considering how understanding or overemphasizing stigma as isolation or social exclusion may obscure Stone's quite nuanced arguments about privilege. I do not think it *wholly* suffices, especially in our own historical moment, to account for Stone's thesis by saying that disability is stigmatized socially and culturally and "privileged" only in relation to the institutions invested in measuring disability to resolve the problem of distributive justice. That particular distinction between where disability is privileged and where it is stigmatized is true, to a large extent, but does not *exhaust* her points — or rather, potentially dilutes them and thereby makes it possible to avoid some more difficult or interesting questions. In 1984, when it was (according to his campaign advertisements) "morning again" in Ronald Reagan's America, one could argue — taking seriously Stone's linkage of disability and privilege — that Stone facilitates a critique of an emergent neoliberalism and attends to the contradictions generated by the necessary simultaneity of exclusion and incorporation (from, but also into, the nation and the state) in ways that queer studies will not fully get around to theorizing until *A Queer Mother for the Nation*, *Terrorist Assemblages*, *The Twilight of Equality*, the homonormativity issue of the *Radical History Review*, and — indeed — *The Straight State*.[19] There is perhaps some of this going on in Rubin's "Thinking Sex," but its explicit focus on the persecution and oppression of nonnormative sexuality (a focus that was, at the time, of course, absolutely crucial) is much more obvious than emergent, neoliberal incorporations.

Cripping the State

For disability studies, even as the field sustains a focus on stigma and exclusion, it is important to keep in view Stone's oft-forgotten points about the centrality of privilege and incorporation. For queer studies, it is important to attend to how a theory of uneven biopolitical incorporation — the incorporation of some bodies (but not others) into the state — has been part of disability studies for as long as we have had Rubin's notes for a radical theory of the politics of sexuality. Queer studies regularly demonstrates, at this point if not in 1984, how both the state and the cultural imagination can deploy sex and sexuality to mask exploitation or oppression in other locations. We are, in other words, used to "thinking sex" in these ways. My intent in conclusion is to push us toward similar ways of "thinking sex and disability" together.

I attempt to exemplify thinking sex and disability in our moment via a brief concluding story of sex surrogacy and the Netherlands (and of course it's much easier to tell the story of sex surrogacy via the Netherlands than it is via the United States — or most other places, for that matter). "Sex surrogacy," where a sex worker either works directly with a disabled person or facilitates that person's sexual interaction with a third party, is a very contested term. I use it here simply to tell this particular story, and I recognize that the language for the processes I discuss is currently in flux.[20]

In 2001 a man named Hennie van den Wittenboer won a seven-year legal fight to get help from the social services department in Tilburg. The Dutch Council in Tilburg agreed to pay for van den Wittenboer to have sex once a month with a sex worker. Van den Wittenboer is disabled and uses a wheelchair and — in a story taken up by Dutch television and newspapers—reported needing less medication and feeling less stress once the state-funded sex surrogacy was in place. Initially, during his legal battle, van den Wittenboer said, "[the council] said sex wasn't part of the primary needs of a human being." "Now," he said in 2001, "there is a lady coming once a month, and I feel much better."[21] Since then, the Dutch government has more consistently codified these services, paying for hetero- and homosexual sexual services for mentally and physically disabled citizens, and, according to Selina Bonnie, "people with significant impairments" have been traveling to the Netherlands "to access sex services, which have been established by the state specifically for disabled people."[22] Although the legal battle prior to 2001 already suggests that the policy was not uncontroversial, it would seem that since then it has both become *somewhat* less so and partly, for some in the Netherlands (and elsewhere, in thought *about* the Netherlands), wrapped up in a national sense of who "we" are: nonplussed about sex, attentive to the health needs of "our" citizens, different from countries that are neither of those, and so forth. Even with the sexualized twist, this Dutch situation fits with one of Stone's other arguments, that national attempts to resolve questions of distributive justice around and through disability get wrapped up almost immediately in national self-definition.[23]

At least two things are interesting to me as disability and sex come together around the state. First, I am interested in how sexualized discourses of "openness" might currently and paradoxically function normatively in the Netherlands (and elsewhere), especially in the wake of Pim Fortuyn's rise to prominence a decade ago. Fortuyn was an openly gay politician running for parliament as a member of the right-wing, anti-immigrant Leefbaar Nederland Party, when he was assassinated by an animal rights activist in 2002. What came to the fore during Fortuyn's campaign (and in some ways after the assassination as well) was how tolerance of sexual diversity and minoritized gay identities could actually be deployed to facilitate xenophobia and Islamophobia. I am not by any means equating the stories of Pim Fortuyn and Hennie van den Wittenboer; instead, I am making a point about dangers that can potentially circulate around sexual identity *or* disability or sexual identity *and* disability: "yes that's who we are as a people" or even "yes that's who we are sexually" and "look to the fairness with which we treat our minoritized citizenry" can coexist with what Jasbir Puar has so effectively analyzed as the targeting of *other* populations for quarantine and death. Puar calls the "securitization and valorization" of certain queer subjects in the contemporary moment "homonationalism" and contends that such securitization is intimately connected to how other subjects (what she calls "terrorist corporealities") are marked as excessive and essentially targeted for death or elimination.[24]

Partly thanks to Puar's important study, we are starting to get used to making these points in queer studies but not so much, I would say, in disability studies, even if Stone's arguments authorized us to do so, at a time when a nascent queer studies really was not. A crip theory of sexuality, then, would insist on thinking seriously about van den Wittenboer's rights and pleasures while being wary of how those *might* get discursively positioned by and around the state. It would, additionally, to use van den Wittenboer's own words, want the sensation of "feeling much better" (in all its resonances) to be autonomous from one's citizen-status (van den Wittenboer seems to have simply evoked the "needs of a human being" that, in his deployment, did not seem to be a category particularly tied to citizen-status). Van den Wittenboer did not necessarily position this as queer or crip theory on the ground, but there is no reason not to.

Second, and this may be why we still have such trouble in disability studies with this kind of analysis around privileged identities, obviously the potential use of disability and sex to shore up who "we" are can and will coexist with plenty of "panic" (to invoke Rubin again), plenty of residual or even dominant discourses that still position disability and desire at odds or, put differently, disability as undesirable: debates in the Netherlands about physician-assisted suicide and, for some, a certain common sense that of course severe disability is cause enough for a state-sponsored exit, coexisted and coexist with the more emergent discourses I have been tracing.[25]

So, to end by repeating one of the questions I identified at the beginning: what if disability were sexy? Of course it already is: crip cultures are as hot and sexy, fierce and happening as queer cultures at their best (and these cultures obviously overlap already and should overlap more). But a crip theory of sexuality is simultaneously hip to how its sexiness might get used, or hip to how disability has already been used in so many problematic ways by the modern state. The sexy queer crip performer Greg Walloch can lead me to a conclusion here. In the 2001 performance video *Fuck the Disabled*, Walloch speaks of perusing bookstore shelves and coming across a Louise Hay book that identifies cerebral palsy as "brought to this earth to heal the family with one sweeping gesture of love." After a pause and deadpan look up at his audience, Walloch continues rapidly, "brought to the earth with one sweeping gesture of love . . . you know, I don't really want that job!"[26] A crip theory of sexuality, thinking and rethinking sex and seeking to feel much better, would push for other sensations, other connections, but would always be attuned to the impossible work that disability has been asked to perform — to resolve questions of distributive justice (with one sweeping gesture of love?) while masking the contradictions inherent in the system that generated those questions of justice in the first place.

Notes

1. Gayle Rubin, "Thinking Sex: Notes for a Radical Theory of the Politics of Sexuality," in *Pleasure and Danger: Exploring Female Sexuality*, ed. Carole S. Vance (Boston: Routledge and Kegan Paul, 1984), 267–319.

2. Anne Finger, "Forbidden Fruit," *New Internationalist* no. 233 (1992): 9.

3. I am taking these two questions, as well as the notion of incongruity that I am considering in these opening paragraphs, from Anna Mollow's and my introduction to the anthology *Sex and Disability* (Durham, NC: Duke University Press, forthcoming).

4. Deborah A. Stone, *The Disabled State* (Philadelphia: Temple University Press, 1984).

5. Abby L. Wilkerson, "Normate Sex and Its Discontents: Intersex, Transgender, and Sexually Based Disability," in McRuer and Mollow, *Sex and Disability*.

6. Despite Wilkerson's generative use of Rubin's "charmed circle" and "outer limits," she is elsewhere critical of how Rubin's theoretical move separates sexual hierarchies from other social hierarchies. See Abby L. Wilkerson, "Disability, Sex Radicalism, and Political Agency," *National Women's Studies Association Journal* 14 (2002): 33–57.

7. Alex Sendham, "Beginner's Sex," in *Queer Crips: Disabled Gay Men and Their Stories*, ed. Bob Guter and John R. Killacky (New York: Harrington Park, 2004), 191–97.

8. Erving Goffman, *Stigma: Notes on the Management of Spoiled Identity* (New York: Simon and Schuster, 1963), 128.

9. Michel Foucault, *Abnormal: Lectures at the Collège de France, 1974–1975*, trans. Graham Burchell (New York: Picador, 2003), 235.

10. "Now No One Is Safe from AIDS," *Life Magazine*, July 1985.

11. Rubin, "Thinking Sex," 299.

12. Rubin, "Thinking Sex," 283.

13. See Audre Lorde, *The Cancer Journals* (San Francisco: Aunt Lute, 1980); and Douglas Crimp, "How to Have Promiscuity in an Epidemic," in *AIDS: Cultural Analysis/ Cultural Activism*, ed. Douglas Crimp (Cambridge, MA: MIT Press, 1987), 237–71.

14. Rubin, "Thinking Sex," 309.

15. Stone, *Disabled State*, 13.

16. Stone, *Disabled State*, 21, 90.

17. Lennard J. Davis, ed., *The Disability Studies Reader* (New York: Routledge, 1997).

18. Paul K. Longmore, *Why I Burned My Book and Other Essays on Disability* (Philadelphia: Temple University Press, 2003), 240.

19. Licia Fiol-Matta, *A Queer Mother for the Nation: The State and Gabriela Mistral* (Minneapolis: University of Minnesota Press, 2002); Lisa Duggan, *The Twilight of Equality? Neoliberalism, Cultural Politics, and the Attack on Democracy* (Boston: Beacon, 2003); Jasbir K. Puar, *Terrorist Assemblages: Homonationalism in Queer Times* (Durham, NC: Duke University Press, 2007); Kevin P. Murphy, Jason Ruiz, and David Serlin, eds., "Queer Futures: The Homonormativity Issue," special issue, *Radical History Review* (2008); Margot Canaday, *The Straight State: Sexuality and Citizenship in Twentieth-Century America* (Princeton: Princeton University Press, 2009).

20. For a now-classic first-person account of his own experiences with sex surrogates in San Francisco in the 1980s, see Mark O'Brien, "On Seeing a Sex Surrogate," *Sun*, May 1990, www.pacificnews.org/marko/sex-surrogate.html.

21. Keith Chalkley, "What a Pleasure," *Dispatchonline*, November 10, 2001, www .dispatch.co.za/2001/11/10/foreign/BWORLD.HTM. The story was reported in the Dutch newspaper *Brabants Dagbland* and then circulated globally in English via "breaking news" Internet sites, largely of two sorts: blogs, sites, and chat forums focused on disability access issues and sensationalizing sites highlighting news of the (supposedly) humorous or bizarre.

22. Selina Bonnie, "Disabled People, Disability, and Sexuality," in *Disabling Barriers, Enabling Environments*, 2nd ed., ed. John Swain et al. (London: Sage, 2004), 129. In the Netherlands, these issues actually predate van den Wittenboer's legal battle, and an organization called Selective Human Relations has offered subsidized sexual assistance for twenty years. See Mutsuko Murakami, "The Right to Sex," *South China Morning Post*, September 11, 2004, 15; Helen McNutt, "Hidden Pleasures," *Guardian*, October 13, 2004, 2; Barbara Smit, "State to Pay for Sex Visits to Disabled Man," *Irish Times*, August 26, 1992, 7.

23. This national self-definition is a discursive formation that then travels beyond the borders of the Netherlands. The cultural work of this discursive formation does not necessarily translate into more sexual freedom on the ground, and, indeed, according to Gert Hekma, the widely accepted idea of Dutch sexual openness has actually inhibited queer radicalism at the turn of the twenty-first century. See Gert Hekma, "Queer: The Dutch Case," *GLQ* 10 (2004): 276–80.

24. Puar, *Terrorist Assemblages*, 3. Puar herself discusses the Fortuyn story and considers briefly some of the ways in which the Netherlands exemplifies the larger processes she is theorizing (19–21).

25. In the United States in 2009, as I was completing this essay, it seems to me that the processes I am sketching remain operative, even though I have chosen in the body of my text to "think disability" (or sex and disability) via another state. The United States remains a location where disabled people's lives are overwhelmingly positioned as undesirable and often, through the corporate (and extremely punitive) insurance-

based health care system, as dispensable. As health care debates raged in the United States during 2009, however (largely over proposals that would clearly not benefit the vast majority of people living with impairment or illness in the United States), certain key disabled figures were brought forward discursively to shore up who Americans as a people are or should be—most notably, Trig Palin, the son of former Alaska governor Sarah Palin, who was used in some of his mother's speeches as a disabled American who would have to stand before "death panels" deciding whether he would live or die if the insurance-based system were to be reformed. Others, sometimes speaking for themselves and sometimes used as examples by family members, occupied similar positions at so-called town hall meetings around the country. My argument is that this particular biopolitical use of disability identity is relatively new and fundamentally antidisabled.

26. Greg Walloch, *Fuck the Disabled*, dir. Eli Kabillio, New York: Mad Dog Films, 2001.

RE: THINKING SEX FROM THE GLOBAL SOUTH AFRICA

Neville Hoad

$\mathcal{T}$here can be no question that Gayle Rubin's widely anthologized 1984 essay "Thinking Sex: Notes for a Radical Theory of the Politics of Sexuality" has been very influential on certain strands in South African scholarship on sex.[1] By South African scholarship on sex, I mean at least two things—scholarship on sex written in South Africa and scholarship on South African sex.[2] To think "Thinking Sex" from South Africa over the twenty-five years of the essay's circulation must raise and beg the problem of a national frame. I think this is a problem that Rubin's essay shares with, and perhaps inherits from, Michel Foucault's equally generative *History of Sexuality*—particularly volume 1.[3] What is the space-time of Rubin's essay? Epistemologically, empirically, in terms of its reception?

At first blush, the essay appears to concern itself with what it calls "Modern Western societies." The geographic designations "North America" and "Western Europe" appear on occasion. The United States is by far the most frequently mentioned nation-state, as well as its individual states, cities, and urban neighborhoods. "The law of God and the law of England" are cited in reference to a 1631 case of the execution for sodomy of the Earl of Castlehaven. In reference to this case and the work of Gil Herdt on the Sambia—"In some New Guinea societies for example—homosexual activities are obligatory for all males"—there is the following delightful sentence: "The New Guinea bachelor and the sodomite nobleman are only tangentially related to the modern gay man" (17). Rubin here implicitly acknowledges that the space-time of her essay is predominantly the United States at her moment of writing. Despite these invocations of other places and times, I think there is a certain U.S. epistemological nationalism in the essay produced by an ethical concern for the locale from which it was written—San Francisco in the early 1980s—which must not be confused with the essay's explicitly

GLQ 17:1
DOI 10.1215/10642684-2010-022
© 2010 by Duke University Press

antistatist politics. Calling the essay "Eurocentric" would be anachronistic and also cannot account for its generative influence on thinking about sex and sexuality in the shifting national frame of South Africa and other places unevenly held under the designation of Euro-America.

Instead, I argue that the reception of the essay in South African sex scholarship reveals something more like what Edward Said has termed "traveling theory."[4] What follows is an attempt to transpose one of the essay's central concepts—"hierarchies of sexual value"—into a necessarily very schematically constructed reading of the politics of sexuality in South Africa in 1984, the date of the essay's original publication and a moment in what Gayatri Spivak has termed "the vanishing present."[5] Sexual politics in contemporary South Africa are a moving target as they shift under the pressures of the HIV/AIDS pandemic and significant migration and immigration, to name just a few variables. My analysis of the present will require continuing updating. The graphic legibility of this concept of hierarchies of sexual value in the two famous figures of the essay—the pie chart of "the charmed circle" of figure 1 ("The Sex Hierarchy: the charmed circle versus the outer limits" [13]) and the walls on a slope of figure 2 ("The Sex Hierarchy: the struggle over where to draw the line" [14]) can be continually redrawn for other space-times. Why? Because they establish the domain of sex as a domain for political inquiry and literally render visible state (at the level of law and policy) and social (institutional and attitudinal) investments in regulating this domain. That national institutions, particularly in moments of crisis—which seem endemic to our present—get worked up over the sexual behavior of their citizen subjects seems to me a relatively obvious universal of global or transnational or neoliberal modernity. Of course, this universal will be differentially experienced, but I think only a fetishistic investment in cultural relativism or national singularity could contest the idea that sexual regulation is a feature of sovereignty—both national and transnational in the world of 2009.

In the national contexts of South Africa in 1984 and 2009, what could get written into the pie chart of the sexual hierarchy would reveal significant similarities and differences. In 1984, in what retroactively can be seen as the dying days of apartheid, the most important addition to the charmed circle would obviously be same-racial classification, with its concomitant cross-racial sex being added to the outer limits. The South African state in its colonial- and apartheid-era incarnations had overriding concerns in regulating sexual behavior in both instrumental and paranoid modes. This has a long history, which could not be captured by the stasis of the chart, but is worth mentioning in truncated chronology here. The apartheid state understood the reproduction of distinct racial groups as essential to its survival and was thus obsessed with regulating interracial heterosexuality. Building on earlier dominion-era laws such as the 1927 Immorality Act, which criminalized sexual activity between whites and Africans, the National Party, which came to power in 1948, instituted the Prohibition of Mixed Marriages Act of 1949, which criminalized sexual conduct outside marriage as well as sex between whites and coloreds, and between whites and Asians, and the Mixed Marriages Act of 1950, which banned marriages between members of different racial classifications altogether, as key early pieces of apartheid-era legislation.[6] The year 1984 is an interesting moment for a snapshot because in 1985 in what was called the dismantling of petty apartheid, then President P. W. Botha decriminalized interracial sex, and the shift of sexual regulation from apartheid cornerstone to petty apartheid tells a story of the changing priorities of the state as it faces its demise. As this speedy history of legislation reveals, the apartheid state was generally more concerned with sex between rather than within its classification of racial groups. This concern has a long and fascinating colonial history. Briefly and brutally, the emerging colonial apparatus in southern Africa had neither the will nor the capacity under policies of what was called Indirect Rule to implement its norms all the way through the social body of the societies it was colonizing. Interested largely in extracting surplus value from these societies first in terms of agricultural and then mine labor, matters of civil law were to be left to the customary law of these societies, and if the customary law was too difficult to ascertain—it could be invented. Either way, its codification represents an intervention. In South Africa Theophilus Shepstone's drafting of an ordinance recognizing Nguni customary law in 1849 can be imagined as a starting point. Indigenous sexual conduct was left to customary law except in instances where it was found to be repugnant to the colonizer's gaze. These repugnancy clauses generally managed to ignore heterosexual so-called offenses—pervasive premarital sex, polygamy, and male circumcision practices, and in southern Africa got worked up over what might be termed indigenous homosexual practices (particularly if a white person was involved as participant or witness) and in East Africa female excision practices. The content of the bricks of the drawing of the line walls of Rubin's figure 2 would have a very complicated history over the course of colonial interventions in sub-Saharan Africa, but the lines were drawn and redrawn, particularly over questions of interracial sex and polygamy, and are being contested again at present.

In 2009 both diagrams could hold their forms as their contents held and shifted. There are at least two major historical and perhaps epochal shifts between 1984 and 2009 that require significant historiographical rethinking: the official end of apartheid and the new democratic constitution of 1994 (ratified in 1996), and the ongoing decimation as part of the largest HIV/AIDS pandemic the world has ever known. The famous equality clause of the South African constitution, which contains an antidiscrimination clause on the grounds of sexual orientation clause, has justly been widely celebrated. The rider that in matters of conflict the equality clause will trump customary law—corrupted as it no doubt is by its colonial- and apartheid-era legacy—is more problematic and to my mind unwittingly evokes the earlier repugnancy clauses this time not in the arbitrary language of moral repugnance but in the language of legal liberalism. I leave this potential conflict between customary and constitutional legal regimes in the impasse of cultural relativism and the difficulty of ethical judgment—even within the circumscribed realm of the legal. The on-the-ground complications of state recognition of cultural sexual practice are overwhelming, especially as the HIV/AIDS pandemic kills up to six hundred South Africans a day.

Both of Rubin's diagrams would have to find a way to represent the fact that South Africa's new president Jacob Zuma, a self-proclaimed "Zulu traditionalist," has five official wives. Where would one put monogamy in a South African sexual hierarchy? Never mind the chatter in Johannesburg and Cape Town and I suspect in the Zuma household itself over which wife will preside at various state functions.[7]

The problems with my confining of Rubin's sexual hierarchy to a national frame become apparent here. National discourses on sex in polyglot, now putatively democratic "liberal" settler colonies like South Africa and the United States, which have as many differences as similarities, are incoherent and fragmentary. In the United States, law offers some measure of determinacy, but as we well know problems of selective enforcement and access make the sphere of the legal a spectacularly uneven measure of social justice. We could consider an identitarian fracturing of the national—would we have to produce, for example, a Zulu charmed circle and how could this be done without invoking the Bantustan legacies of apartheid? The emergence of a global, transnational human rights discourse on sexual rights in which the South African constitution participates breaks the frame at the other end of the scale.

In this sense, I think the fuzziness of what I termed at the outset the essay's epistemological U.S. nationalism is more of a utility than a problem. The world has changed considerably since 1984, and not, so has the United States, so has South Africa, but "Thinking Sex: Notes for a Radical Theory of the Politics of Sexuality" remains an essay we should be thankful for. I teach it in any introduction to sexuality studies class. I teach it in a class on the literature and culture of the sub-Saharan HIV/AIDS pandemic. In this brief essay, I moved one of its central claims/concepts/questions — the sexual hierarchy — into a national context that the essay itself does not really imagine, and in the long temporality and strange spatialities of an idea, the political work of the idea of a sexual hierarchy held, both analytically and descriptively. In conclusion, I would like to suggest that the form our gratitude should take for those of us who work inside and outside the modern West, which given the unevenness of the political economy of global capitalism might be all of us, is to hang on to the essay's central impulses, to ask the questions of the connections between sex and politics, and to learn something perhaps about the nature of theory itself. Rubin's essay reminds us that theory is produced in and out of a space-time, with political allegiances to that space-time, and that while any theory of sexuality risks reifying and universalizing its space-time, it can be adapted, reworked, and embraced as it travels, and travel it will.

Notes

1. Gayle S. Rubin, "Thinking Sex: Notes for a Radical Theory of the Politics of Sexuality," in *The Lesbian and Gay Studies Reader*, ed. Henry Abelove, Michèle Aina Barale, and David M. Halperin (New York: Routledge, 1993), 3–44. Hereafter cited by page number.

2. There is simply too much scholarship to cite or synthesize here. Rubin's essay is invoked by leading South African sexuality and gender scholars in diverse political, historical, and policy contexts. Highlights could include Jacklyn Cock and Alison Bernstein, *Melting Pots and Rainbow Nations: Conversations about Difference in the United States and South Africa* (Urbana: University of Illinois Press, 2002); Deborah Posel, "Sex, Death, and the Fate of the Nation: Reflections on the Politicization of Sexuality in Post-Apartheid South Africa," *Africa* 75, no. 2 (2005): 125–53; Vasu Reddy and Theo Sandfort, "Researching MSM in South Africa: Some Preliminary Notes for the Frontier of a Hidden Epidemic," *Feminist Africa* 11 (2008): 29–54. In the essay itself, Rubin implicitly and polemically invokes the South Africa of the time of the essay's writing: "At their worst, sex law and sexual regulation are simply sexual apartheid" ("Thinking Sex," 21).

3. Michel Foucault, *An Introduction*, vol. 1 of *The History of Sexuality*, trans. Robert Hurley (New York: Vintage, 1990).

4. Edward Said, "Traveling Theory," in *The World, the Text, and the Critic* (Cambridge, MA: Harvard University Press, 1983), 243–47.

5. Gayatri Chakravorty Spivak, *A Critique of Postcolonial Reason: Toward a History of the Vanishing Present* (Cambridge, MA: Harvard University Press, 1999).

6. Neville Hoad, introduction to *Sex and Politics in South Africa: The Equality Clause/ Gay and Lesbian Movement/the Anti-apartheid Struggle*, ed. Neville Hoad, Karen Martin, and Graeme Reid (Cape Town: Double Storey, 2005), 15–16.

7. In a fascinating article, Judith Stacey and Tey Meadow examine a comparative history of polygamy and same-sex marriage in the legal and political contexts of the United States and South Africa. Both polygamy and same-sex marriage are legal in South Africa, though the legal regime has trouble imposing its will on social formations and public attitudes. The authors argue, however, that the inverse pertains in the United States, that "social and material conditions make it easier to practice family diversity in the U.S. than in South Africa," and that "when it comes to the lived experience of family diversity . . . the United States has few peers. No society has generated more extensive grassroots movements to transform intimacy than the United States" (Stacey and Meadow, "New Slants on the Slippery Slope: The Politics of Polygamy and Gay Family Rights in South Africa and the United States," *Politics and Society* 37 [2009], 167–202).

SEXUAL HEALING

Lisa Henderson

September 2009, U.S. These are tough times. The thrill of Obama's election hangs in the balance, the Iraq and Afghanistan wars carry on, and political bad faith swells against so essential a provision as health care. Jobs are few and bailout money unaccounted for. In academe, everything is up for grabs, save casualization, sponsored research, and cutbacks presented as entrepreneurial opportunity. It is a hard time to write lovingly about anything, and thus all the more striking that Gayle Rubin's work evokes love and possibility even as much of her writing documents hostility, oppression, and loss in the history of U.S. sexuality and sex scholarship. I would like to write to that evocation, not just as a matter of my personal sensibility or Rubin's but as a feature of her scholarly project and style.

Rubin is precise about her intellectual indebtedness, which I think means our indebtedness comes to her as a bit of a surprise. I am indebted to Rubin for many intellectual orientations, three in particular that are critical to my research and teaching: her long scholarly memory and archival imagination, her commitment to living and dying sexual populations and their breathtaking variety of human sexual practice and alliance, and her enduring attention to questions of class as part of the project of studying sex.

Memory

Rubin has cultivated a personal archive of documents and ephemera that deserves a professional staff to care for it, and her writing is distinguished by old-school scholarly regard and a deep incorporation of the work of others. She also attunes her readers to the long *durée* of risks taken and institutional prices paid by those who came before her, whose curiosity about the social and cultural character of sex and whose conscious opposition to sexual moralism took root long before sex scholarship would be rewarded with a trace of academic glory or capital. Those

GLQ 17:1
DOI 10.1215/10642684-2010-023
© 2010 by Duke University Press

scholars include, for example, Clellan Ford and Frank Beach, anthropologists and authors of the 1951 compendium *Patterns of Sexual Behavior*; Donald Marshall and Robert Suggs, also anthropologists and authors of *Human Sexual Behavior: Variations in the Ethnographic Spectrum* (1971); Nancy Achilles, author of perhaps the first bar study, "The Development of the Homosexual Bar as an Institution," published in William Simon and John Gagnon's edited collection *Sexual Deviance* (1967); the British historian of sexuality Jeffrey Weeks; the U.S. community historian Jonathan Ned Katz, and many early-twentieth-century sexologists. I came to sexuality studies as a reader (not yet a researcher) in the mid-1980s and didn't encounter some of these authors until the publication of Rubin's essay "Studying Sexual Subcultures" in 2002. It is not that I couldn't have, but that, with the exception of Weeks and Katz in some contexts the work of these authors did not circulate in the United States as the foundation or the emerging pantheon of contemporary sexuality studies.[1]

To recognize Rubin's attention to colleagues whose work precedes hers, however, is less to heroicize Rubin than to socialize everyone else. It is also to bear in mind continuities in the history of sex scholarship and sexual politics, as early work sought, if unevenly, to destigmatize sexual variation through research. By the 1970s, moreover, many sexuality scholars were also political activists radicalized by 1960s social movements. The political sociability of Rubin's work has influenced my own efforts to tease out some of the hostility and opposition between (nonqueer) Left and queer intellectual politics since the early 1980s, in the interest of imagining the terms of queer Left political friendship.[2] Despite the obvious antagonisms of a contemporary period—the 1980s—in which straight Left hostility to queer identity produced some unlikely formulations ("identity politics killed the Left"), queer and Left dispositions are deeply connected.

In Rubin's writing, this connection surfaces as a labor of scholarly memory and accountability. With historical and anthropological imagination, she narrates coming of age in the wake of Left and antiwar social movements as an undergraduate at the University of Michigan in the late 1960s and early 1970s. At Michigan, she also cultivated a feminist critique of gender value amid evolving feminist theory and sometimes competing feminist theorists.[3] In that context, the articulation of labor activism and feminism also became visible to her, for example, in the work and company of the Ann Arbor activist Carol Ernst, a proponent of matriarchal theory and "the idea that women had political power in societies that worshipped female deities."[4] These were not ideas that Rubin had much truck with, but Ernst went to work in a massage parlor and organized the workers there, several of them lesbians. Later, when the parlor was busted and many in the Ann Arbor lesbian community discovered that their local heroes had been arrested for prostitution, a routine response was that they should not have been doing patriarchal sex work in the first place. But those arrested organized the Prostitution Education Project and launched a series of critical questions: How was what they did so different from what anyone else did for a living? Why was it "more feminist to work as secretaries and for longer hours and less money?" "They demanded," says Rubin, "that we deal with prostitution as a work issue rather than a moralistic one. They brought in Margo St. James and had a big hookers' ball to raise funds for the legal defense."[5]

Sex as work is a formulation long familiar to Rubin's readers, though it bears repeating given the terms of the recent renewal of feminist politics against sex work and "porn culture."[6] More to my point, however, is that those readers most familiar with Rubin's monumental essay "Thinking Sex" might be surprised to discover that indeed she had had to learn Ernst's position.[7] I was.

Rubin's response to Ernst fills in a key analytic transition from "The Traffic in Women" to "Thinking Sex," a transition initiated when Rubin was still an undergraduate student.[8] She tells the story of her early political formation at Michigan through the unadorned recognition that we are intellectually made, not born; we take shape in an alchemy of time, place, disposition, and those others with whom we come to recognize common cause. Such memories are reminders that, like sex itself, theory arises in situ. Theory is a social practice deserving of a practice account, and in that account we have the finest chance of seeing the ground against which any new figure moves into high relief. It is a constructionist's view, not collapsing sex, politics, and sexual theory but putting them together in dialogue and living suspension.

I routinely draw students' attention to this gesture on Rubin's part. Whether she is quoting Esther Newton on Newton's appreciation of the encouragement she received from her academic supervisor David Schneider to study drag queen performance, or narrating her own happenstance encounter with Michel Foucault in the Bibliothèque nationale de France, the stop-start character and the sociability of intellectual formation come into view and into the record.[9] This is an essential contribution in sexuality studies, a field with a rich twentieth-century history but barely the institutional firmament to ensure retrievability and development without reinventing existing insight. Rubin herself made this point in her 2003 David R. Kessler Lecture at the Center for Lesbian and Gay Studies in New York, where she appealed to the virtues of bureaucracy—for example, in the forms of real estate, archives, programs, and institutions—for sustainability in the study of sexual subcultures, however mismatched sexual radicalism and bureaucracy might, at first blush, seem to be.[10]

Living Sexual Populations

As an anthropologist, Rubin has been duly skeptical about attributing to sexual practitioners and scenes those illuminations and conclusions arrived at through criticism or theory.[11] As critic and ethnographer, I find the boundaries leakier than Rubin does, since, like most of us schooled in post-structuralist cultural studies, I need a critic's skill in reading genre and cultural tradition to interpret the worlds of cultural production and the uses of cultural materials in everyday life. I heartily agree, however, that recognizing discourse is not an invitation to bypass people in favor of exemplary texts as evidence of social practice or disposition. But, in almost any field save anthropology and some versions of sociology, the academic conditions of long-term interaction with living populations are being squeezed, not expanded, even as the virtues of fieldwork are recognized by nonfieldworkers among cultural scholars. Fieldwork takes time to learn and to do, and demands an investment in uncertainty—resources at odds with academic economies of labor, appointment, and tenure. It also usually means leaving wherever you already are, whether or not you have to cross a territorial or linguistic border. Even anthropology has its tradition of nonrecidivist fieldworkers, who collect field materials at the dissertation stage and later return to those same contexts but who do not undertake new projects with new populations. As fieldworkers (and adjunct faculty) know, relocation can be a very hard way to live.

As a longtime San Franciscan and one-time urban migrant from South Carolina, Rubin has lived and undertaken fieldwork in the same place, a circumstance enabled (or enforced) by the absence, until recently, of continuing academic employment. From her writing and speaking, those of us not already inside the gay men's leather culture of San Francisco's Tenderloin district—Rubin's "beloved Tenderloin"—have come to understand the history, social network, sexual styles, and symbolic universe of a population rooted in place, but whose world has been painfully vulnerable to political and police control, HIV/AIDS, and strategies of urban development that priced out all but the wealthiest citizens of San Francisco (and those, like Rubin, who bought early in parts of the city that came late to upmarketeering).[12]

There is nothing like social and sexual curiosity devoid of investigative judgment: people spring to life; the long and deep reach of community practice in sex, politics, work, retail, and residential organization becomes visible; and the tight boundaries of repressive moralism give way to social alternatives that make sense in their own terms. This is a kind of research opening seen time and again in the history of U.S. urban ethnography, especially those strands that sought to recast familiar forms of social exclusion and familiar projections of deviance and stigma, authored, as Rubin points out, by such early sociologists as Robert Park and by a postwar generation that included Erving Goffman and, still writing, Howard Becker.[13] In gay anthropology, such worlds are beautifully visible in the work of Esther Newton, both her groundbreaking ethnography, *Mother Camp*, and her later book *Cherry Grove, Fire Island*.[14] They are visible again in Anglo-American urban history by such authors as George Chauncey and, in monographs from the University of Chicago Press, Mark Stein, David K. Johnson, and Matt Houlbrook; in analyses of diasporic New York from the anthropologist Martin Manalansan; and, recently, in an account of the rural Midwest, from the communication scholar Mary L. Gray.[15] Rubin's work stands handsomely at the core of that tradition, both at its radical conceptual center and extending forward from the historical middle of urban sexual scholarship in the United States. From "Thinking Sex" to "Of Catamites and Kings," her attention to living populations invites a welcome sense of ordinariness, a practical and ethical description of people and groups who are still easy to demonize and scapegoat in an official culture quick to sell sex in some forms but hostile to the principle of human sexual diversity, and even in the defensive sectors of nondominant sexual communities.[16]

Sex and Class

Rubin's work on sex cuts across questions of social class in two key ways: first, schooled in Left intellectual tradition, Rubin has long been accustomed to thinking about class as a key part of social organization, including within the sexual subcultures she and others have written about; second, her critique of sexual value, memorably articulated in "Thinking Sex," speaks directly to questions of class value. Like sexual value, class value can be arrayed from the "charmed circle" to the "outer limits" of social regard and enfranchisement.

Rubin's 2002 essay on studying sexual subcultures offers many examples of the place of class in sexual cultures, among them the work of Newton on urban drag scenes in the 1960s. Rubin pays close attention to the distinction Newton introduced between "overts" and "coverts" among drag performers and nontheatrical cross-dressers or street fairies. Covert status—where drag performers are careful to restrict their practice to their performance life and to conceal it in their civilian work life in heterosexual contexts—was typically aligned with higher status and class distinction in 1960s Kansas City and Chicago. Overt status, in contrast, was for street fairies, some of them sex workers, who neither concealed their practice and identity in straight public environments nor cultivated cross-dressing as stagecraft, with all the status, propriety, and hauteur that stage-craft conveys. Within gay drag scenes in that time and place, then, alongside their challenges to sexual and gender norms, a class hierarchy keyed to overtness and covertness was enacted and regulated.[17] That hierarchy has echoed through the decades since, as gay people have sought, and sometimes found, conditional social acceptance but usually at the expense of those unable, or uninclined, to pay the tithe of concealment or conformity.

Beyond class as dependent and independent variable, however, are the ways in which Rubin's social theorization of sexual value offers a homology for understanding class value and distinction as they are culturally expressed and institutionally levied. The claim of homology is mine, though Rubin anticipates it in her discussion of the emergence in history and the social sciences of the social constructionist approach to sexual variation. Arguments in the late 1970s and 1980s between "social constructionism and essentialism vis-à-vis sexuality," she argues, "are conceptually similar to those [in the 1950s and 1960s] in economic anthropology between substantivism and formalism," the latter claiming a "universal set of economic motivations shaping economic behavior," the former claiming that "economic motivations were a product of social institutions and varied accordingly."[18] In matters of sexual and economic practice, Rubin is a confirmed constructionist, and so am I. Given their institutional character, sexual and economic formation can be examined together as parallel and reciprocal social forces, and the cultural idioms of each are likely to bear on the other.

Consider Rubin's famed mapping of the charmed circle of socio-sexual propriety, authority, and privilege as both sexual and class framework. In the charmed circle, sex is good, normal, natural, and blessed, in contrast to the outer sexual limits, where it is bad, abnormal, unnatural, and damned. In the early 1980s, sex in the charmed circle meant heterosexual, married, monogamous, procreative, noncommercial, paired, relational, intragenerational, private, no-porn, bodies-only, vanilla sex. Sex at the outer limits meant homosexual, unmarried, promiscuous, nonprocreative, commercial, solitary, group, intergenerational, public, porn- and toy-centered, and sadomasochistic sex. The point was not to assert an absolute hierarchy but to chart the historical valuation and devaluation of sexual practice and subjectivity from religious, medical, and popular points of entry. Over time and place, items would move from the outer limits toward the charmed circle (and haltingly, or subculturally, in the other direction), and the borders themselves would be cast on new ground. But such a schematic, amid the theoretical narrative that surrounded it, would sustain a consciousness of the social construction of sexual value that even radicals had strained to articulate, as well as a model for the relationship between sexual value and stigma. As a historical gesture, moreover, it would provoke questions of what, when, where, and who. What practices and persons, when and where, with what effects? One could no longer project sexual judgment of any kind without recognizing — if you were honest about it — one's participation in a field of value.

The charmed circle and the outer limits can be brought to bear in theorizing class value and demonization, and this is where Rubin's work on sexuality has cut across my own on queerness and class. It isn't at all hard to see where the items in each list in 1984 could be rewritten as expressions of class hierarchy and of the class markers of queer worth. In thinking about queer class cultures, I would find myself in a project of mapping the movable borders between the charmed and its outside, stricken by the ceaseless engines of the social project of distinction and its hierarchies, provisions, and deprivations; stricken by the ease and consistency with which embodiment and sex — always articulated to race as root and branch of class difference — are deployed to mark class worth in almost every form of social good from jobs to things to relationships; and stricken by the ease with which class and status hierarchies are wielded again and again against sexual and gender outsiders as a matter of both misrecognition and maldistribution, usually through common registers of excess and shame. To paraphrase Stuart Hall et al.'s famous articulation about race in *Policing the Crisis*, sex is a mode through which social class is produced.[19] In feminist scholarship this is called intersection, but I remain rooted in the neo-Marxist expression of overdetermination, to bring multiplicity but also distributions of force or effect to any given intersection.[20]

Solidarity

At "Rethinking Sex," my comments focused, first, on the character of friendship I find in the grain of Rubin's work and that of two of her contemporaries, the historian Allan Bérubé and the novelist Dorothy Allison. Separately and together — as friends themselves — Rubin's, Bérubé's, and Allison's writing conveys the value of friendship in the history of sexual politics and sexuality studies since the 1970s, and the strength of friendship in some of the harshest social contexts documented in their writing, and some of the most generative: the barracks, the waterfront, police stations, hospitals and psychiatric interviews, the Marine Cooks and Stewards Union, the writer's workshop, the bathhouse and leather party, the army love affair. In the press of academic distinction and employment — a press that has served me, all things considered — such founding forms of queer solidarity are at risk, which is what makes Rubin's attention to memory, living populations, and the reciprocity of queerness and class so loving. As I reread her essays and interviews, I find that these gestures acknowledge and welcome interdependence in a harsh world of sexual and academic formation. They take on, rather than evade, the impossible contradictions of life as it is lived and lost, and they enable close witness to change. They form a scholarly language of attachment that is available to theorizing and even to a bureaucratic language of policy, and they reflect and preserve a history of studying sexual subcultures from the inside and out. As Rubin herself said in her "Rethinking Sex" keynote address, the attacks she suffered from antipornography feminists, among others, following "Thinking Sex" and her participation in the lesbian S/M circle Samois, have left a punishing imprint on her intellectual past. That imprint can eclipse what else is so formative for so many about her work. Rubin's beautiful contrariness to shaming is solidarity — with her teachers, her communities, and her intellectual traditions. It hasn't been made easy, which makes Rubin's openness remarkable, a model; in anthropology's terms, a gift.

Notes

Many thanks to Heather Love for her invitation to "Rethinking Sex" and to Liliana Herakova for careful editorial assistance.

1. See Gayle Rubin, "Studying Sexual Subcultures: Excavating the Ethnography of Gay Communities in Urban North America," in *Out in Theory: The Emergence of Lesbian and Gay Anthropology*, ed. Ellen Lewin and William L. Leap (Urbana: University of Illinois Press, 2002), 17–69.

2. Lisa Henderson, *Love and Money: Queers, Class, and Cultural Production* (New York: New York University Press, forthcoming).

3. Judith Butler, "Sexual Traffic: An Interview with Gayle Rubin," *differences* 6, nos. 2–3 (1994): 62–98.

4. Rubin, "Studying Sexual Subcultures," 73.

5. Rubin, "Studying Sexual Subcultures," 74.

6. For example, the Stop Porn Culture movement launched in 2006 by Gail Dines, Robert Jensen, and Rebecca Whisnant. See www.stoppornculture.org.

7. "Thinking Sex" appeared first in *Pleasure and Danger: Exploring Female Sexuality*, ed. Carole S. Vance (Boston: Routledge and Kegan Paul, 1984) and has since appeared in many anthologies worldwide.

8. Gayle S. Rubin, "The Traffic in Women: Notes on the 'Political Economy' of Sex," in *Toward an Anthropology of Women*, ed. Rayna Reiter (New York: Monthly Review, 1975).

9. Rubin, "Studying Sexual Subcultures," 46; Butler, "Sexual Traffic," 83–84.

10. Gayle Rubin, "Geologies of Queer Studies: It's Déja Vu All Over Again," *CLAGSNews* 14, no. 2 (2004), web.gc.cuny.edu/clags/archives/Summer04. pdf.

11. To quote Rubin's comment from the audience microphone in response to a presenter at "Rethinking Sex": "Thank you for talking to people."

12. See Gayle Rubin, "Sites, Settlements, and Urban Sex: Archaeology and the Study of Gay Leathermen in San Francisco, 1955–1995," in *Archaeologies of Sexuality*, ed. Robert Schmidt and Barbara Voss (London: Routledge, 2000), 62–89; Rubin, "The Miracle Mile: South of Market and Gay Male Leather in San Francisco, 1962–1996," in *Reclaiming San Francisco: History, Politics, Culture*, ed. James Brook, Chris Carlsson, and Nancy Peters (San Francisco: City Lights, 1998), 247–73.

13. Rubin, "Studying Sexual Subcultures," esp. 21–35.

14. Esther Newton, *Mother Camp: Female Impersonators in America* (Chicago: University of Chicago Press, 1972); and Newton, *Cherry Grove, Fire Island: Sixty Years in America's First Gay and Lesbian Town* (New York: Beacon, 1995).

15. See George Chauncey, *Gay New York: Gender, Urban Culture, and the Making of the Gay Male World, 1890–1940* (New York: Basic Books, 1994). From the University of Chicago Press, see Mark Stein, *City of Sisterly and Brotherly Loves: Lesbian and Gay Philadelphia, 1945–1972* (2000); David K. Johnson, *The Lavender Scare: The Cold War Persecution of Gays and Lesbians in the Federal Government* (2004); Matt Houlbrook, *Queer London: Perils and Pleasures in the Sexual Metropolis, 1918–1957* (2005). See also Martin Manalansan IV, *Global Divas: Filipino Gay Men in the Diaspora* (Durham, NC: Duke University Press, 2003), and Mary L. Gray, *Out in the Country: Youth, Media, and Queer Visibility in Rural America* (New York: New York University Press, 2009).

16. "Of Catamites and Kings: Reflections on Butch, Gender, and Boundaries" illustrates Rubin's truly extraordinary skill in describing gender variation and expression and her humane and sensible caution against community hostility to gender and sexual category trouble (in this case levied in lesbian communities against masculine gender variance). The essay first appeared in *The Persistent Desire*, ed. Joan Nestle (Boston: Alyson, 1992), 466–83, and is reprinted in *The Transgender Studies Reader*, ed. Susan Stryker and Stephen Whittle (New York: Routledge, 2006), 471–82.

17. Rubin, "Studying Sexual Subcultures," esp. 45–53.

18. Here, Rubin draws from the economic historian and theorist Karl Polanyi, in his 1957 book with Conrad Arensberg and Henry Pearson, *Trade and Market in the Early Empires: Economies in History and Theory* (Chicago: Gateway, 1957). See Rubin, "Studying Sexual Subcultures," 41.

19. Stuart Hall, Chas Critcher, Tony Jefferson, John Clarke, and Brian Roberts, *Policing the Crisis: Mugging, the State, and Law and Order* (London: Macmillan, 1978).

20. Many authors turn to Rubin's work in articulating sexual dissidence and social

class. See, e.g., Laura Kipnis's analysis of *Hustler Magazine* in her book *Bound and Gagged: Pornography and the Politics of Fantasy in America* (Durham, NC: Duke University Press, 1999), where Rubin meets Peter Stallybrass and Allon White (*The Politics and Poetics of Transgression* [Ithaca: Cornell University Press, 1986]) on the class affront of hypersexual humor; Michael Warner in *The Trouble with Normal* (New York: Simon and Schuster, 1999), where Rubin meets Goffman in Warner's analysis of stigmaphilia and stigmaphobia; Carolyn Kay Steedman, *Landscape for a Good Woman: A Story of Two Lives* (New Brunswick: Rutgers University Press, 1994), where Rubin meets Sigmund Freud and Steedman's mother in 1950's England, in an analysis of the trade value of working-class motherhood and the psychosocial power such value confers, and Katherine Sender in *Business, not Politics: The Making of the Gay Market* (New York: Columbia, 2004), esp. chap. 7, where Rubin meets Pierre Bourdieu in an analysis of "moral capital" in the development of the gay market.

THINKING TRAFFICKING, THINKING SEX

Carole S. Vance

Gayle Rubin's importance as a theorist of heterosexuality has been underappreciated. Although "Thinking Sex" is often recognized as foundational to lesbian/gay and queer studies, the essay, along with the earlier "The Traffic in Women," is a long rumination on the political economy of heterosexuality, sexual hierarchies, and sex law that portion out "natural" forms of heterosexuality from the "unnatural," and moral panics that selectively mobilize and direct public attention and outrage to particular forms of sexual danger while ignoring others.[1] The tools offered in "Thinking Sex," along with the title "The Traffic in Women," deliciously borrowed from the work of turn-of-the-century anarchist Emma Goldman, bring us full circle to the growth and intensification of trafficking, particularly of women, as a contemporary global concern and riveting issue of social justice.[2]

Rubin's homage to Goldman recognizes how their projects overlap, though separated by over seventy years. Like Goldman, though with considerably more theoretical sophistication and ethnographic depth, Rubin locates the subordination of women in the most conventional and socially valued form of heterosexuality, the exchange of women in marriage. Goldman's essay mocked the newfound tabloid fascination (circa 1911) with the "social evil" of prostitution (184), railing against the industrial system of wage slavery and low pay for women that made prostitution a more attractive economic alternative. Along the way, she attacks Victorian hypocrisy, the double standard of sexual conduct for women and men, the denial of women's sexual pleasure, and the socially respectable forms of traffic in women—that is, marriage—in which sexual services are exchanged for livelihood and resources. Goldman gives a final rhetorical kick to the "righteous" who "cry against the white slave traffic" and the ever-present moral entrepreneurs, "parasites who stalk about the world as inspectors, investigators, detectives, and so forth" (184).

GLQ 17:1
DOI 10.1215/10642684-2010-024
© 2010 by Duke University Press

Goldman's energetic and irate essay argues that late-nineteenth-century crusades against "white slavery" and the "traffic in women" (prostitution) were misguided sideshows, which diverted attention from and action against the underlying causes of women's oppression: marriage, the family, and political economy. Rubin develops these themes, but her witty borrowing of the title "The Traffic in Women" pokes fun at the then-archaic and quasi-comical specter (for the reader in 1975) of late Victorian social purity crusades. Rubin trusted the reader to get the joke, given how these crusades had faded from public attention, having eventually been discredited by popular media at the time and by later scholarship.[3] But now, the joke is on us, since new crusades against trafficking, hyperfocused on women and prostitution, have reappeared, capturing popular imagination and outrage, while instigating changes in national and international law and policy. The new antitrafficking campaign reanimates archaic narratives and interventions while also inventing novel frameworks for identifying and remedying social injustice.

The internal contradictions and incoherence of the antitrafficking campaign make it a capacious home for reactionary and progressive impulses and groups alike. In addition, the favorite narrative form for telling trafficking stories, the melodrama, diverts attention from larger structures of exploitation. It focuses instead on individual actors: an innocent female victim crying out for rescue from sexual danger and diabolical male villains intent on her violation. The plot may feature excess, extremity, and sensation, but what is at stake — as in the sexual purity campaigns of the early twentieth century — is normative heterosexuality and its sexual arrangements.

Far from stable, the nature and terms of heterosexual sex have been the subject of ferocious social and political struggle in the past two hundred years, far overshadowing debates about homosexuality. The "lower orders" in Rubin's sexual hierarchy contained disreputable forms of heterosexuality, too: premarital heterosex, nonreproductive heterosexual practices ("unnatural sex"), heterosexual transactions for money, and excessive forms of sexual desire, particularly for women. The normative elements of heterosexuality have long been disputed in highly public controversies about the purpose of marital sex (procreation or intimacy and pleasure); the means to effect nonprocreative sex (information and technologies for birth control and abortion); the right to engage in premarital heterosexuality (repeal of criminal laws against fornication); the double standard of sexual judgment for men and women (social purity campaigns directed against prostitution and venereal disease); and the ways that naturalized heterosexuality functions as a site of gender inequality and violence (the growth of consent as a standard of sexual value, and reforms that criminalized marital rape). Expansion of the terms of heterosexuality for women, particularly in regard to safety, nondiscrimination, and pleasure, has been the subject of major political battles in the past two centuries, especially for feminism.

The massive and enduring social purity campaigns of the late nineteenth and early twentieth centuries—against prostitution ("trafficking"), venereal disease, the double standard—were interventions into heterosexuality. The overt objective of these campaigns was to rein in and transform male heterosexual behavior, but the focus on prostitution emphasized male behavior in the public, extrafamilial realm. Although the tragic narrative of a brothel patron transmitting venereal disease to his unsuspecting wife and child was a staple of antiprostitution broadsides and identified a clear link between male sexual privilege and the home, the connection remained abstract; the connective tissue was disease, not sexual violence and women's conjugal duty. Critics of prostitution, especially women, might rail against the "social evil" and condemn the harsh treatment of young women, forever cast out as "fallen" while their male partners remained respectable, but the question of whose husband frequented prostitutes remained unasked, though probably not unthought. Lacking legal personhood, the right to property and the vote, and with feeble means of economic independence, married women's ability to expose and challenge male sexual privilege in marriage was limited and perhaps more safely displaced onto crusades against trafficking.

In the late nineteenth and early twentieth centuries, the term *trafficking* meant prostitution (of women and girls).[4] National laws and early international conventions against trafficking criminalized prostitution, chiefly the selling of sex but also related services and activities (running a brothel, renting rooms to prostitutes, living off the earnings of prostitutes, or assisting in transporting persons for the purpose of prostitution). The criminal offense violated morality: sexual exchange and behavior outside marriage injured society. For this reason, the actual conditions of sexual exchange were irrelevant: voluntary or coerced selling of sexual services was equally criminal. Early international conventions are explicit that the consent of the prostitute is to be disregarded.[5]

Although not all Euro-American nations prohibited prostitution through criminal law (some permitted it through various forms of administrative regulation), those who criminalized the selling of sexual services arrested, detained, and prosecuted the overwhelmingly female sellers, not the overwhelmingly male buyers. Thus, the contradiction inherent in suffragist-driven campaigns against trafficking: their efforts to renarrate the story of prostitution (that is, to decry male lust and misbehavior, while defending and "rescuing" downtrodden women and girls) collided with a legal regime that criminalized women's part of the transaction but not men's and a symbolic regime that cast women selling sex as debased temptresses, unnatural women, and latter-day Eves.[6] In either case, Goldman's point rang true: in the furious campaigns about trafficking, questions about women's position in marriage and wage labor gained little traction, while mobilizations about trafficking resulted in increased criminal penalties and state control for prostitutes but few improvements in women's livelihood and legal personhood.

By the 1920s, public campaigns against white slavery faded and antitrafficking laws fell into relative disuse, only for the issue to be revived in the 1990s by concerns about transnational migration, exploitation of migrant workers, and human rights.[7] By the start of the twenty-first century, however, newly enacted laws on trafficking offered a transformed definition of the nature and harms of trafficking. In both the new international law (Protocol to Prevent, Suppress and Punish Trafficking in Persons, Especially Women and Children, 2000) and U.S. law (Trafficking Victims Protection Act of 2000 and subsequent reauthorizations, trafficking no longer focuses exclusively on prostitution, but instead on all extreme forms of labor exploitation.[8] Both laws make clear that any type of person can be trafficked (man, woman, or child) into any type of work (factory, farming, fishing, sexual services, domestic labor, to name a few). The UN Protocol echoes past conventions by naming the "exploitation of prostitution" as a marked category, but it also makes clear that states ratifying the Protocol are free to handle prostitution in any way they see fit (including permitting it); they are obligated only to criminalize the "exploitation of prostitution," parallel to exploitation of other types of labor.[9] Although the crime of trafficking is no longer synonymous with prostitution in international law, these more capacious and exploitation-based definitions compete with popular and media portrayals, which overwhelmingly favor the nineteenth-century story of sexual danger and rescue.

New antitrafficking laws target the most heinous and extreme forms of labor exploitation, not garden-variety and everyday exploitation (e.g., underpayment or denial of benefits). In addition, the definition of trafficking requires that three tightly linked elements be demonstrated: (1) an action (recruitment, transportation, transfer, harboring, or receipt of a person), (2) the use of specific methods (force, fraud, abuse of authority, etc.), (3) with the intent to place a person into a condition of exploited labor.[10] These required elements set a high bar for proving the crime, while making a sharp disjunction, of the kind Goldman was eager to dissolve, between extraordinary (criminal) and ordinary (legal) exploitation.

Recent antitrafficking law is impressive on paper: trafficking has been completely recast. The crime is no longer understood as a moral offense against society committed through prostitution but as harm to an individual committed through extreme exploitation in any type of work. In the case that the coerced work is criminalized (as prostitution may be), the trafficked person is to be treated as a victim of crime, deserving of social services, rather than a criminal.

Despite the radical revision in trafficking's definition, these new laws have been disappointing in their implementation.[11] They have also been disappointing in their vulnerability to capture by antiprostitution activists (both evangelical and feminist) and late nineteenth-century frames of melodrama.[12] If the implementation and interpretation of the new law has been weak, however, the flood of documentary, exposé, investigation, and made-for-TV dramas about trafficking has been robust and the structure for telling the alleged story—melodrama—excessive.

Virtually unchanged from its nineteenth-century versions, the modern melodrama of trafficking performs various reductions that erode the innovations of international law: trafficking again means prostitution (forced or voluntary); the trafficked person is a woman or female minor; the danger and injury are sexual; and the nature of the crime is an offense against society and morality (for evangelical activists) or against women's equality (for antiprostitution feminists).[13] With its compelling narrative of sexual danger, drama, sensation, furious action, wild applause, and most important, clearly identifiable victims, villains, and heroes, the antitrafficking melodrama remains highly effective in mobilizing public opinion. Classic melodrama's anticipation of and satisfaction with rescue as the plot's denouement is most compatible with the state's rescue of women through criminal law and increased state power. The ubiquitous antitrafficking melodrama displaces modern concepts of extreme labor exploitation and rights violations, replacing them with scripts of male lust endangering innocent women. It also replaces the trafficked person's claim to multiple rights with a single remedy, the right to be rescued.[14]

Melodrama is a very flexible narrative form, and the antitrafficking melodrama can be and is set in any global location—Nepal, Moldova, Nigeria—with small changes in costumes, background scenery, and names, which nevertheless lend local color and "authenticity." Although the antitrafficking melodrama invokes contemporary issues like globalization, poverty, and gender inequality, these gestures are sketchy at best. Antitrafficking melodramas offer minimal exploration of political and social factors in specific locations. Remedies are generalized across all places: one-size-fits-all. Melodrama is about people, not states, institutions, or structural conditions.[15] The focus on individual actors guarantees that structural factors cannot be portrayed (since they are not persons and do not have emotions). The emphasis on individuals and nefarious motivations is echoed by new antitrafficking tools and conventions, given their predilection for criminal law and prosecution of individuals.

As in the previous century, antitrafficking discourses, both vernacular and legal, are contradictory and displaced conversations about heterosexuality. Who are the bad men — immoral, sex-driven, or nonegalitarian, depending on the standards of sexual legitimacy and value being employed? How can they be recognized, as individuals or as members of dangerous social, racial, or ethnic collectivities? Do the bad men comprise a distinct minority? Or are they everywhere? Are women likely to encounter them when alone, unmarried, adventuring, at work, far from home, or not in the family? Or are the behaviors of such men more likely to be encountered in ordinary heterosexuality and marriage, Goldman's *ur*ground of trafficking? To the extent that new ideas about trafficking as labor exploitation gained any traction, what kinds of work and exchange (sexual and nonsexual) occur in heterosexuality? Is this work exploitative? Furthermore, what is the relationship between forms of sexual and nonsexual exploitation, as well as between exploitation in intimate and nonintimate spheres? To the extent that ideas about female culpability in prostitution and trafficking into forced prostitution remain powerful, if less blatant, discussions of trafficking also admit the specter of the bad woman and raise questions about what is to be done with her — arrest, rehabilitation, or rescue? Such questions are present, explicitly or spectrally, in virtually every legislative debate, law, report, witness testimony, or dramatization about trafficking into forced prostitution.

Sexuality remains a potent terrain for political and social struggles. Like dangerous radioactive substances, trafficking has a long half-life. The resurgence of campaigns against trafficking, still popularly understood as women forced into prostitution, makes clear that archaic battles return in new forms, with some, if not all, of the same underlying stakes. That heterosexuality is interrogated and challenged is not a bad thing, but the examination of heterosexuality needs to be at once closer to home, scrutinizing normative and everyday heterosexualities and marriages rather than distant and extreme cases of sexual danger, and more in the world, foregrounding the political and social architectures — many of which are nonsexual — that limit human flourishing more effectively and cruelly than all the villains of twenty-first-century antitrafficking melodramas combined.

Now is still a good time "to think about sex."[16]

Notes

Thanks to Heather Love and the University of Pennsylvania for organizing and supporting the conference "Rethinking Sex" at which this paper was given. For encouragement and suggestions regarding this essay, thanks to Heather Love, Gayle Rubin,

Ann Snitow, and the editorial staff of *GLQ* and Duke University Press. Thanks to Alice Miller for a decade of conversations.

1. Gayle Rubin, "Thinking Sex: Notes for a Radical Theory of the Politics of Sexuality," in *Pleasure and Danger: Exploring Female Sexuality*, ed. Carole S. Vance (Boston: Routledge and Kegan Paul, 1984) 267–319; Rubin, "The Traffic in Women: Notes on the 'Political Economy' of Sex," in *Toward an Anthropology of Women* ed. Rayna Reiter (New York: Monthly Review Press, 1975) 157–210.

2. At the end of a long list of acknowledgments, Rubin thanks "Emma Goldman for the title" (Goldman, "The Traffic in Women," in *Anarchism and Other Essays* [New York: Mother Earth Publishing Association, 1910], 183–200; hereafter cited by page number).

3. Gretchen Soderlund, "Covering Urban Vice: *The New York Times*, 'White Slavery,' and the Construction of Journalistic Knowledge," *Critical Studies in Media Communication* 19, no. 4 (2002): 438–60; Mark T. Connelly, *The Response to Prostitution in the Progressive Era* (Chapel Hill: University of North Carolina Press, 1980); Judith R. Walkowitz, *City of Dreadful Delight: Narratives of Sexual Danger in Late-Victorian London* (Chicago: University of Chicago Press, 1992).

4. The International Agreement for the Suppression of the "White Slave Traffic" (1904); the International Convention for the Suppression of the White Slave Traffic (1910); the International Convention for the Suppression of the Traffic in Women and Children (1921); and the International Convention for the Suppression of the Traffic in Women of Full Age (1933) address "women and girls" as the victims of trafficking, although the 1921 convention also applies to "children of both sexes." It is not until the Convention for the Suppression of the Traffic in Persons and of the Exploitation of the Prostitution of Others (1951) that the victim is imagined as a "person" ("procures, entices or leads away, for purposes of prostitution, another person").

5. For example, the International Convention for the Suppression of the White Slave Traffic (1910) states: "Whoever, in order to gratify the passions of another person, has procured, enticed, or led away, even with her consent, a woman or girl under age, for immoral purposes, shall be punished" (Article 1), www1.umn.edu/humanrts/instree/whiteslavetraffic1910.html. Similar language is found in the International Convention for the Suppression of the Traffic in Women and Children (1921); The International Convention for the Suppression of the Traffic in Women of Full Age (1933); and the Convention for the Suppression of the Traffic in Persons and of the Exploitation of the Prostitution of Others (1951).

6. For this reason, some social purity reformers attacked state licensing or regulation of brothels, without necessarily supporting criminal laws that targeted prostitutes. As the strength of the social purity movement grew, however, this nuanced strategy was overtaken by more comprehensive programs to eliminate prostitution using any and all available tools.

7. Antitrafficking laws remained a powerful tool for persecution and selective prosecu-
    tion. In the United States the federal Mann Act (1910), aimed at stopping the inter-
    state or foreign trafficking of women for "immoral purposes," was used to prosecute
    the African American boxer Jack Johnson, the actor Charlie Chaplin, and the Uni-
    versity of Chicago sociologist William I. Thomas, widely viewed as payback for their
    violation of racial and sexual conventions. See David J. Langum, *Crossing over the
    Line: Legislating Morality and the Mann Act* (Chicago: University of Chicago Press,
    1994).

8. Protocol to Prevent, Suppress and Punish Trafficking in Persons, Especially Women
    and Children, Supplementing the U.N. Convention against Transnational Organized
    Crime, G.A. Res. 55/25, Annex II, U.N. GAOR, 55th Sess., U.N. Doc. A/55/383
    (Nov. 15, 2000) (hereafter cited as UN Protocol); Trafficking Victims Protection Act
    of 2000, Pub. L. No. 106–386 §2A, 114 Stat. 1464 (2000) (hereafter cited as TPVA),
    as supplemented by the Trafficking Victims Protection Reauthorization Act of 2003,
    Pub. L. No. 108–193, 117 Stat. 2875 (hereafter cited as 2003 TVPRA), the Traffick-
    ing Victims Protection Reauthorization Act of 2005, Pub. L. No. 109–164, 119 Stat.
    3558 (2006) (codified at 22 U.S.C. §7101) (hereafter cited as 2005 TVPRA), and
    the William Wilberforce Trafficking Victims Protection Reauthorization Act of 2008,
    Pub. L. No. 110–457, 122 Stat. 5044 (2008) (codified at 22 U.S.C. §7101) (hereafter
    cited as 2008 TVPRA).

9. Ann Jordan, The Annotated Guide to the Complete U.N. Trafficking Protocol
    (Washington, DC: International Human Rights Law Group, May 2002 [updated
    August 2002]), 4. www.globalrights.org/site/DocServer/Annotated_Protocol.pdf
    ?docID=2723.

10. For example, the UN Protocol defines trafficking as "the recruitment, transportation,
    transfer, harbouring or receipt of persons, by means of the threat or use of force of
    other forms of coercion, of abduction, of fraud, of deception, of the abuse of power or
    of a position of vulnerability or of the giving or receiving of payments or benefits to
    achieve the consent of a person having control over another person, for the purpose of
    exploitation. Exploitation shall include, at a minimum, the exploitation of the prostitu-
    tion of others or other forms of sexual exploitation, forced labour or services, slavery
    or practices similar to slavery, servitude or the removal of organs."

11. The notion that trafficked persons are crime victims needing social services turns out
    to be an expensive project. Recognizing the potential cost, the UN Protocol *recom-
    mends* that states provide such services but does not *require* them to. Similarly, the
    U.S. Congress, alarmed by the prospect that hordes of undocumented migrants could
    attempt to claim continued presence and costly services, instituted an onerous vetting
    process to prove that one was a "victim of severe forms of trafficking," while restrict-
    ing the number of visas for trafficked persons to no more than five thousand per year.
    The narrowness of the eye of the needle is further illustrated by the fact that from

2001–2009, only some two thousand of these visas have been approved. For details about implementation and benefits under the US law, see Alicia W. Peters, "Trafficking in Meaning, Law, Victims, and the State" (PhD diss., Columbia University, 2010).

12. Typical melodramatic examples include Nicholas Kristof's many journalistic exposés of trafficking in the *New York Times*: "Girls for Sale," January 14, 2004; "Bargaining for Freedom," January 21, 2004; "Going Home, with Hope," January 24, 2004; "Loss of Innocence," January 28, 2004; and "Stopping the Traffickers," January 31, 2004. See also *The Selling of Innocence*, an Emmy Award–winning film depicting the trafficking of girls from Nepal to India (dir. William Cobban, Elliott Halpern, and Simcha Jacobovici [Ruchira Gupta, field researcher], Canadian Broadcasting Company, 1997), and the two-part television drama "Human Trafficking," with Mira Sorvino and Donald Sutherland, which aired on *Lifetime* (2005).

13. On the history of melodrama and melodrama as a generic form, see Peter Brooks, *The Melodramatic Imagination: Balzac, Henry James, Melodrama, and the Mode of Excess* (New York: Columbia University Press, 1985); and James Redmond, ed., *Melodrama* (Cambridge: Cambridge University Press, 1992). For an example of the nineteenth-century deployment of this rhetoric, see W. T. Stead, "The Maiden Tribute of Modern Babylon I," *Pall Mall Gazette*, July 6, 1885. For an analysis, see chapter 4, "The Maiden Tribute of Modern Babylon," in Walkowitz, *City of Dreadful Delight*, 81–120.

14. For a more detailed analysis of the work of antitrafficking melodramas, see Carole S. Vance, "'Juanita/Svetlana/Geeta' Is Crying: Melodrama, Human Rights, and Anti-Trafficking Interventions," Owens Lecture, University of Rochester, December 1, 2006, and "Hiss the Villain: Depicting Sex Trafficking," Lecture, School for American Research, Santa Fe, May 2005.

15. Melodrama does not easily incorporate structural analysis: for example, how would the World Bank or U.S. opium-eradication policy (which impoverished Thai farmers and drove their daughters into being trafficked into forced prostitution) appear in the plot? See David Feingold, "The Hell of Good Intentions: Some Preliminary Thoughts on Opium in the Political Ecology of the Trade in Girls and Women," in *Where China Meets Southeast Asia: Social and Cultural Change in the Border Regions*, ed. Grant Evans, Christopher Hutton, and Khun E. Kuah (New York: St. Martin's, 2000), 183–204.

16. Rubin, "Thinking Sex," 267.

LOVE AND ANGER

Scenes from a Passionate Career

Lisa Duggan

$\mathcal{G}$ayle Rubin exudes a cool brilliance. But she contains multitudes, and beneath the surface of her analytic prose and courtly presence, passionate engagements have shaped her career. Her emergence into political and academic superstardom began in 1972, with a section of her senior honors thesis in women's studies at the University of Michigan that would become her classic 1975 article "The Traffic in Women: Notes on the 'Political Economy' of Sex." Though she has said she initially expected perhaps fifty people to read that article, as we all know it blew into feminist theory with hurricane force. The reason? That cool, analytic brilliance of course. The article introduced the concept of historically and geographically varying "sex/gender" systems, grounded in Rubin's innovative combination of insights from anthropology and psychoanalysis. The argument was elegant, and it was groundbreaking. But more than that, Rubin's work on that article reflected her profoundly passionate engagement with the conundrums of feminist politics at a moment of ferment. She found a way out of the limits of Marxist theory without dismissing it, because she applied that cool intellect to the hot campaigns and conundrums of feminist organizing around her, especially the efforts to organize massage parlor workers in her college town of Ann Arbor.[1] Passionate engagements, the working out of problems that matter in the political world, can infuse scholarly work with a connected presence that energizes as well as enlightens readers.

The success of "The Traffic in Women" catapulted Rubin into the academic limelight at a time when she was a graduate student in anthropology, still at the University of Michigan. The transformation from student to major figure in feminist theory had to have been jolting, but it was overall a positive event (for all of us, as well as for her). But by the time she came out with her second blockbuster article in 1984, "Thinking Sex: Notes for a Radical Theory of the Politics of Sex-

GLQ 17:1
DOI 10.1215/10642684-2010-025
© 2010 by Duke University Press

uality," the tone of her reception had begun to shift into more mixed affective registers. The passionate engagements in sexual politics that led Rubin to write the article were polarizing as well as energizing for readers. "Thinking Sex" fell into the vortex of a sex panic that the article itself sought to analyze. Rubin was attacked, personally and viciously, as well as celebrated. Some activists demonized her while others hung on her every word; some academics condescended to or dismissed her while others elaborated eagerly on her insights. Her until then presumptively golden career path took a difficult turn.

In the world of activist politics, these vicious attacks, demonization, efforts to defeat a political position through personal smears of its advocates are familiar enough. During the 1980s the widespread employment of these modes of discourse in feminist precincts was nonetheless shocking to some of us. During the 1980s Rubin became one of the central targets of antipornography feminists who objected to her analysis in "Thinking Sex." But her article was seldom analyzed and refuted. Instead, she was more often attacked for her membership in the San Francisco–based lesbian S/M group, Samois, that she had helped found in 1978.[2]

The attacks drew on the deep wells of stigma attached to S/M sexual practices. At the same time, attackers generally misunderstood those practices, equating them with coercion and violence, as well as the forms of dominance and submission that underpin inequalities in the social and political world. Ignoring the history of a sexual subculture that emphasizes consensual power play and that features women as dominants more centrally than men, attackers simply and unequivocally equated lesbian S/M with patriarchal and racist violence and inequality. Aside from the general political antagonism, antipornography activists singled out individuals for sexual shaming. Rubin was a key target. Her assumed sexual desires and practices were invoked, publicly and repeatedly, to disqualify her not only as a feminist but also as an advocate for social justice. Rubin herself never spoke publicly or wrote about her personal sexual history, so her desires and practices were extrapolated by assumption from her membership in Samois and from her political positions. Such sexual shaming in the context of a public dispute cuts far more deeply than intellectual or political vituperation alone can. Public sexual shaming, for desires and practices already drenched in stigma and freighted with a history of misunderstanding and persecution, constitutes a kind of trauma. In the context of the feminist "sex wars," lesbianism shed its wider social stigma to become a valorized index of egalitarian sexuality, but only if properly embodied and performed according to "feminist" standards of sisterly romance. Lesbian S/M, in the rhetoric of antiporn activists, signified the reviled outer edge of queerness tied to all the violence and inequality that feminism opposes. And there stood Gayle Rubin, in that place of intersecting personal shaming and political attack.[3]

In academic settings, such direct personal attacks are generally (although not entirely) taboo. Academics and many other intellectuals responded to her work in more distanced ways. Some embraced "Thinking Sex," others dismissed it, often by positioning it at some "extreme" against which they might appear as "moderate." In academic circles she acquired another layer of superstardom among an emerging cohort of "sex radical" feminist and queer studies scholars.[4] But at the same time, the stigma attached to her dissertation research on the gay male S/M scene in San Francisco persisted, taking distanced or coded forms. Within academia, affect is subtly but assiduously policed. Contempt and condescension are acceptable, as professors compete for places at the top of the (manufactured) scarcity economy of smartness. Hero worship is permissible in the form of uncritical citation of broadly certified authorities. Passive aggression is a pervasive affective mode, acted out within the boundaries of professional civility. But passionate engagements that might be called *love*, or reactions to unfairness recognizable as *anger*, are deeply suspect.

I want to argue here that Gayle Rubin should, on a just planet, have an endowed chair at a major university, with busloads of research money and a light teaching load. She should be paid enormous sums to grace our lecterns. Not that this is what she seeks; such careerist rewards have never been her primary motivation. But I'm talking about justice. Her two classic field-changing articles alone are worth piles and piles of books by ordinary academic intellectuals. Her contributions to the feminist and queer academy are as great as those of anyone living. I believe that the reason she has not been so rewarded is not only the obvious one—that she hasn't yet published the required monograph. Exceptions to this requirement are rare, but possible. The less obvious reason, I believe, is that Rubin's academic career has been haunted by the stigma attached not only to the topic of her dissertation but also to the affective surround in which she finds herself post–sex panic.[5] Her passion—both the clear love for her comrades and subjects that lives beneath the cool prose, and the anger, suppressed by her courtliness, that nonetheless animates her accounts of the years of sex panic—makes academics uncomfortable. The very qualities of her writing that gave "Traffic" and "Thinking" such powerful multiple lives—the passionate engagements that infuse them, their address to both activist and academic readers, the ways that they *matter* in the world—are also barriers to full recognition in academic quarters. Their brilliance just isn't *dry* enough.

I first encountered Rubin at an academic conference, and my friendship with her was shaped and punctuated over time at a series of such conferences. They provide me with snapshots of crucial moments that help illuminate the vicissitudes of her career.

"The Second Sex": Thirty Years Later, New York University, 1979

I came to New York City from my native Virginia in 1976 to enroll as an MA student in women's history at Sarah Lawrence College. By fall 1979 I was beginning to apply to PhD programs. I was twenty-five years old, and "The Second Sex" conference at New York University was my first major academic conference. The conference was overflowing with well-known feminist intellectuals, and mobbed by wannabes like me. It was full of intensity and controversy. Audre Lorde delivered her lecture "The Master's Tools Will Never Dismantle the Master's House" at a panel called "The Personal Is Political," where she generated intense responses during the speak-out at the microphone that passed for a question and answer period.[6] I remember sitting on the floor in a large public space between panels, organizing my notes, when Rubin walked through the room in a motorcycle jacket. The effect on the assembled conference goers was electric. Already a superstar as a graduate student, read, cited, and admired by nearly everyone there, her appearance nonetheless stirred up powerfully mixed responses in that setting. She was an openly butch dyke in leather, not exactly a professorial look in 1979. There were rumors about her involvement in lesbian S/M politics in San Francisco. She was *hot* in a very challenging way. I was smitten.

I went to her panel, "Sexuality, Feminism, and Culture," with talks by Carole Vance and Ellen DuBois as well as Rubin. I remember Vance's talk as hilarious and sharp, DuBois's as earnest and pointed, and Rubin's as . . . well, I can't say I really remember the talk itself, an early working through of the issues analyzed in "Thinking Sex." I was taking in her presence on some other level. I was impressed by her humility, her generosity (she credited *everyone* she had drawn ideas from), her soft southern accent. She didn't take up the huge ego space that academic rock stars usually occupy. She gathered up ideas, worked with them, and distributed them back — a kind of agricultural model of intellectual production. I was struck by the contrast between the earlier electric impact of her hot leather-clad dyke presence and her gentle, collaborative, *warm* mode of panel participation.

The Scholar and the Feminist: The Barnard Sex Conference, 1982

By the time I got to Barnard for the Scholar and Feminist IX conference, "Towards a Politics of Sexuality," in 1982, I was nearing the end of my PhD course work and heading into my comprehensive exams in history at the University of Pennsylvania. But I was an ambivalent academic, not at all sure that I wanted to be a professor. Political activism and journalism were calling my name at increasing volume. When I walked into the Barnard conference that year, I felt like I was walking into my own split engagements. A planning group of intellectuals and artists had organized a genial environment to consider sexual politics in the overlapping arenas of history, art, literature, and feminism. But the maelstrom of debate within activist circles literally walked in the door and took over, creating intensities of conflict that live now in infamy. At this conference, I went again to hear Rubin.[7]

At her panel, Rubin presented a working version of "Thinking Sex," complete with handouts of the drawings of "the sex hierarchy" and "the charmed circle" of sexual respectability. Like the anthropologist that she is, Rubin coolly analyzed the strange sexual beliefs of Americans. She proceeded methodically to lay out and pick apart the assumptions governing the very stigma that would soon wash over her own career like a tsunami. The workshop was fascinating, but low-key, though I do remember noticing the vitality of her language, the glee with which she explained "the domino theory of sexual peril" and "the fallacy of misplaced scale." She was not only brilliant and prescient (one of the earliest U.S. adopters of Foucault's *History of Sexuality* — the first time I saw the book was in her hand), but she was innovative and funny, passionately engaged and full of herself. Outside the doors of the workshop, though, she was increasingly under personal attack.

In the wake of that Barnard conference, I dropped out of graduate school to become a full-time activist and journalist. My first big publication was a 1984 story on the cover of the *Village Voice* about the antipornography ordinances passed in Minneapolis and Indianapolis. I got to know Rubin then through my activism — we worked together through the Feminist Anti-Censorship Taskforce, meeting and planning in both New York and San Francisco. The academic context fell away for nearly a decade.

The Australian National University, Canberra, 1993

By 1993 I had returned to finish my PhD and was a visiting assistant professor in American studies at Brown University. I was thrilled to be invited to be a visiting fellow at the Humanities Research Centre (HRC) at the Australian National University in Canberra that summer. The Australians had invited six North Americans involved in LGBT studies to come to what we referred to as queer summer camp (though it was winter in Australia) — Cindy Patton, Henry Abelove, Rubin, John D'Emilio, Vance, Dianne Chisholm, and me. (There were other fellows and visitors in residence at different, overlapping times.) We were still mired in the sex panic focused on pornography, S/M, and butch/femme roles, and there were many moments when we were attacked for our sexual politics.[8] But I remember the good times more clearly — the twice daily breaks for tea and cookies, the two-hour dim sum lunches, the hikes to see kangaroos and koala bears, the apartments we all lived in with rainfall showerheads, the talks we each gave at the HRC. Rubin gave a lecture based on her dissertation research, including a slide show of the images and artifacts she had collected in the South of Market (SOMA) San Francisco neighborhood where the gay S/M scene was located during the 1980s.

Rubin's lecture provided a richly documented ethnographic portrait of the SOMA scene during the late 1970s and early 1980s. But her demeanor, her affective surround, had shifted significantly since her Barnard conference workshop. She was more somber, less animated, and much more defended. I think there were at least two reasons for that. Many of the men who were subjects of her research had died of AIDS since the mid-1980s, so the lecture had the tone of a eulogy. She clearly loved the men she had known as well as studied. The scene she was re-creating for us, in vivid detail, had died as well. There were many moments of humor, but sadness infused Rubin's talk. In addition, by this time Rubin and her political comrades had been under attack for so long that the habit of defending herself and her work had settled into her manner of presentation. Constantly challenged to explain the etiology of S/M, Rubin constantly resisted those questions to emphasize the historical and cultural contexts for "erotic speciation." It seemed to me that, under the surface of humility and graciousness that always marks Rubin's public appearances, she was angry. Who wouldn't be? And who among us who has not been attacked the way she was for so many years has any real idea what impact such sustained hostility has on one's psyche and one's work? I can only guess, but my guess is that the cost of absorbing hurt and anger over time leads to various kinds of paralysis, the kind of paralysis that might significantly delay or derail that required monograph.

"Rethinking Sex," University of Pennsylvania, 2009

What an exciting event—a gathering of scholars influenced by Rubin's work, a chance to express collective gratitude and appreciation. The spring 2009 conference "Rethinking Sex" showcased the broad impact of "Traffic" and "Thinking," and also illuminated the new directions that feminist theory and queer studies have taken over the past decade. Finally, work that draws from critical race theory and embraces a transnational frame has come to occupy the center of gender and sexuality studies. The sparkling new work now called "queer of color critique," new queer approaches to the study of affect, queer studies intersecting with disability studies, and research that connects sexuality to political economic formations (such as neoliberalism), was on display. Rubin's work has been taken along, by emerging scholars, in these new directions. Twenty-five years after the publication of "Thinking Sex," there is a lot to celebrate about the growth of this motley field.

Rubin's keynote lecture at this conference, "Blood under the Bridge: Reflections on 'Thinking Sex,'" offered reflections not only on the article but on the political climate from which it emerged. Never one to congratulate herself for her own brilliance, Rubin characteristically credited a long list of scholars and the historical moment more broadly for the creativity that produced "Thinking Sex." She re-created the scene of the 1980s sex wars for her audience. There is no way not to recognize it as a scene of trauma, the kind of scene that generates painful, repetitive revisiting. I circled the words laden with affect on my copy of the speech: "public enemy," "intimidate," "chorus of indignant condemnation," "vilification," "bitterness," "panicked," and more. Some refer to the attacks, some to her responses, and all together they pop off the pages. I arrived in Philadelphia for "Rethinking Sex" as a full professor at NYU, with something of a checkered career behind me—in and out of academia, in and out of various political conflicts, with some scars and some bitterness still marking the intense moments. But I was never under the kind of attack that Rubin (and a few others, including Dorothy Allison and Amber Hollibaugh) endured during the sex wars. I wonder how recognition of the probable impact of such trauma can influence how we shape our academic institutions in the twenty-first century? Can we recognize the stigma against the kind of work Rubin does on sexuality (not abstract, but focused concretely and specifically on a sexual subculture) and push back against it? Can we see the taboo on love and anger in academic scholarship, and violate it? Do we have the collective power and resources at this point in time to create places for major figures like Gayle Rubin, who violated all the rules making work that actually matters?

Notes

1. Gayle Rubin, "The Traffic in Women: Notes on the 'Political Economy' of Sex," in *Toward an Anthropology of Women*, ed. Rayna Reiter (New York: Monthly Review, 1975), 157–210. Rubin describes the political scene in Ann Arbor surrounding her work on this article in her interview with Judith Butler, "Interview: Sexual Traffic," *differences* 6, nos. 2–3 (1994): 62–99.

2. Gayle Rubin, "Thinking Sex: Notes for a Radical Theory of the Politics of Sexuality," in *Pleasure and Danger: Exploring Female Sexuality*, ed. Carole S. Vance (Boston: Routledge and Kegan Paul, 1984), 267–319. Rubin describes the attacks on her after the publication of this article in "Blood under the Bridge: Reflections on 'Thinking Sex,'" in this issue.

3. Vance's *Pleasure and Danger* covers these issues in the included articles and also appends an account of the personal sexual attacks launched by antipornography feminists at the 1982 conference at Barnard. See also Robin Ruth Linden, *Against Sadomasochism* (East Palo Alto, CA: Frog in the Well, 1982); and ed. Lisa Duggan and Nan D. Hunter, *Sex Wars: Sexual Dissent and Political Culture* (New York: Routledge, 1995).

   I use the term *trauma* here not in the specific psychoanalytic sense, or in reference to the psychic residue of physical attacks and injuries, but to designate the pain and damage generated by public shaming and humiliation aimed at stigmatizing individuals in deeply personal ways, in the context of a political conflict. For a related expansion of the meaning of the term *trauma*, see Ann Cvetkovich, *An Archive of Feelings: Trauma, Sexuality and Lesbian Public Cultures* (Durham, NC: Duke University Press, 2003).

4. The appearance of "Thinking Sex" as the lead article in *The Lesbian and Gay Studies Reader*, ed. Henry Abelove, Michèle Aina Barale, and David M. Halperin (New York: Routledge, 1993) indicates its impact and importance nearly ten years after its first publication.

5. By "affective surround," I mean the unarticulated mix of feelings and reactions that pervade an event or collect around a figure, in either physical or virtual space. Rubin and her work exist within a complex and shifting affective surround that is rarely, if ever, described or mentioned in academic contexts. One of my goals in this essay is to describe this changing affective surround and begin to analyze it.

6. Audre Lorde, "The Master's Tools Will Never Dismantle the Master's House," in *Sister Outsider: Essays and Speeches* (Trumansburg, NY: Crossing, 1984). The scene at the conference, and the controversy it generated, is described from a position some-

what hostile to Lorde in Jessica Benjamin, "Letter to Lester Olson," *Philosophy and Rhetoric* 33, no. 2 (2000): 286–90. "The Master's Tools" has had a long career, from controversial conference event to influential publication, similar to that of "Thinking Sex."

7. An account of this conference is available in Vance, *Pleasure and Danger.*

8. Rubin describes some of those attacks in Australia in "Blood under the Bridge."

QUEER STUDIES IN QUEER TIMES

Conference Review of "Rethinking Sex," University of Pennsylvania, March 4–6, 2009

Regina Kunzel

*I*n 1984 Gayle Rubin published "Thinking Sex: Notes for a Radical Theory of the Politics of Sexuality," and in fifty-two pages of historical analysis, closely argued propositions, some brilliant turns of phrase, and two memorable diagrams, opened new worlds of possibility — politically, intellectually, and institutionally.[1] Published in the ferment of the feminist sex wars, Rubin's argument that feminism alone was inadequate as a mode of analysis to explain the production of sexual hierarchies is among the essay's key legacies (and sometimes a lightning rod for its misreading). More broadly, Rubin called for new theoretical tools and optics that might help us grasp what she termed the "fallacy of misplaced scale" that burdened nonnormative sexual practices with the weight of other social anxieties and made sex more generally a locus of oppression, marginalization, and persecution.

In the twenty-five years since its publication, "Thinking Sex" has circulated widely and promiscuously. The generative power of Rubin's invitation to explore "the political dimensions of erotic life" and her inspiration to scholars in a range of fields were in abundant evidence at "Rethinking Sex," a conference organized by Heather Love and held at the University of Pennsylvania, March 4–6, 2009.[2] Setting out to mark the twenty-fifth anniversary of the publication of Rubin's essay and to use that occasion to consider the "state of the field" of gender and sexuality studies, Love expressed the hope that we might "honor the contributions of Rubin and others to the making of our field, and . . . imagine new solutions to the challenges of the global present."[3] In two days and twelve panels, some thirty invited participants and more than five hundred attendees responded to the

GLQ 17:1
DOI 10.1215/10642684-2010-026

conference's invitation from a variety of angles, demonstrating the expansive reach and range, and attending to the possible limits, of queer studies in queer times.

"The Time Has Come to Think about Sex"

Central to Rubin's "Thinking Sex" are claims about time—about the urgency of sexual politics in the late 1970s and early 1980s, when she conceived and wrote the essay, and about how understanding the logic and dynamics of sex panics in the past might help us recognize and resist their iterations in the present. Rubin looked to the logics of late-nineteenth-century antiprostitution, antimasturbation, and anti-obscenity crusades and 1950s sex-psychopath scares to understand late-1970s panics about S/M and pornography and early assaults on gay rights ordinances. The 1980s scandals involving sexual abuse of children in day care, sex education in schools, and the more-generalized panic surrounding HIV/AIDS followed earlier scripts and bore out Rubin's warnings, and then some. Today, Rubin's analysis brings into focus the panicked thinking of our own historical moment, manifest in newly expansive sex offender laws, narratives about sex trafficking, as well as the more insidious ways in which fears and fearmongering around sex and sexuality snake their way through the agendas of the post-9/11 security state.

Rubin's powerful opening exhortation—"The time has come to think about sex"—was echoed by many conference presenters who wrestled with its meaning for our current moment.[4] Rubin wrote "Thinking Sex" at a time she identified, with some restraint in retrospect, as one of "great social stress," when the rise of the New Right, the election of Ronald Reagan, the culture wars, an emergent neoliberalism, and the HIV/AIDS epidemic were converging to transform the political landscape. In an interview with Judith Butler published in *differences* in 1994, on the tenth anniversary of the publication of "Thinking Sex," Rubin commented on her aims: "I approach systems of thought as tools people make to get leverage and control over certain problems."[5] A new "radical theory of sex," she proposed, might expose sexuality's centrality to politics and challenge the operations of privilege and stigma that structure thinking about sex and sexuality.

To what extent has the field delivered on that promise? How are we to understand our present moment, and what systems of thought might offer traction on its problems and expand its opportunities? Gathering in the late winter of 2009, "Rethinking Sex" participants considered the profound stresses of the moment and the meaning of contemporary political transformations for the future. The compounded effects of the global financial collapse and its assault on neoliberalism's market fundamentalism, the election of Barack Obama, and the continuing wars in Iraq and Afghanistan have produced what Lisa Duggan characterized as "a particularly stark moment of unknowing," inspiring an on-the-spot contest among conference participants and attendees to "Name That Era" and eliciting a more serious effort to grapple with the current moment's complexity and contradictions. If recent conferences, journal special issues, and anthologies have explored queer pasts and debated the notion of queer futures, "Rethinking Sex" participants pondered the contours, challenges, and possibilities of our queer present.[6]

The dominant American political culture currently summons us to hope, the election year's ubiquitous, if now tarnished, appeal. But conference participants on the queer left, wary of the normative assumptions and vacuous optimism that can lie within hope's most conventional scripts, struggled over their relationship to political hope and hopefulness. The power of the Christian Right, so dominant in the reactionary politics of the past three decades and so important for setting the stigmatizing terms of public discourse on gender and sexuality, as Rubin recognized presciently in 1984, may be waning. But in a talk that considered "Why Obama Doesn't Want to Think about Sex," Janet Jakobsen (in a paper written jointly with Ann Pellegrini) proposed that Obama's "working alliance" with moderate evangelicals and a broader Christian-inflected secularism contributed to his reticence about engaging gender and sexuality. Jakobsen drew attention in particular to Obama's ostensibly rationalistic, nonpartisan, and secular appeal to "responsibility," a keyword whose Christian and American genealogy is freighted with pernicious, blame-the-victim implications for sexual and racial politics, and in so doing complicated a narrative that links secularism, modernity, and progressive change.

Other putatively progressive legal changes, popular narratives, and institutional developments came under critical scrutiny as well. A central focus of Rubin's analysis of sexual persecution in 1984, sodomy laws were struck down in the 2003 *Lawrence v. Texas* ruling, but Nan Hunter noted that the state has not retired from the business of sexual regulation. New, more refined forms of regulation and surveillance, Hunter warned, might emerge in unlikely places. Hunter offered an analysis of adultery laws, operating in ways parallel to sodomy laws in promoting self-governance and regulatory discipline around a practice broadly viewed as illicit and illegitimate, even where legal. Dean Spade also raised caution about change assumed to be progressive, expressing concern in particular about how the "non-profit industrial complex" that has emerged to serve trans-identified people inhibits radical possibilities and falls sway to the "liberal and neo-liberal fantasies" of the virtues of visibility and inclusion. Thinking beyond a liberal political framework and drawing instead from the insights of critical race theory and Foucauldian biopolitics, Spade suggested, might help illuminate and resist the functions of the state — surveillance, profiling, detention, and deportation, certainly, but also the state's ostensibly benign projects that sort populations and establish the identities of its residents — that incorporate certain subjects into its security and life-promoting fold and exclude others. National and international laws against "trafficking" passed in 2000 made promising changes in recognizing that men, women, and children can all be trafficked and that people can be trafficked into a range of exploitative labor sectors. But Carole Vance exposed how the laws as practiced collapse all forms of trafficking into sexual trafficking and associate all forms of prostitution with trafficking's coercions, echoing arguments made by antipornography feminists and sustaining the hierarchies that Rubin elaborated in "Thinking Sex," in which sex for pay lies outside the sexual value system's "charmed circle."

Trafficking and its representations traverse a global landscape, and in her analysis Vance moved beyond the national frame of Rubin's "Thinking Sex." While Rubin charted the peculiarly American intensities of the sexual politics of the late 1970s and early 1980s, several conference presenters accepted Love's invitation to consider the urgencies of "a global present." Neville Hoad, Martin Manalansan, Gayatri Gopinath, and Lisa Rofel joined Vance in tracking how sexual knowledges, ideologies, and hierarchies are produced in various geopolitical locations under globalization and neoliberalism. Together with early works in black feminism, Gopinath noted, Rubin's "Thinking Sex" has offered scholars powerful theoretical tools with which to comprehend the centrality of sexuality within histories of colonialism, nationalism, racialization, and globalization. This crossing of queer studies with postcolonial, diaspora, and area studies, David Eng suggested, might be understood as a new kind of intersectionality, one that expands outward to consider how migration and immigration determine sexual citizenship and its exclusions. At the same time, Eng suggested, new scholarship that brings together postcolonial and queer studies usefully "provincializes" queer studies by calling into question its unthinking universalisms.

"Rethinking Sex" considered the importance of contemporary biopolitics as well as geopolitics to our global present in Steven Epstein's examination of the sexual politics of biomedical exclusion in the recent marketing of the human papillomavirus (HPV) vaccine. Locating biomedicine as a domain in which sexual and biological citizenship are "jointly claimed and jointly contested," Epstein analyzed the research and marketing rationale of the HPV vaccine Gardisil, targeted to the parents of (presumptively heterosexual) teenage girls and to young women. Epstein tracked how new claims on the part of gay men for protection against

HPV ran up against heteronormative medical assumptions that rendered anal cancer both stigmatized and invisible, as well as the exclusion from biocitizenship of queer youth.

In thinking about how to gain political purchase on our own vexed and urgent moment, many "Rethinking Sex" participants evinced a suspicion toward conventional strategies of opposition and resistance on the part of the Left, even the queer Left, as rooted in normative teleologies of progress and modernity or as trapped in binary logics of mastery/enslavement or activity/passivity. Some found resources for a more expansive, emancipatory, and possibly redistributive politics in the alternative intimacies and collectivities modeled in queer life. Duggan and Muñoz, in a collaborative presentation, queried the dialectic of hope and hopelessness and located possibilities for an "educated," "grounded" form of hope, unbuoyed by optimism and undisciplined by developmental progress narratives, in the alternative intimacies — nonprocreative, nonfamilial, beyond the couple form — of queer modes of sociality. Jasbir Puar speculated that an ethical orientation she termed "conviviality" might offer a more hopeful politics than the conventional stances of oppositionality, resistance, subversion, or transgression.[7] Lisa Henderson also made an appeal for the possibilities of friendship as a form of attachment that might hold untapped political and cultural resources. Two dialogic presentations at "Rethinking Sex," by Duggan and Muñoz and by Lauren Berlant and Lee Edelman, performed the possibilities of queer collaboration and friendship in scholarly work and perhaps beyond, against the grain of academic practice in the humanities that rewards and valorizes single-authored scholarship.

Others took a more critical position on the conventional vocabulary and strategy of political action and the tendency of queer studies to celebrate transgression and resistance. Leo Bersani, drawing from his collaboration with Ulysse Dutoit, found a model for eluding the seemingly elemental and inevitable links between and among knowledge, desire, and mastery in his reading of Claire Denis's 1999 film *Beau travail*. The film's choreographed study of French legionnaires stationed in East Africa, its refusal of the family drama and of deeply psychologized renderings of relationship and desire, to Bersani, offered an alternative to the aggression and desire for the mastery of difference at the center of Enlightenment epistemology. Inspired by Bersani's rewriting of the psychoanalytic narratives of intimacy and by Love's provocation to attend to the bad feelings — "nostalgia, regret, shame, despair, *ressentiment*, passivity, escapism, self-hatred, withdrawal, bitterness, defeatism, and loneliness" — that arise from a queer history of social exclusion, J. Jack Halberstam likewise critiqued conventional calls to action, resistance, and mastery and questioned queer studies' investments in self-congratulatory and heroic narratives of queer oppression, met with resistance, and followed by near-victory (and repeat).[8] Instead, Halberstam pressed the counterintuitive possibilities of a "radical form of radical passivity" — embodied in moments and performances of failure, unbecoming, and masochism — which might allow for political alternatives beyond those embedded in the dichotomies of colonizer/colonized and master/slave.

Taken together, "Rethinking Sex" participants speculated about the promise of nonoptimistic, noncelebratory, nonteleological, nonheroic, "sideways" forms of politics that might sidestep the unwitting collusions and dead-ends of liberal and Left politics.[9] These proposals were cautious, circumscribed, and caveated, and provoked discussion about whether the time of large political gestures is over and about the value of what seemed to be a turn inward — toward the eclectic, the prosaic, and the provincial — at a moment that calls for outward action. They also raised questions about the dangers of a mistaken (or false) notion of queer exceptionalism and about the pitfalls of new norms or erasures that might lurk within assumptions that equate the queer and the antinormative or within assertions of a special queer purchase on friendship. Less fully explored at the conference but invited by its discussion was the question of whether an emphasis on the antinormativity of queer evades questions of privilege. Many conference participants, of course, reside within the "charmed circle" of tenured academic life and are recipients of academic sanction and reward. How might we think through an antinormative politics that works against Left vanguardism and romance and questions a too-easy equivalence of the queer and the antinormative?

State of the Field?

"Rethinking Sex" stated its ambition in its subtitle — "Gender and Sexuality Studies, State of the Field Conference" — and in its impressive roster of senior scholars whose work (with that of many others) has shaped the field. In writing this review, I have used "sexuality studies," "gender and sexuality studies," and "queer studies" nearly interchangeably, echoing the slippages in the many presentations at "Rethinking Sex" but communicating different histories of and trajectories for the field. But what do we mean by "the field"? And what does the field look like, twenty-five years after Rubin offered scholars the inspiration, some of the tools, and (at least as important) the courage to think critically about sexuality?

While Rubin called in 1984 for an analysis of sexual oppression as distinct from gender oppression, Love's organization of a conference on "gender and sexuality studies" reflected the influence of scholarship in the intervening years, especially the emergence of transgender studies, which has challenged the incorporation of gender variance under a more-overarching rubric of sexual dissidence. If "Thinking Sex" posed a challenge to feminism, Susan Stryker proposed, transgender studies has posed a challenge to queer studies, asking whether it adequately accounts for transgender subjectivities, experiences, and politics, or whether a new "system of thought" is required. Joanne Meyerowitz also underlined the inseparability of gender and sexuality as domains of analysis and experience, reflecting on her own work on the history of transsexuality and offering a nimble reading of Earl Lind's sensational life narrative *Autobiography of an Androgyne* (1918), a text that has been mined both by historians of early-twentieth-century fairy life and gay community in New York City and by historians of gender variance, but one that demonstrates gender and sexuality's deep entanglement.

In "Thinking Sex," Rubin referenced race by way of analogy to sex. Like race, she proposed, sexuality is given life and meaning by culture and history, not by biology. Sexual morality, Rubin argued, was akin to "ideologies of racism" in its hierarchies of value and devaluation and in its disbursement of privilege and disfranchisement.[10] In the intervening twenty-five years, scholars have explored the constitution of sexuality and sexual hierarchies through intersections of race, class, region, (dis)ability, nation, geopolitical location, and other axes of power and disempowerment. Several conference presentations, building on work by Cathy Cohen, Eng, Roderick Ferguson, Robert Reid-Pharr, Siobhan Somerville, and others, made clear the degree to which critical sexuality studies has been enriched by thinking about the integral links between regimes of gender and sexuality and other categories as mutually constitutive systems of power.[11] In a panel on "Rethinking Intersectionality," Robert McRuer declared that "the time has come to think about disability" and joined Puar in considering subjectivities produced through the intersections of queer and disabled—in Puar's words, the "historical entwinement that has produced disabled bodies as queer and queer bodies as intrinsically debilitated." These and other presentations showcased the value of placing multiply marginalized people at the center of queer analysis.

Writing in 1984, Rubin anticipated some of the connections made in recent studies of sexuality to other, seemingly unrelated phenomena that have expanded the reach and relevance of the field. "Once sex is understood in terms of social analysis and historical understanding," Rubin wrote, "one may then think of sexual politics in terms of such phenomena as populations, neighborhoods, settlement patterns, migration, urban conflict, epidemiology, and police technology."[12] At a time when a well-developed interdisciplinary field devoted to the critical study of sexuality was barely thinkable, Rubin envisioned its engagement with the meta-frames of governance and securitization and with the more granular features of everyday life.

The field that has emerged since "Thinking Sex" can lay claim to the richness and expansiveness that Rubin imagined and helped usher into being. "Rethinking Sex" was one of the first efforts in many years to bring together scholars in gender, sexuality, and queer studies from a wide range of disciplines and interdisciplines and with a variety of methodological and theoretical commitments. Scholars representing domains of knowledge and theory infrequently brought into conversation — critical science studies, psychoanalysis, ethnography, border studies, disability studies, critical race studies, media and cultural studies, transgender studies, history, visual culture, literary studies, postcolonial studies, critical legal studies, intersections and combinations of the above, and more — shared space on panels organized around broad themes and questions ("Bodies, Media, and Politics," "Rethinking Intersectionality," "Living with Neoliberalism," and "Globalizing Sex" among them). Unlike queer studies conferences of the past two decades, which came to devolve around disciplinary divides and more recently have been organized in such a way as to sidestep altogether the challenges of inter- and cross-disciplinary conversation, "Rethinking Sex" was bold in its effort to take a broad survey of the field and to spark unlikely exchanges. In her welcoming introduction, Love asked conference participants and attendees to consider together, "What's exciting about the field, what's wrong, what's difficult, what's necessary, and what can we build together?"

"Rethinking Sex" was enlivened by many of the key issues and questions that have animated critical gender and sexuality studies and queer studies of the past decade: the contingencies of gender and sexuality in a global and transnational world, queer temporality and political futurity, critiques of homo- as well as heteronormativities, and the affective valences of queer life and politics. The conference showcased a field of study boasting a wide range of methodological and theoretical approaches, in vibrant conversation with transnational cultural studies, disability studies, critical race studies, and studies of empire and diaspora. At the same time, no consensus emerged in response to Love's questions. Rubin lamented the lack of a "coherent and intelligent body of radical thought about sex" in 1984; twenty-five years later, an unruly and ranging field has taken shape.[13] Its state, as registered by "Rethinking Sex," is neither coherent nor bounded. In fact, my effort here to bring together the ideas presented at the conference under some organizing narrative and thematic logic thins and flattens their heterogeneity. Presentations were offered in different scholarly and activist vernaculars, using different methodologies, and guided by different and sometimes implicitly opposing ideas about what was wrong, difficult, or necessary, and what might be possible to build together.

Rather than coherence or consensus, what emerged from these exchanges was a desire to enlarge the frame of the field still further and to shift and unsettle its terms and orthodoxies. *Agnotology*, a concept Epstein called on to analyze the gaps in biomedical knowledge and "undiscussed queer issues" generated in relation to the new vaccine against the HPV virus, might be more broadly applied to the field as assessed at "Rethinking Sex." Developed by the historian of science Robert N. Proctor, agnotology moves beyond the traditional questions of epistemology and the study of "how we know" to ask "why don't we know what we don't know?"[14] In some respects, of course, the cultural production and maintenance of ignorance in relationship to sex and sexuality has been a guiding question in critical sexuality and queer studies. Eve Kosofsky Sedgwick's interrogation of the "regime of the open secret" and "the privilege of unknowing" has inspired queer studies' inquiries into heteronormativity and queer inquiries more generally. Her absence from "Rethinking Sex," at which she was scheduled to speak but unable to attend because of illness that would take her life less than two months later, was sadly observed and deeply felt.[15] "Rethinking Sex" participants reflected on agnotology's slipperier meanings for the state of the field: What forms of knowledge does our current understanding of the field foreclose? What unwitting exclusions does it perform? What modes of living, forms of intimacy, and ways of distributing resources—in the past and in the contemporary world—does it keep us from seeing? And what forms of unknowing might be worth cultivating?

Presentations that considered these questions of the field's agnotology included Sharon Holland's reflection on violent crimes against transgender people of color, largely neglected and almost all unsolved, and her question about how queer studies' putative object might prevent it from recognizing such subjects. Those questions were present in other ways in Michele Mitchell's speculations about the body as an elusive and possibly rich archive, bearing the traces of sexual trauma, desire, pleasure, and memory untraceable in the conventional archive and accessed through such unlikely sources as early-twentieth-century photographic racial taxonomies. They were implicit in Berlant's and Edelman's challenge to take seriously the undoing nature of sex, in the face of impulses to aestheticize, harmonize, and order it (including impulses present in the constitution of a field of study or a conference assessing the state of that field). And they were present in Halberstam's reminder of the "sexual rabble" assembled in Rubin's expansive rendering of sexuality's "outer limits," including sex workers, the promiscuous, the unmarried, the nonprocreative, the cross-generational. It is time to return to those surprising and unpredictable groupings, Halberstam proposed (recalling Cohen's now long-standing challenge to queer studies and queer politics to recognize the links between the marginalization of "punks, bulldaggers, and welfare queens"), in order to think in new ways about the vectors of sexual oppression and privilege.[16] Questions of the field's agnotology, finally, inspired incitements to investigate its alternative and often erased genealogies, in black feminism and queer of color critique in particular, that might further decenter sex and sexuality.

Some conference participants attended to subjects farther beyond the analytic frames of gender and sexuality studies. Jennifer Terry's analysis of "object-sexuality"—as represented by the people who feel love for and erotic connection to objects and in reality television's exoticizing and sensationalizing representations of them—exposed contemporary moral pieties and mandates about who and what are proper objects of desire and "real love." Meyerowitz's consideration of how Lind's eroticized identification as a "baby" exceeded the more familiar analytic categories of gender and sexuality and the more intelligible sexual subjects imagined to be encompassed by "LGBT" reminds us of the limits of our categories to capture the strangeness and capaciousness of the past (and, by extension, of the present).

It is impossible to do justice in this review to the range of methodologies, approaches, and challenges represented at "Rethinking Sex." The conference made few pronouncements or definitive statements about "the field"; instead, it posed questions and suggested alternative ways to conceive of and multiply it. If conferences can have affects (and of course they do), the affective register of "Rethinking Sex" was generous, tentative, and quirky. Participants seemed willing to live with the field's discontinuities, unhurried about resolving problems or winning a debate (or even setting the terms of one), and disinclined to resolve contradictions. The sum effect of "Rethinking Sex" was to enlarge the frame of the field; to question its terms, concepts, and orthodoxies; and, at points, to look beyond it.

Notes

1. Gayle Rubin, "Thinking Sex: Notes for a Radical Theory of the Politics of Sexuality," in *Pleasure and Danger: Exploring Female Sexuality*, ed. Carole S. Vance (Boston: Routledge and Kegan Paul, 1984), 267–319.
2. Rubin, "Thinking Sex," 310.
3. "Rethinking Sex," conference program, 1.

4. Rubin, "Thinking Sex," 267.

5. Judith Butler, "Interview: Sexual Traffic," *differences* 6, nos. 2–3 (1994): 90.

6. See, for example, David L. Eng, Judith Halberstam, and José Esteban Muñoz, eds., "What's Queer about Queer Studies Now?" special issue, *Social Text*, nos. 84–85 (2005); Kevin P. Murphy, Jason Ruiz, David Serlin, eds., "Queer Futures," special issue, *Radical History Review*, no. 100 (2008).

7. See Jasbir K. Puar, "Prognosis Time: Towards a Geopolitics of Affect, Debility, and Capacity," *Women and Performance* 19 (July 2009): 161–72.

8. Heather Love, *Feeling Backward: Loss and the Politics of Queer History* (Cambridge: Harvard University Press, 2007), 4; Leo Bersani and Adam Phillips, *Intimacies* (Chicago: University of Chicago Press, 2008).

9. For different considerations of the potential of "sideways" as a queer analytic practice, see Siobhan Somerville, "Queer Loving," *GLQ* 11 (2005): 335–70; Kathryn Bond Stockton, *The Queer Child, or Growing Sideways in the Twentieth Century* (Durham, NC: Duke University Press, 2009).

10. Rubin, "Thinking Sex," 283.

11. See Cathy J. Cohen, *The Boundaries of Blackness: AIDS and the Breakdown of Black Politics* (Chicago: University of Chicago Press, 1999); David L. Eng, *Racial Castration: Managing Masculinity in Asian America* (Durham: Duke University Press, 2001); Roderick A. Ferguson, *Aberrations in Black: Toward a Queer of Color Critique* (Minneapolis: University of Minnesota Press, 2004); Robert Reid-Pharr, *Once You Go Black: Choice, Desire, and the Black American Intellectual* (New York: New York University Press, 2007); Siobhan B. Somerville, *Queering the Color Line: Race and the Invention of Homosexuality in American Culture* (Durham: Duke University Press, 2000).

12. Rubin, "Thinking Sex," 277.

13. Rubin, "Thinking Sex," 274.

14. Robert N. Proctor, "Agnotology: A Missing Term to Describe the Cultural Production of Ignorance (and Its Study)," in *Agnotology: The Making and Unmaking of Ignorance*, ed. Robert N. Proctor and Londa Schiebinger (Stanford: Stanford University Press, 2008).

15. See Eve Kosofsky Sedgwick, *Epistemology of the Closet* (Berkeley: University of California Press, 1990); and Sedgwick, "The Privilege of Unknowing: Diderot's The Nun," in *Tendencies* (Durham, NC: Duke University Press, 1993).

16. Cathy J. Cohen, "Punks, Bulldaggers, and Welfare Queens: The Radical Potential of Queer Politics?" *GLQ* 3 (1997): 437–65.

QUEER MEDIA LOCI

$\mathcal{W}$e are thrilled to inaugurate Queer Media Loci in this issue of *GLQ*. A new, ongoing series for the Moving Image Review, Queer Media Loci is designed to present a cross-sectional analysis of queer media at a specific location. As issues of globalization, border crossing, migration, and diaspora are increasingly being addressed in queer scholarship, we want to situate discussions around queer media production, exhibition, and reception within these debates and to shift the focus away from what remains a predominantly European-American context. In the Queer Media Loci series, we ask the following questions of each of our authors: What makes the chosen geographic location distinct? What kinds of queer media activities happen there? How do these media activities define or describe this locus? And how are they produced by, and how do they in turn produce, media representations of the locus?

In the series, we define a locus as a specific place — a city, town, village, neighborhood, region, or, in some cases, a country — that perceives itself as distinct and projects a distinct culture or identity to the world at large. Instead of presenting generalized surveys and lists of organizations, festivals, and other venues for exhibition and production, our cross-sectional approach encourages our authors to examine a broader, representative range of images and interpretations created through close reading, thick description, and an insider's perspective. We ask our authors to consider queer media activities that range from commercial and industrial productions to underground, local, and grassroots activities, as well as events and cultural phenomena that do not necessarily manifest as conventional festivals or screenings, including online spaces and new media productions. The methodologies used by authors will vary by loci. Each locus, with its own social, cultural, political, and historical context, will require an approach that is appropriate to its circumstances. Thus, we anticipate commissioning studies from scholars, curator/programmers, activists, and other practitioners who are trained in different disciplines and have different expertise. Queer Media Loci presents a series of specific, in-depth case studies that can help sketch out a larger picture of the queer media being produced, consumed, debated, and censored in locations that are increasingly visited and inhabited by queers, but not necessarily looked at or studied as centers of queer media production. In this sense, our use of the term *locus* is crucial in that its deployment signals the undoing of the relation between cities (the established, First-World queer capitals of San Francisco, New York, London, Paris, Berlin, and Amsterdam) and nation or region, and opens up into the less restrictive and non-Eurocentric category of place or location.

In conceiving the series, we are also aware of its potential dangers. We are wary of producing a queer touristic discourse — a sex tour of queer media in exotic locales, or an Atlantic or Olivia cruise with movies, as it were. We therefore encourage our authors to challenge and interrogate colonial and capitalist tendencies within their and our communities. In fact, queer sex tourism and the larger issue of queer touristic discourse are confronted directly in our inaugural project on Bangkok by Dredge Käng. As mentioned above, we also encourage our authors to examine other forms of intercultural communication, including migration, border crossing, and diaspora, and to look at how these transnational and global flows of information and bodies are expressed in and through queer media. We are interested in pursuing how these issues help define or disrupt a sense of place, focusing in particular on queer media that can construct or challenge nationalistic ideologies or other forms of localized group identity.

We are extremely pleased that Käng has taken up our challenge and produced an inaugural contribution to Queer Media Loci that exemplifies our goals for the series as a whole. His multifaceted analysis of the queer mediascape in Bangkok — a locus that is very much queer-identified but also visited and at the same time "othered" in relationship to the aforementioned First-World queer centers — examines diverse media forms, from Internet blogs to television and film to street protests. Käng's essay performs important interventions in the popular (queer) media representation of Bangkok as a "gay paradise," a "land of smiles" populated by Thai "boys" and "ladyboys" who are always eager to satisfy the sexual needs of visiting foreigners. Turning his ethnographic lens not on the "natives" but on gay tourists and ex-patriots, Käng analyzes the queer media they produce and consume as sites of anxiety over authenticity and postcolonial sexual exploitation. Media by and for locals, on the other hand, reflects much more complex expressions and receptions of queer sexuality. In some of the case studies Käng analyzes, queer media becomes the unwitting catalyst for debates on national identity and globalization. In sum, his survey of Bangkok queer media shows us examples of complex local and international attitudes and reactions to queer media, in ways that exceed what we had hoped for in conceiving this series. We look forward to further developing Queer Media Loci with upcoming contributions from Israel/Palestine, Brazil, India, Vietnam, Africa, and Eastern Europe.

—Alexandra Juhasz and Ming-Yuen S. Ma

DOI 10.1215/10642684-2010-027

QUEER MEDIA LOCI IN BANGKOK
Paradise Lost and Found in Translation

Dredge Byung'chu Käng

It's summer 2009 in Bangkok, the newsstands at Silom Complex are carrying *Slim Up*, with *kathoey* supermodel Ornapa Krisadee seminude on the cover as the main feature, offering to share her beauty secrets.[1] On a different rack one finds Worapoj Petchkoom, an Olympic silver medal–winning boxer, as the centerfold model of *Stage*, one of several magazines in the gay soft-core section.[2] Close by on another rack, *@tom act*, a "tomboy lifestyle magazine," can be seen.[3] On the wall of one of the many tourist agencies lining Silom Road, just down the block and across the street from the newsstand, images from Calypso, the most famous of the "lady-boy" cabarets in Bangkok, are juxtaposed next to glossy posters of the Grand Palace. Alongside temples, snakes, crocodiles, elephants, and beaches, *kathoey* have come to represent one of the natural, scenic, and "amazing" wonders of Thailand.[4] Just a little farther down the street, the gay bars in Soi 4 offer free magazines with local information, event listings, maps, puff pieces, and event photos. The covers are adorned with male models in Speedos lounging at the beach, pool, or spa.

At the Telephone Bar, a group of Singaporeans sits down and orders a beer tower, a tall three-liter beer tap made to look like six by filling the core with ice. The appearance of excess is delightful, and they squeal when it arrives. All around are groups of men and male couples. Single men are often greeted by a young Thai man who would like to sit with them. No one needs to stay alone for very long. Drop an ice cube in your glass of whisky and soda, and you can almost hear the carbonation say, "Ahh! Welcome to (gay) paradise!"

I take a photo of my Thai friend home from college in the United Kingdom. One Singaporean sneers, "Tourists, I wish they would go home!" and his group toasts him. A gray-haired *farang* walks up to the bar.[5] He plops down on a stool and waits for the bartender to turn around. "Thailand, this is paradise!" he exclaims. The bartender squints his eyes. "Really? This life more hell than heaven." The *farang* frowns: "What do you mean?" The bartender pauses, then replies: "What you like drink?" What is lost in translation is the idea of "paradise" from a Theravadan Buddhist perspective, which is not of this world, but freedom from the existence of this world, its sensuality and materiality.[6] Furthermore, what might be idyllic to a tourist is labor to those who make the pleasures of this world possible.

This is a glimpse into the representations and experiences that construct and contest Bangkok as a gay paradise. These scenarios raise the question: paradise for whom, in what manner, and to what extent? A survey of media and an analysis of select cases will demonstrate how Bangkok is portrayed as a gay paradise by foreigners and the limits of such a representation for local discourse and experience.

Imagining Paradise: Queer Mediascapes in Bangkok

Bangkok is saturated with queer (gay, *kathoey*, and *tom*) representations that construct what we see as queer Bangkok.[7] The media differs depending on whether it is intended for a local or foreign audience. In the Western popular imagination, Bangkok is a "gay paradise," a city that affords cheap and easy access to exotic "boys."[8] This reputation for sex tourism and a social tolerance for homosexuality and transgenderism is a common representation of queer Bangkok in English-language media. Yet Thai media imagery eclipses this one-dimensional portrayal. Here, I present several articulations within the queer mediascapes of Bangkok, including blogs, film and television, YouTube videos, and political demonstrations, to recontextualize the foreign gaze that constructs Bangkok as a gay paradise. Focusing on the media's relationship to macrosocial changes and everyday experience builds on previous scholarship on Thai and Asian transgenderism and same-sex eroticism by showing the diversity of depictions and the complex forces that shape the competing ways through which queer Bangkok can be imagined. I argue that lack of access to Thai media perpetuates *farang* belief in their centrality to Thai desire. Additionally, Western gazes that depict Thailand as especially tolerant of homosexuality and gender variance may in fact inhibit the free expression of male-bodied effeminacy. Finally, I argue that the hypersexualization of Thais and new regional alignments are molding local desires and subjectivities away from the West. Relationships with *farang* are increasingly stigmatized in favor of relationships with East Asians. *Farang* partnerships can carry a stigma because the Thai partner is visually marked as a potential sex worker (money boy, kept boy, etc.) and thus of low social status. This is particularly salient because of Thailand's reputation for sex tourism.[9] At the same time, the figuring and enactment of desire for East Asian partners has been enabled by the circulation of media, Internet sites such as fridae.com, and the proliferation of discount airlines that makes regional communication and travel possible.

Sexpatriotism: Sex, Expatriates, Foreign Advice

A variety of media, inside and outside Thailand, create the image of Bangkok as a gay-friendly tourist destination. The advent of online media has provided a new vehicle for disseminating information and advice. Blogs, YouTube, and other new media have become major sources for the imagining of Thai queerness from afar and the construction of local queer subjectivities. Such resources are more current and accessible than traditional print or moving image media; allow for greater interaction in their coproduction, circulation, and consumption; and can provide a sense of camaraderie, confidence, and intimacy. Web sources are highly trusted by tourists coming to Bangkok because they are easily compared and because participants on sites will provide their own commentary, giving them the appearance of greater objectivity compared to guidebooks, magazine articles, or tourist maps that provide recommendations in a singular voice.

In foreign online blogs and forums, what distinguishes Bangkok's interpenetration of the cultural and the sexual is the fact that online media tend to reduce the local populace to the status of potential sexual partners.[10] A fifty-something white American man living in Bangkok writes the "Rice Queen Diary" (RQD) blog to offer his "experiences and perspectives [to] those considering a long or short-term stay in Thailand." The blog, initially devoted to the topic of sex, now covers broader issues such as "culture and communication."

> At first, sex in Thailand was a prominent topic of my blog. One of the great things about this place, particularly at my age, is the sex. On arrival I had more sex here, in one month, than in the previous 10 years! While my earlier posts read more like a kid in a candy store, I think the blog has evolved, as I have. The sex is still an important topic, but I believe my focus has shifted more to culture and communication, particularly as it relates to interacting with the boys.[11]

The blogger uses the topics of culture and communication to obtain and maintain sex and companionship. He distinguishes his blog from other tourist sources that "sugar-coat" Thai life and fail to provide a "street wise" perspective on living in Thailand. He notes, for example, that his "experiences are predominantly with lower class boys." As the blogger points out, most Westerners initially do not realize that the Thais they are interacting with in sexualized settings generally come from poor rural backgrounds and do not represent all Thai people, although they are a large segment of the population. Sex tourists often make the assumption that the behavior of sex workers is representative of Thai behavior in general, which is not the case at all, since sex workers are often breaking cultural rules around "appropriate" social interactions. This is particularly true in Bangkok, where there is a large middle class that is often publicly prudish and often differentiates itself from the poor by avoiding romantic relationships with *farang*. It is clear, however, that while claiming to demystify Thailand as a gay paradise, RQD reinforces the idea that sex is easily obtained, even for those who would only be competitive in specialized sexual markets at home (e.g., rice queens, daddies, bears). In an entry titled "Show No Interest," he writes, "The difference in age and looks are not a huge factor in Thailand. A lot of Thais have a daddy complex. Some will even call you daddy in bed. . . . Similarly, a lot of Thais are into Bears, including the younger 20's guys." Such an assessment portrays young Thai men as nonsubscribers to gay North American beauty standards centered on an aversion to those who are older, large-bodied, or hairy. Taking up the role of foreign observers, RQD identifies a "cultural difference." Yet intergenerational partnership and patronage are nothing new to either queer Western male or Thai cultures. Their taken-for-granted status, however, fails to engage the social and economic factors that make pairings between older white men and younger Thai men both feasible and desirable.

While the blog has changed its focus to "culture and communication . . . as it relates to interacting with the boys," miscommunication continues to occur. In a post titled "Thai English," the blogger describes Tinglish (Thai English) with the goal of helping foreign gay men interpret it for both relationships and everyday life.[12] What is highlighted is the inadequacy of the Thai language and the difficulties Thais have with English, the latter represented as a marker of their inferiority. Such pronouncements, however, also point to the blogger's limited understanding of the Thai language. He writes:

> Thai is not a wordy language, so what might seem choppy, broken, or even a bit rude, may be a result of direct translation. That, and the fact their vocabulary is extremely limited, means a lot of words will be used when, in

proper English, there is a more accurate, or polite, way to communicate it. To understand what the boy is really trying to say, you want to avoid taking things too literal [*sic*].

Problems occur because most sexpatriates expect all their communication in Thailand to be conducted in English—which is an assertion of their privilege in sexual negotiations, where their needs are accommodated first and foremost. Phil, one of the commenters, reposts some Tinglish translations:

> Copied from Pattaya Boys Talk
>
> 1. Today him holiday = He is with another customer
> 2. Him go home stay mother = He is in prison
> 3. You han-sam man = My rent is due
> 4. Him no working = He is a kept boy now
> 5. Excu me I go toilet = I have a short time customer waiting upstairs[13]

These sarcastic interpretations reduce Tinglish to common "money boy" phrases and address another side of Thai-foreigner relations, that of deception. In fact, online foreigner advice focuses on warnings for the *farang* about the "annoyances" of living in Thailand. These generally fall into two themes: identifying whether a boy "really" loves him or just wants to be financially supported, and paying more for a sexual experience than is expected or "fair."

Thailand's largest expatriate Web site (Thaivisa.com) hosts a "Gay People in Thailand" forum. Posts frequently complain about Thai men, their inscrutability, and the difficulties of living as a foreigner in Thailand. Regardless of domain, any inexplicable difference can be reduced to a few pat phrases such as "This is Thailand" (TIT for short) or "welcome to the LOS (land of smiles)." Yet posts generally come to the conclusion that regardless of the difficulties of living in a country where one does not know the language, does not understand the cultural norms of relationships (especially kinship), and does not read emotions successfully, the situation is still better than in the poster's home country.[14] In summary, expatriate Web sites, blogs, and forum threads promote and reinforce the image of Bangkok as a place of sexual plenitude. The key is to learn how to navigate its treacherous terrain in order to sift out the good and authentic (the gracious and pliable) from the bad and corrupted (commercialized and agentive) "Thai boys." A *farang*'s verbal dismissal of "paradise," however, is often contradicted by his action of staying put.

In contrast to foreigner sites that focus on Thais, the Thai queer online world renders tourists and expats relatively invisible. Thais generally express little interest in reading *farang* forums, and Thai forums rarely discuss issues related to foreigners. They focus instead on music (especially K-Pop), celebrity and porn pics, relationship problems (with other locals), places to cruise men, and gossip about who was seen where doing what. *Kathoey* forums also focus on body modification, beauty contests, and issues related to civil rights. These sites are usually inaccessible to foreigners as they require Thai literacy. This lack of Thai interest in *farang* decenters the Western gaze, particularly in representations that construct Bangkok as a sexual haven.

There are numerous online cruising sites for Thai gay men and, to a lesser extent, *kathoey*. Camfrog is a webcam chat site immensely popular with Thai gay youth who chat with each other in Thai online slang. Other multilingual sites, such as GayRomeo.com, provide avenues for Thai-Thai, Thai-*farang*, and Thai-Asian interaction while the Hong Kong/Singapore-based fridae.com is used primarily by Thais to interact with East Asians. These sites differentiate audiences along the lines of age, race, ethnicity, geography, and language. In so doing, they allow most Westerners to feel central to Thai desire, as *farang* illiterate in Thai are linguistically excluded from sites in which they are not sought. At the same time, middle-class Thais remain acutely sensitive to their depiction as sexualized subjects. They thus avoid situations that potentially mark them as sex workers and thereby lower their social standing.

Centering the Metropolis of Angels: A Brief Demography and Queer Geography

Krungthep (Thai shorthand for Metropolis of Angels, the Thai name for Bangkok), Thailand's capital, mediates between the "other provinces" and the world-at-large in the production of its own distinct locality.[15] The city is a major tourist destination. It draws economic and queer migrants from throughout the country and Thailand's poorer neighbors as well as professional workers and retirees from the developed world. The city's multiple-lane boulevards, many of which used to be canals, are clogged with traffic. Lined with shop houses, malls, office buildings, and condominiums, the roads are fed by an endless stream of *soi*, or small lanes, where most Thai people live and go about their everyday lives. What makes Bangkok distinctive to those visiting for the first time are the contrasts — skyscrapers rise above the sky train, while on the asphalt below, peddlers push carts and carry baskets slung on their shoulders with bamboo poles.

Most of Bangkok's approximately 250 gay venues are found in the anonymity of a *soi*.[16] Yet the extensive queer scene makes it a major destination for gay tourism and guarantees its "iconic status as a place of imagined sexual tolerance and liberality."[17] When people say there are a million gays in Bangkok, that figure may not be so far from the truth. There are approximately seventeen thousand *kathoey* among approximately half a million Thai males who have sex with males (MSM).[18] This scale and the city's status as a cosmopolitan hub holding large populations of foreign workers, expatriates, and tourists mean that social spaces and commercial establishments are highly differentiated and segregated along axes of gender presentation, class, nationality, and partner preferences.

Gay Bangkok is linked with Southeast and East Asian cities including Tokyo, Taipei, Hong Kong, Singapore, and Kuala Lumpur via large circuit parties attracting thousands of participants. These linkages are symptomatic of a greater trend toward regional integration in Southeast and East Asia (ASEAN +3: China, Japan, Korea).[19] In Thailand, Japan alone invests more than double that of all European, North American, and Australasian countries combined. With Japanese restaurants supplanting American fast food chains, eating Japanese signifies modernity and wealth. East Asian media is dramatically shaping Thai aesthetics and fashion. The Korean Wave, in particular, has become a dominant source of television series, movies, and music.[20] At gay bars, one will typically hear more Korean than Thai songs. Cosmetic procedures and devices, like eyelash extensions or big-eye contacts imported from Korea, are popular among gay/*kathoey*. At the same time, Thailand exports media to neighboring countries, and art films in particular are gaining attention internationally. Bangkok is central to a new queer Asian regionalism in which capital, media, commodity, and human flows are circumventing Western gay forms and fashioning new queer subjectivities.[21]

An Excess of Sissies: Stereotypical Representation and the Disciplining of Normative Masculinity

Examination of Thai television and film reveals the complexity of queer representations and their local contestations. Thai television is awash in male-bodied effeminacy. Thai television programming contains queer content almost every night. In 2004 the visibility prompted former Prime Minister Thaksin Shinawatra's minister of education to call for a reduction in queer characters on television, as they were believed to provide poor role models for children. The rationale was that any representation on television, because of its glamorous associations, would be emulated. This positions queerness as simultaneously fashionable and contagious.

However, North Americans or Europeans would not consider these representations "positive" portrayals. Typically, *kathoey* and effeminate gay men are cast as comic relief characters or as criminals with lives mired in tragedy, not unlike historical American images of sissies, drag queens, and other queers.[22] While contemporary Thai images of queers on television should not be read as historically backward, such imagery counters any claims that Thais express no negative sentiment about homosexuality and transgenderism.

These media are constructing diverse and contradictory images of gay and *kathoey*. Television and film producers are creating more complex and varied representations of gay and *kathoey* on their own accord. In the summer of 2009, the Rainbow Moon (พระจันทร์สีรุ้ง phrachantha sirung) drama series focused on a storyline in which a *kathoey* raises a child. To give the son a better life, she sacrifices her transgender identity by reverting to living as an effeminate man. Thai commercial and public television have entertainment programs and talk shows hosted by gays and *kathoey*. *Kathoey* increasingly participate as guests on talk shows, not as entertainers but as activists, researchers, and transgender rights advocates. The transsexual celebrity Nok Yollada sells diamonds on cable television. Television and print news incorporate queer content, typically controversies about the excesses of effeminate male behavior. These stories act to discipline queerness and warn the general population about its dangers. When *kathoey* appear in the news, the theme is generally crime or the bizarre. The year 2009 produced controversies about inappropriate sexual behavior and sex work between monk novices and older monks and *kathoey*, effeminate Reserve Officers' Training Corps (ROTC) students who lure their peers into unseemly acts, and flamboyant monk novices.[23] The novice monk behavior deemed inappropriate included wearing false eyelashes, using blush and lipstick, and tying monk's robes to produce empire and kimono-style waistlines. Such controversies produce national identity as it is articulated through a reinforcement of traditionalized religion and morality, thereby policing gender expression and sexuality based on a heteronormative standard.[24] *Kathoey* are simultaneously portrayed as ugly and beautiful, traditional and modern, backward and cosmopolitan.

As the U.S. market for international gay films has grown in the past decade, many queer North Americans have come into contact with representations of Thai queerness through Thai films. These films generally represent Thailand as tolerant of homosexuality and transgenderism. Yet the stories often mask the complexity of the films' local reception and queer Thai lived experience. With films such as *Iron Ladies* (2000), *Beautiful Boxer* (2003), and *Tropical Malady* (2003) playing in art cinemas in the United States and others, such as *Bangkok Love*

Story (2007) and *Love of Siam* (2007), available on DVD, Thailand is represented as a fantastic place where even transgender women are able to become national men's sports champions. The teen romance *Love of Siam* won Best Picture in all major Thai awards that year and was submitted by Thailand for consideration at the 2009 Academy Awards. These critical accolades, however, are attenuated by the film's popular reception. Many Thai viewers took offense at the boy-boy love story. Advertisements for the movie featured two heterosexual couples with no hint that the boys would become paired. When *Love of Siam* was broadcast on Thai cable television, the kissing scene between the boys was cut, but subsequently, the censored kissing scene proliferated via many postings on YouTube. Many Thai gay men relate specifically to *Love of Siam* because they consider its ending realistic: family takes precedence over a romantic relationship. The boys are not coupled in the end. Even the feel good, wildly popular, "based on a true story" *Iron Ladies*, the second- highest grossing movie of all time in Thailand at the time of its release, occludes the eventual real-life outcome. Stating that they would have to prove that they were really men, the secretary-general of the Volleyball Association of Thailand disqualified team members who were not deemed masculine enough from international competition, as this would embarrass the nation. Gender and sexuality are indeed objects of governmental and media control and discipline. The representation of Thai masculinity and the national pride associated with it is at stake in these controversies.

Without access to information about their local reception and the realities of queer lived experience, these films can be read like documentaries of exotic, faraway places. Viewing the queer Thai films available in the United States, audiences are led to imagine a land of unparalleled gay and transgender social acceptance. Additionally, the Thai films that U.S. audiences see are already filtered through international art and queer cinematic lenses. Approximately 10 percent of commercially released Thai films are queer-themed or feature queer characters. Yet a large proportion of Thai queer films are never distributed abroad. Many of these, such as 2009's *Sassy Players* (แต๋วเตะตีนระเบิด Taew Te Teen Rabert: literally, sissies kicking with explosive feet), about a group of queeny boys who play soccer (a high school version of the *Iron Ladies*) or *Haunting Me* (หอ แต๋วแตกแหกกระเจิง Hor Taew Taek Haek Krajerng: literally, sissy dorm shattered, sissies scattered), both directed by Poj Arnon, would be considered stereotypical and offensive by Western standards. However, they are popular both with mainstream and with queer audiences.[25] Thus, while there is an extensive range of queer media, the sheer volume masks both the complexity of the content, its reception, and the varied discourses around its circulation. Portrayals that seem socially enlightened from afar can actually be either mundane or controversial. Male-bodied effeminacy can be displayed on-screen for a laugh, but such characters should not come to represent the nation.

Wonder Gay: We're Already Too Gay

The production, consumption, and contestation over queer representation in Thailand shows the regulatory pressure placed on gender expression and same-sex eroticism. Thais are keenly sensitive about being seen as "too gay" by the rest of the world. Wonder Gay provides a particularly salient example from 2009 that exemplifies the limited acceptability of male effeminacy in popular Thai discourse and how Thai national identity is articulated through discourses of gender and sexuality.

The Wonder Girls are an award-winning South Korean girl band that swept the charts in many Asian countries. They were the first Korean group listed on *Billboard*'s Hot 100. The Wonder Gay is a group of five Thai high school students whose impersonation of the Wonder Girls catapulted them to celebrity status in Thailand. In their viral YouTube video, the Wonder Gay lip-synch and dance to the Wonder Girls song "Nobody." Each member of Wonder Gay copies the movements and takes on the persona of one of the Wonder Girls. Garnering approximately one-third as many hits as the official Wonder Girls' "Nobody" YouTube video, the Wonder Gay's "Nobody — Ouz Wonder Girls (cover)" video is the most popular YouTube video from Thailand to date. Wonder Gay discussions are prevalent on many Thai Web discussion boards, both mainstream and queer. In general, Web forum threads tend to start positively, with early adopter fans posting enthusiastic comments. But as the threads progress and the audience grows, the comments become more critical.

The Thai television interview with the Wonder Gay on เจาะข่าวเด่น (*Jao Khaow Den*, Breaking News) starts with opening text scrolling onto the screen. After noting that 1,300,000 people have seen the Wonder Gay "Nobody" video, Wonder Gay are referred to as the "Third Gender Wave" (กระแสเพศที่ 3, krasae phet thi 3) using terminology reminiscent of the "Korean Wave" (กระแสเกาหลี krasae kao li). The host then begins the program by making the following statement:

> This is an interview with a group of high school students that one day wore their school uniforms and used a school stage to perform a dance using the Wonder Girls' song "Nobody," and they posted the clip on YouTube. The Susan Boyle clip was seen by more than 150,000 people. But this group's

clip was seen by more than 1,300,000. Their clip has been posted since last February. There is something special that draws people to watch this clip. And now, a music company has asked them to be singers. So some people accept this hot topic, others are against it. They are good students and have good exam scores. Society is already more open but some people ask why they behave this way. And this may lead others to copy them.[26]

The opening statement highlights the social concerns of Wonder Gay's critics, namely, that they are inappropriately representing Thai-ness (i.e., performing in school uniforms on a school stage in front of a flagpole, flamboyantly) and that their popularity will encourage other boys to become effeminate/homosexual like them.

After the introduction, the interview shifts to the members' academic performance. All members of the Wonder Gay have a GPA of over 3.0. Thus they are established as good students, which suggests that they are moral teenagers and that they can be good role models.[27] The members emphasize that they are not addicted to drugs or involved in other deviant behavior. But the focus on academic performance as a measure of "goodness" presumes that their effeminacy makes them already corrupt; the result is the policing of Thai masculinity. The host then concludes with the statement: "This group is still young. They don't look very mature like in their clip. They just get together and do what they like, and now it depends on society whether to accept them or not."

Online, however, reception of the Wonder Gay video follows a different logic. In Thai forums the response increasingly shifts from congratulatory to disapproving as the audience broadens. The same pattern is observed on YouTube. I elaborate on the comments written by Thais on YouTube because they specifically address an international audience as opposed to a national one.[28] By October 14, 2009, there were 2,949 YouTube comments on the Wonder Gay's initial "Nobody" clip. These comments are overwhelmingly favorable (the clip has a 4.5 out of 5 rating based on 2,754 ratings), yet the critical comments, as might be expected, stand out. Wonder Gay's dancing and singing ability, their gender presentation, and their appropriateness as representatives of Thailand constitute the main issues. However, it is also important to note that they are, as a queer phenomenon, attractive because of their difference, which is often interpreted as humorous and entertaining. Their "strange" behavior is what garners attention. In this sense, they commodify the novelty of Thai gender difference to sell their music.[29]

Thais constitute the early consumers of the "Nobody" video clip. As the clip's popularity increases, the audience becomes more global. Internationalization of the audience brings to the fore issues of national representation, and Wonder Gay's queerness is the primary concern. Much of the YouTube commentary points to the reputation of Thailand as a country with an exceedingly large gay and transgender population. The following exchange from YouTube comments discusses Thailand's reputation for being gay and the role of queers as entertainers.

> *IHyRaXI* -4
>
> yeah thai kids are known to be gay. did you know there the tranny capital of the world?
>
> i mean come on how could these boys actually do this?? for a girl ok, but highschool biys?? just wow . . .
>
> *ThaiSouljaBoi* 0
>
> u got caught hating again dawg lol come on now.. lol u dont like these fags or u do.. whatever . . . let it go lol me persoanlly dont really like these kinda people that much, but i dont say shit to them. You said u dont hate all Thais, so come on dawg, do what u said. Be an example
>
> *IHyRaXI* -1
>
> ahahha come lol i knew youd see this comemnt anyways but i jsut ahd to say somthin cuz it was so gay lol!!!! haha
>
> i know not all thai ppl are gay, jsut these kids are so funny though hahaha
>
> *ThaiSouljaBoi* 0
>
> well keep it on the low, that will be good. Come on, i know u dont like people makin fun of u, do u ? lol
>
> but anyway, these kinda people r like jukebox for us, so its good to have them around, just something to laugh at.[30]

Here ThaiSouljaBoy defends the Wonder Gay because they are Thai. While acknowledging their queer presence, he nominally accepts them for their entertainment value, as objects of ridicule.

The representation of gay and *kathoey* in media that are accessible abroad, such as film and online sources, influences how Thais come to see their country as well as its status for outsiders. For example, labchaeong states: "after watching this vid i realise why thailand never develop [*sic*]."[31] That is, excessive male effeminacy and the lack of talent of the performers are associated with an inability to progress as a nation. Wonder Gay are controversial not only as queers but also as Korean imitators.[32] Thai popular music and other media borrow heavily from the West. However, copying the East, and in such a wide-scale fashion, reignites anxieties about the loss of Thai-ness (ความเป็นไทย khwampenthai). Because the Wonder Gay are situated as a Thai sissy group, they come to represent a nation

Figure 1. Red Shirt protest march in Pattaya, February 22, 2009; photo by Käng. Sign portrays the prime minister as a *kathoey*: "I [pronoun used by girls] want to be prime minister. Suthep [the deputy prime minister] is my husband."

that is already overly queered, and one that can only mimic others without producing anything original. They become a source of national shame.

The Politics of Pride: The Censure and Contest over Visible Evidence

While the Wonder Gay case exemplifies the limits of acceptable representation on the Web, the contestation of queer visibility also occurs in everyday life. One example of such anxiety erupting in the political arena is in Red Shirt (National United Front of Democracy against Dictatorship, or UDD) politics, when queers became a target of Red Shirt protest.[33] Chiang Mai's second gay pride march in 2009 was violently disrupted by Red Shirt protesters and others, who claimed that Lanna (northern Thai) culture does not support such displays. Red Shirt rhetoric excises queerness from local tradition, even though some *kathoey* trace their origins to the Lanna tradition. Red Shirt propaganda also portrays current Prime Minister Abhisit Vejjajiva and other political leaders as *kathoey* to discredit them (see figs. 1 and 2). Such moves do not deny the existence of gays/*kathoey* in UDD politics. Gays/*kathoey* were active protesters in the rallies, and *kathoey* entertain-

Figure 2. Red Shirt protest encampment in Bangkok, April 18, 2010; photo by Käng. Poster, one of many in a series displayed as an art exhibit satirizing Thai politicians as queer, portrays the prime minister as a *kathoey* sex worker: "Daddy [slang for an old, fat, rich man who likes to have sex with young girls/boys; probably a reference to General Prem Tinsulanonda, the sixteenth prime minister of Thailand, who is widely rumored to be gay and the mastermind of the 2006 coup] come, help Mark [Abhisit's Engligh name]!! It'll slip through the prime minister's fingers soon." This idiomatically means the prime minister will lose his position soon. The sticker reads: "Abhisit Murderer."

ers performed at the main stage at Ratchaprasong during the encampment at that area in March–May 2010.[34] *Kathoey* who preened and posed for pictures in front of the Louis Vuitton store just next to the main stage did not fear reproach. Rather, the Red Shirts use homosexuality/transgenderism as a tactic of political shaming. That is, while individuals are allowed to act out their queerness, the concept of queerness is still illegitimate. English-language news reports generally portray the Red Shirts as the rural poor, ignoring the complexity of the UDD constituency. These reports also did not cover the political use of queer imagery and therefore do not impinge on foreigners' views of gay/*kathoey* representation. Thus an image of unequivocal Thai acceptance of homosexuality and transgenderism is preserved.

The UDD protests are not the only venue in which queerness is made politically visible. In Bangkok, clashes among activists, community organizations, and

Figure 3. Phuket, September 9, 2009; photo by Käng. Prem, a *kathoey* researcher and activist, and Luk Yi, a former *kathoey*, in front of a hotel sign: "Prohibited from Entry: Transgenders [*kathoey*], Sissies [young effeminate gay men], Bar Girls. Entry Only for Those with Proper Manners."

commercial interests have put the "pride" march, which incorporates Thais and foreigners, on hiatus. Yet there is an annual "human rights" march, with related events focusing on the Thai queer community, that takes place during the last weekend in November. In 2009 the march occurred in Siam Square, in the heart of Bangkok's shopping district on a Saturday afternoon. Simultaneously, male and transgender sex workers staged a condom fashion show at Hua Lamphong, Bangkok's central train station. Earlier that same morning, a forum including a former Human Rights Commission officer on the topic of กะเทยห้ามเข้า (Kathoey Ham Khao: No entry for *kathoey*) was attended by approximately two hundred participants (see fig. 3).[35] The next day, a festival commemorating World AIDS Day and human rights for sexual minorities brought all these groups and other organizations together in Chatuchak Park. This festival occurred on the footpath between the sky train station and Chatuchak Weekend Market, perhaps the busiest area in Bangkok on a Sunday afternoon. Although gay pride events have ended in Bangkok and were disrupted in Chiang Mai in 2009, they still continue in Pattaya and Phuket. Expressions of queer pride are both suppressed and supported, contingent on local politics and circumstances. Yet the UDD use of transgender imagery for political defamation clearly points to the disgrace that can be evoked by gender nonconformity. As Peter Jackson argues, the Thai situation can best be described as "tolerant but unaccepting."[36]

Paradise: Lost, Found, and Reinvented

The notion of a prelapsarian "gay paradise" in Bangkok is clearly limited, but not entirely unfounded. The complex situation of queer representation in Bangkok points to how thoroughly portrayals of Thai gender and sexuality have been constructed through the sometimes contradictory forces of anticolonial rhetoric, politics, tourism, commodity flows, and other forms of transculturation. Analysis of Thai media shows that there are intense social anxieties about queerness and its relationship to the national body. There is great concern, in a country overdetermined by sex tourism and male-bodied effeminacy, about how the nation appears to non-Thais. Thus foreign portrayals of Thailand as a "gay paradise" may unintentionally incite animosity toward gay/*kathoey*, who, in their excessive sexualization, are seen to defame the nation. Ironically, the portrayal of "gay paradise" may indeed call for the suppression of the very groups that supposedly make Thailand a paradise. Nevertheless, queer Thais themselves refer to the situation as "better here than elsewhere." If you ask Thais why there are so many gay/*kathoey*, the typical answer is that "we accept them."[37] After all, why do so many Western and East Asian gay men come here? Why has Bangkok become the capital of gender-transformation surgery? The economic imbalance that makes Thailand a bargain is key. However, social tolerance toward homosexuality and transgenderism is clearly another primary factor for gay and transgender travelers. The visibility of queerness is high and rarely attracts negative attention. Though there are few legal rights granted to queers (e.g., *kathoey* cannot change their sex on national identity cards), social tolerance for them makes life relatively easy compared with the situation in other countries. Transgenderism and effeminacy are seen as more humorous and "cute" than "sick" or deranged. Compared with East Asian cultures, in Thailand there is less pressure to marry and have sons. Even if one cannot be "open" or "reveal" oneself verbally (เปิดเผย poetphoei), one can "show" (แสดงออก sadaeng ok) oneself visually with little condemnation and live a queer life relatively comfortably.[38] Thai queers say that their situation is better than that of their Asian neighbors.

New geopolitical alignments are also structuring queer subjectivities and cultural trajectories. With increasing economic development and Asian regionalism, there is an increasing shift away from the West. Rather than a unifying teleological force, globalization and modernization also produce local difference. For example, new non-Western sexual subjectivities in Bangkok, such as *"tom"* and *"dee,"* are produced through the same market mechanisms that create "global gays."[39] Indeed, a gender-based model of same-sex female sexuality, which is constructed against local understandings of Western lesbianism, has developed throughout Southeast Asia and Greater China.[40] While some critics have suggested that the situation in queer Asia is like that of the United States in the past, the Thai situation is not behind developmentally but rather a different articulation of queer modernity. Indeed, Thai gay cultures evolved concurrently with Western ones, not after them.[41] Contrary to global gay predictions, gender-stratified *kathoey* have proliferated alongside globally identified gay men.[42] One major difference from the West is in the relative visibility of *kathoey* compared with gay men.[43] In fact, gayness is said not to "show" the way that being *kathoey* usually does. With the growing use of surgical procedures among *kathoey*, however, their visibility decreases as they increasingly pass. As Thai gender and sexuality work through and alongside different cultural logics, evolutionary comparisons with the West are both inadequate and faulty.

Queer Thais themselves, especially those from the middle classes, are creating distinctive desires that are meaningful for them within the context of a middle-income country striving to join the developed world.[44] New consumptive practices and partnership patterns position queer Thais as desiring subjects for whom the Western ideological framework of egalitarian homosexuality takes a backseat to neoliberal economics and their countercurrents.[45] Depictions of sex tourism in particular have shaped how middle-class Thais increasingly display cosmopolitanism by avoiding personal relationships with *farang*. The Internet, regional flows of media, and a rise in regional travel made possible by discount airlines have simultaneously made East Asians desirable and accessible romantic partners. Middle-class Thai gay men often avoid white partners, and other Thais, in staking a claim to an Asian gay cosmopolitan identity. They profess a desire for East Asian partners, and particularly those from wealthier countries. For whom, to what extent, and in what manner is Bangkok a paradise? The answer is that paradise itself does not exist, and paradise is relative to one's social positioning. For many queer Thais, expatriates, and tourists, however, Bangkok is as close as a city gets to being one.[46]

Notes

1.   See www.magazinedee.com/main/magpreview.php?id=6535. In general Thai usage, "*kathoey*" (กะเทย) refers to anyone with nonnormative gender presentation or sexuality, or any variation beyond heterosexual male or female. Here it is used, as in Bangkok, to refer specifically to male-to-female transgender persons. I use the term "ladyboy," which is a common English translation of "*kathoey*," only when it occurs in original text sources, as some *kathoey* consider it offensive.

      Nouns from Thai are not modified to express plural form, thus the plural of "*kathoey*" is "*kathoey*." Unless a common or preferred transliteration exists, all renderings of Thai in roman alphabet use the Royal Thai General System. All translations are mine.

      This article focuses on gay and *kathoey* populations in Bangkok, which have relatively little interaction with *tom*. (These populations have greater interaction outside of Bangkok.) Additionally, much information about gays and *kathoey* is available because of HIV-related research and their common classification as MSM in public health discourses.

      MSM is a public health term that includes gay-identified men and youth, bisexual males (males who have sex with males and females), male-to-female transgenders, male partners of transgenders, male sex workers, and other males who engage in same-sex sexual activity.

2.   See www.magazinedee.com/main/magpreview.php?id=6599. In this article, there is no lexical differentiation made between the English "gay" and the Thai loan "เกย์" (ke), which some scholars italicize (*gay*) to highlight the different meanings and conceptualizations of the word. "Gay" here, and in Thai usage refers only to males. In Thai and other Southeast Asian languages, "gay" is used as an adjective or as a noun. (In this article I use an unitalicized "gay" for convenience.)

      Worapoj was temporarily barred from boxing for his *Stage* modeling.

3.   "*Tom*" refers to masculine women who engage in same-sex relationships. Their counterparts are "*dee*," feminine women in relationships with "*tom*." The terms are derived from the English "tomboy" and "lady."

4.   Third-World women are often equated with the natural resources of a holiday destination. *Kathoey* images for tourists not only naturalize them as local resources but additionally work to construct Thailand as exotic, having a "third" gender.

5.   *Farang* is the term Thais generally use for white foreigners. Like *kathoey*, it can be used as a slur.

6.   Approximately 90 percent of Thais practice Theravada Buddhism.

7.   Thais rarely refer to themselves as "queer." I use it here as a convenient umbrella term for nonnormative gender presentation and same-sex eroticism. Thai academics use the term as in the West.

8. In much of the gay foreigner discourse, Thai males are generally referred to as "boys."

    The "ladyboy" market is primarily targeted toward heterosexually identified men. Listings of *kathoey* go-go bars appear within lists of female go-go bars. *Kathoey* bars are generally not included in lists of gay bars or male go-go bars.

9. Though East Asians probably constitute a larger population of sex tourists to Thailand than white Westerners, being seen in public with another Asian is generally not stigmatizing. Other Asians can be interpreted as friends, while *farang* are more likely coded as sexual partners.

10. I have argued elsewhere that a critique of "rice queens" and sex tourists ignores their local circumstances. They are often marginalized from their communities of origin because of their attractiveness, body size, age, and other characteristics (Dredge Byung'chu Käng, "Reconsidering the Rice Queen" [paper presented at Sexualities, Genders, and Rights in Asia: First International Conference of Asian Queer Studies, Bangkok, Thailand, July 7–9, 2005]; Käng, "Beauty and Its Other: Body as Resource, Sex Tourist as Foil" [paper presented at the annual meeting of the Society for Applied Anthropology, Santa Fe, New Mexico, April 5–10, 2005]).

11. Anonymous, Rice Queen Diary, "About My Blog, August 18th, 2007," www .ricequeendiary.com/about-my-blog/.

12. Anonymous, Rice Queen Diary, "Thai English, December 30th, 2007," www .ricequeendiary.com/thai-english/.

13. Phil, Rice Queen Diary, "Thai English, December 30th, 2007," posted January 30, 2009, 10:37 p.m., www.ricequeendiary.com/thai-english/. The original source, Pattaya Boys Talk, is no longer available online.

14. One bias when looking at forums on sites such as thaivisa.com is that they are skewed toward retirees who are receiving their pensions in Thailand. Retirement visas are among the easiest visas to obtain in Thailand.

15. Nicknames for Bangkok include "Sin City."

16. Frits van Griensven et al., "Evidence of a Previously Undocumented Epidemic of HIV Infection among Men Who Have Sex with Men in Bangkok, Thailand," *AIDS* 19 (2005): 521–26.

17. Peter A. Jackson, "Capitalism and Global Queering: National Markets, Parallels among Sexual Cultures, and Multiple Queer Modernities," *GLQ* 15 (2009): 370.

18. Various studies have estimated 3–17 percent of young men in Thailand are MSM. The estimates for the number of MSM are based on behavioral surveys, primarily of military recruits from the northern provinces. There is no estimate for the size of the self-identified gay population. Estimates for the population of Bangkok range from 6 to 12 million (The Thai census is conducted via household registration, and approximately half the city population is not registered as living in Bangkok). These values create a range of between 90,000 and 1,020,000 MSM in Bangkok. The estimate for *kathoey* in Bangkok is extrapolated from venue-time sampling at shopping malls. See

Sam Winter, "Counting Kathoey" (2002), web.hku.hk/~sjwinter/TransgenderASIA/paper_counting_kathoey.htm.

19. The Association of South East Asian Nations is a political organization of Southeast Asian countries that is increasingly developing economic ties with Japan, Korea, and China.

20. The Korean Wave or *Hallyu* refers to the immense popularity of Korean mass media (i.e., television drama series, pop music, film) and popular culture in Asia and other parts of the globe.

21. Ara Wilson has called for studies that highlight the regional influences that Asian nations exert on each other rather than position Asia as a recipient of flows from the West (Ara Wilson, "Queering Asia," *Intersections: Gender, History, and Culture in the Asian Context* 14 [2006]: intersections.anu.edu.au/issue14/wilson.html). Existing accounts of Thai gender pluralism and same-sex eroticism focus on the interaction between autochthonous, national, and Western influences. Little is known about the impact of East Asian capital, media, and tourism on Thai gender and sexuality. Yet the examples cited above clearly demonstrate that East Asia is a significant source of Thai queer modernity.

22. Vito Russo, *The Celluloid Closet: Homosexuality in the Movies* (New York: Harper and Row, 1981); Thomas Waugh, *The Fruit Machine: Twenty Years of Writings on Queer Cinema* (Durham: Duke University Press, 2000).

23. This latter story was brought to the attention of the media by the Task Force for the Preservation of Civilization, including the prominent and controversial gay activist Natee Teerarojjanapongs. From Natee's perspective, such behavior both demeans traditional religious institutions and portrays gays negatively, as immoral and irresponsible citizens.

24. Thailand has a long history of disciplining gender. Early efforts to prevent Western colonization included the transformation of Thai gender to meet the expectations of Western civilization, as transforming barbaric gender and sexual practices was one of the justifications for colonization (Peter A. Jackson, "Performative Genders, Perverse Desires: A Bio-History of Thailand's Same-Sex and Transgender Cultures," *Intersections: Gender, History, and Culture in the Asian Context* 9 [2003]: intersections.anu.edu.au/issue9/jackson.html); Penny van Esterik, *Materializing Thailand* [Oxford: Berg, 2000]).

25. There are, of course, gays and *kathoey* who find such representations offensive. As few of the actors are gay, their gay performances are exaggerated. However, the vast majority of viewers, whether queer or not, find these representations humorous and fun, nothing requiring serious examination.

26. My translation. The figure for the Susan Boyle clip given by the reporter seems too low. However, multiple versions of clips are often posted on YouTube, and thus the statistic given might refer to a clip that was not Boyle's most popular clip.

27. There is also a stereotype that gays are smarter and better behaved in school than heterosexual boys.

28. YouTube comments are left in English, Thai, Thaiglish (identifiable through online idioms such as "555" [i.e., ha ha ha] or a phonetic rendition of Thai in Roman alphabet), Tagalog, Chinese, Korean, and Japanese.

29. For a discussion of the commodification of *kathoey* in selling products, see Prempreeda Pramoj Na Ayuttaya, "The Kathoey as a Product" (2003), web.hku.hk/~sjwinter/TransgenderASIA/paper_the_kathoey_as_a_product(thai).htm; also available in English at web.hku.hk/~sjwinter/TransgenderASIA/paper_the_kathoey_as_a_product.htm.

30. Text from YouTube is reproduced exactly as rendered online, and all spelling and grammatical mistakes have been retained. I have removed the dates of the comments and the voting links. The number following the handle of the poster represents the positive or negative votes the comment received.

31. The profile for labchaeong identifies him/her as from Afghanistan, but the fact that the profile is written in Thai suggests that the author is either Thai or Thai living abroad.

32. Wonder Gay follow other Thai imitators of K-pop, such as the all-*kathoey* group Venus Flytrap, modeled after the transgender Korean group Lady and the girl band 7 Days, modeled after the Korean girl band Girls' Generation. Such mimicry questions Thai originality at the same time that it poses a competition between countries. Most Thais do not realize that the Wonder Girls' song "Nobody" re-creates a Motown aesthetic.

33. The Red Shirts are a populist political organization composed mostly of the rural and urban poor that support former Prime Minister Thaksin. They claim the current administration came into power illegitimately and thus call for the dissolution of the government and new elections.

34. Ratchaprasong is the name of the intersection of Rama I and Ratchadamri Roads. The Red Shirt camp was centered at this intersection, where the main stage was set up. This intersection is also the center of high-end shopping in Bangkok.

35. Many commercial establishments, especially hotels and night clubs, do not admit *kathoey*. The rationale is that they are sex workers or thieves who will steal from other guests.

36. Peter A. Jackson, "Tolerant but Unaccepting: The Myth of a Thai 'Gay Paradise,'" in *Genders and Sexualities in Modern Thailand*, ed. Peter A. Jackson and Nerida M. Cook (Bangkok: Silkworm Books, 1999), 226–42.

37. Thais often refer to queerness as something that is more acceptable in Thailand than elsewhere. Typically, they will say that Thais "ยอมรับ" (yom rap: accept) homosexuality and transgenderism while other countries are "ปิด" (pit: closed, concealed) or queers there must be "อับอาย" (apai: ashamed). However, this refers specifically to everyday life and the openness one can show in publicly displaying male-bodied effeminacy. Thais often believe that queers have more rights overseas, for example,

the right to marry. This is often exaggerated. For example, some believe that same-sex marriage exists throughout the United States rather than in specific states.

38. As in other parts of Asia, there is not an emphasis on "coming out" in Thailand. However, unlike more Confucianist East Asian societies, there is less emphasis on hiding one's gender and sexual nonconformity. For *kathoey*, transgenderism is generally made visible via sartorial practice, cosmetic use, bodily comportment, and language (Thai uses gendered particles that mark the speaker as male or female). Effeminate gay Thais (who generally would not describe themselves as "men") will often state that everyone knows about their sexual orientation, even if they have told no one.

39. Dennis Altman, "Global Gaze/Global Gays," *GLQ* 3 (1997): 417–36. However, capitalism does not produce the same results wherever it trespasses. For a case related to Thai *tom* and *dee*, see Ara Wilson, *The Intimate Economies of Bangkok: Tomboys, Tycoons, and Avon Ladies in the Global City* (Berkeley: University of California Press, 2007).

40. Megan Sinnott, *Toms and Dees: Transgender Identity and Female Same-Sex Relationships in Thailand* (Honolulu: University of Hawai'i Press, 2004); Evelyn Blackwood and Saskia E. Wieringa, "Sapphic Shadows: Challenging the Silence in the Study of Sexuality," in *Female Desires: Same-Sex Relations and Transgender Practices across Cultures*, ed. Evelyn Blackwood and Saskia E. Wieringa (New York: Columbia University Press, 1999), 39–63.

41. Peter A. Jackson, "An American Death in Bangkok: The Murder of Darrell Berrigan and the Hybrid Origins of Gay Identity in 1960s Thailand," *GLQ* 5 (1999): 361.

42. Stephen O. Murray's taxonomy of homosexualities describes modern Western homosexuality as egalitarian in that both partners are more or less equal in status and similar in gender presentation, compared with other systems in which age difference, gender-transformation, or other factors structure homosexuality (Stephen O. Murray, *Homosexualities* [Chicago: University of Chicago Press, 2000]).

43. At least in central Bangkok, one could argue that *tom* and *dee* are more visible than gay men, in that they are often seen holding hands as couples. Typically, couples are easily identifiable, as one woman will have long hair and be very feminine while the other will have short hair and masculine gender presentation. They are, however, generally not considered threatening to normative gender the same way that male same-sex couples are, as female same-sex sexuality is referred to as a kind of "play." Same-sex male couples rarely hold hands or are affectionate in public.

44. Lisa Rofel notes that gay men in China avoid white partners to demonstrate belonging to the nation (*Desiring China: Experiments in Neoliberalism, Sexuality, and Public Culture* [Durham: Duke University Press, 2007]), 88.

45. Murray, *Homosexualities*, 2–5.

46. Perhaps in reaction to the representation of Thailand as a "gay paradise," particularly

in popular literature, academics have emphasized the faultiness of such a portrayal, pointing to the complex and contradictory nature of homosexuality and transgenderism in Thailand. The academic literature focuses on negative events and aspects of intolerance to sexual diversity. However, queer Thais themselves, especially *kathoey*, typically frame their situation in Thailand as better than in other countries.

DOI 10.1215/10642684-2010-028

QUEERING THE BLACK ATLANTIC, QUEERING THE BROWN ATLANTIC

David L. Eng

Pedagogies of Crossing: Meditations on Feminism, Sexual Politics, Memory, and the Sacred
M. Jacqui Alexander
Durham: Duke University Press, 2005. 410 pp.

Impossible Desires: Queer Diasporas and South Asian Public Cultures
Gayatri Gopinath
Durham: Duke University Press, 2005. 247 pp.

At a recent state-of-the-field queer studies conference hosted by the University of Pennsylvania to mark the twenty-fifth anniversary of Gayle Rubin's groundbreaking essay "Thinking Sex," it became clear to me that the critique of the normative, which we might describe as queer studies' most important epistemic as well as political promise, is currently in the intellectual custody of three dynamic fields: transgender studies, disability studies, and area studies. For this review, I focus on area studies—more specifically, on the intersectional and interdisciplinary encounter among area studies, diaspora studies, and postcolonial studies. M. Jacqui Alexander's *Pedagogies of Crossing: Meditations on Feminism, Sexual Politics, Memory, and the Sacred* and Gayatri Gopinath's *Impossible Desires: Queer Diasporas and South Asian Public Cultures* are two important books that illus-

GLQ 17:1
DOI 10.1215/10642684-2010-029
© 2010 by Duke University Press

trate the critical stakes in bringing together queer theory with area, diaspora, and postcolonial studies. Along with several other prominent scholars, Alexander and Gopinath have helped forge out of this encounter the burgeoning field of "queer diasporas." Emerging most forcefully in relation to South Asian, East Asian, and Latin American studies, queer diasporas as a method demands immediate and sustained attention to how diaspora has traditionally relied on a "genealogical, implicitly heteronormative reproductive logic" (Gopinath, 10) to shore up conventional structures of family and kinship. In this manner, diaspora has reinforced dominant sexual and gendered ideologies of the nation-state that constitute it as the site of not only purity and origin but also exclusion, racial tension, and political, economic, and social strife in the West, as elsewhere.

Yet if "'diaspora' needs 'queerness' to rescue it from its genealogical implications," Gopinath observes, "'queerness' also needs 'diaspora' in order to make it more supple in relation to questions of race, colonialism, migration, and globalization" (11). Indeed, considering queerness and diaspora together offers, in the broadest sense, important new ways to approach some of the critical aporias in all these fields. More specifically, it offers a rethinking of a long history of Euro-American modernity, sexual politics, racial formation, political economy, and migration in relation to the advent and rise of colonialism, the subsequent dilemmas of postcoloniality and decolonization in the Third World, and the current proliferation of U.S.-led global capitalism and the militarization of everyday life.

In Alexander's estimation, a certain brand of post-structuralism has had the "effect of constructing queer theory in a way that eviscerates histories of colonialism and racial formation, frameworks that could themselves point the way to a radical activist scholarship in which race, sexual politics, and globalization would be understood together rather than being positioned as theoretical or political strangers" (70). A queer diasporic methodology maps the theoretical and political itineraries of such a critical proposition. In short, it illustrates what is at stake when disparate bodies and sexualities travel in the global system—across the Black Atlantic to the Caribbean in Alexander's case and across the Brown Atlantic to various locales of the South Asian diaspora in Gopinath's study.

Thus, for example, in terms of normative morality, homosexuality is conventionally characterized as "immoral" and "lewd"—"primitive" and "uncivilized"—in the West. Yet, paradoxically, homosexuality (and tolerance of it) becomes a marker of modernity and civilization when applied in non-Western contexts and to non-Western cultures. Often considered a poor imitation of more advanced Western models of social life, a recognizable gay identity becomes, Gopinath suggests, "intelligible and indeed desirable when and where it can be incorporated into [a] developmental narrative of modernity" (142). In a transvaluation of the same logic, when taken up by conservative postcolonial and neocolonial native elites and administrations, homosexuality is often denounced and disavowed as a degenerate Western import, thus rescripting and reifying heteronormativity as the prerequisite for nation and empire, for racial purity and moral rectitude, for good citizenship and social belonging—for social life itself.

On both sides of this debate, sexuality appears as a fixed identity and property belonging to a group of authorized citizen-subjects residing in the global North, while continuing to evolve and develop elsewhere. Heightened attention to how queer diasporas complicate such fixed notions of ownership and belonging illustrates how sexuality continually exceeds its conventional boundaries in a Euro-American tradition of liberal modernity and its rights-based identity claims. Hence we witness the transformation of sexuality, as it migrates in the global system, into many other things: a discourse of development; a dialectic of Enlightenment; a geopolitics of the civilized and the primitive; a tale of racial, religious, and cultural barbarism; a story of democracy and progress; and, most recently, an index of self-determination and human rights.

Pedagogies of Crossing and *Impossible Desires* carefully unfold the manifest contradictions and intricacies of sexuality in the diaspora as it travels across different locales, public and private zones, and political and cultural fissures—indeed, helping construct and define through its various movements these locales, zones, and fissures themselves. Paying particular attention to queer diasporas as they cross not only geopolitical but also institutional boundaries, often abruptly and impolitely, Alexander's and Gopinath's projects disrupt and denaturalize given ways of knowing and being "over here" as well as "over there." To borrow a concept from the postcolonial historian Dipesh Chakrabarty, they provincialize queer studies, area studies, and diaspora studies, as well as a host of other interlocking and interconnected fields, including postcolonial theory, transnational feminism, ethnic studies, and Marxism, to name some immediate examples.

Alexander's *Pedagogies of Crossing* consists of seven chapters, divided into three sections. As she explains in the book's opening pages,

> *Pedagogies'* central metaphor is drawn from the enforced Atlantic Crossing of the millions of Africans that serviced from the fifteenth century through the twentieth the consolidation of British, French, Spanish, and Dutch empires. At the time I conceived of the book in 2000, the world had not yet witnessed the seismic imperial shifts that characterize this moment. In one

> sense, then, *Pedagogies* functions as an archive of empire's twenty-first-
> century counterpart, of oppositions to it, of the knowledges and ideologies
> it summons, and of the ghosts that haunt it. (2)

Alexander's three sections cover a wide historical range — from the Spaniard
Vasco Nuñez de Balboa's colonial conquest of the New World and his feeding of
forty Indian "cross-dressers" to his dogs in 1513; to the criminalization of lesbian
and gay sex by neocolonial administrations in Trinidad and Tobago in 1986 and
1991 and in the Bahamas in 1991; to our contemporary neo-imperial moment of
U.S. empire, the Defense of Marriage Act, and the Patriot Act, in which "hegemonic heterosexual masculinity wishes to assert a Pax Americana through imperial violence undertaken within its own borders as well as in different parts of the
world" (183).

Drawing attention to how imperialism and heterosexuality have been historically welded together by both state and corporate interests, Alexander also
examines the remarkable contemporary shifts in global capitalism that mark "a
systemic, interdependent relationship between heterosexual capital and gay capital" reminiscent of how "black capitalism has been called on to do a similar kind
of work for white capital" (66). In the first section of *Pedagogies*, "Transnational
Erotics: State, Capital, and the Decolonization of Desire" (chapters 1–2), Alexander explores this convergence in the phenomenon of gay tourism in the Bahamas
and other sites in the Caribbean, investigating how capitalism reformulates sexuality and sexual desire to meet its ever-expanding needs. Gay tourism illustrates
the flexibility of global capitalism. Its particular significance, Alexander notes,
"lies in its ability to draw together powerful processes of sexual commodification
and sexual citizenship" (27).

Alexander deftly examines the contemporary production of the rights-
based consumer citizen embodied in the figure of the gay white tourist. She notes
that while "citizenship based in political rights can be forfeited, these rights do not
disappear entirely. Instead, they get reconfigured and restored under the rubric of
gay consumer at this moment in late capitalism" (71). As brown bodies from the
global South move north to take up employment as domestic labor, in agricultural
sectors, and in service industries, white bodies in the global North move south in
search of leisure and pleasure. In the process, they expand networks of capital, I
might note, from general tourism into areas of sex tourism and medical tourism as
well as related industries such as artificial reproductive technologies (e.g., "womb
renting"), transnational adoption, and organ trading.

Alexander's study of gay tourism thus provides one early and important genealogy for the current historical emergence of what I have elsewhere described as queer liberalism. Queer liberalism marks a coming together of economic and political spheres that now forms the basis for liberal enfranchisement and inclusion of particular U.S. (as well as other Western) gay and lesbian citizen-subjects petitioning for rights and recognition before the law. In this regard, Alexander's study of tourism charts the shifting legacies of colonialism and colonial travel literature and their transformations under the shadows of global capitalism. It underscores how "racialization and colonization are being consistently written into modernity's different projects. . . . [and] occasioned by the uneven class relations and differentiations produced by neo-liberal capital's dispersions" (194).

At the same time that Alexander considers how the shifting routes of global capitalism work to fold once dissident U.S. gay and lesbian citizen-subjects into its economic and political mandates, she also analyzes how these movements invoke homophobic responses by postcolonial and neocolonial administrations. That is, she illustrates how gay and lesbian tourists from the global North are being conscripted by neoliberal framings of capital, welfare reform, and sexual normalization (in the form of marriage, adoption, inheritance, etc.) as exemplary consuming citizen-subjects, even as these neoliberal mandates travel and are transformed in the diaspora into debates about postcolonial independence and heteronormative self-determination. In this manner, while gays and lesbians in the metropolitan North are being unevenly incorporated into the cultural imaginary of "We the People," citizenship in places such as the Bahamas continues to be "premised in heterosexual terms. . . . Lesbian and gay bodies are made to bear the brunt of the charge of undermining national sovereignty, while the neocolonial state masks its own role in forfeiting sovereignty as it recolonizes and renarrativizes a citizenry for service in imperial tourism" (11).

Alexander presents us with a provocative history of the present in which sovereignty is waged in the domain of sexuality and sexual regulation and asymmetrically on the backs of racialized queer immigrant bodies. Hannah Arendt famously noted that citizenship is nothing less than the "right to have rights."[1] However, Alexander concludes, critical attention to the problematic of citizenship, immigration, and alienage in queer diasporas reveals how the category of formal citizenship is simply too fragile, too fraught, and "far too subject to state manipulation and co-optation for it to become the primary basis on which radical political mobilization is carried on" (249).

If section 1 of Alexander's book presents the various movements of crossings past and crossings present that produce authorized and dissident bodies in the global system, section 2 (chapters 2–5) of her study, "Maps of Empire, Old and

New," focuses on the "pedagogies" part of the book's main title. Here, Alexander focuses on how we might "teach for justice"—how we might effectively and ethically intervene in state power, a project "fundamentally at odds with the project of militarization, which always already imagines an enemy and acts accordingly to eliminate it" (92). Contesting the privileged connections among capitalism, democracy, and freedom, Alexander explores how we might contest the state and corporate production of citizenship normalized within the prism of heterosexuality, a normalization whose ideological consolidation, as Louis Althusser notes, is largely the responsibility of the school in secular societies.[2] Alexander wonders, "What is democracy to mean when its association with the perils of empire has rendered it so thoroughly corrupt that it seems disingenuous and perilous even to deploy the term. Freedom is a similar hegemonic term, especially when associated with the imperial freedom to abrogate the self-determination of a people" (17). Through heightened attention to these particular pedagogical queries, Alexander shows "how free-market democracy might stand in the way of justice [and] how legacies of transformational struggles in the academy may not be reflected in the everyday life of an institution" (92).

Alexander presents numerous examples of such pedagogic initiatives, drawn from real-life examples of political intervention into the production of knowledge and the contestation of state power: from her musing on the social contract and John Locke ("We can't get to liberalism and rights without John Locke, but we can watch him as he gazes at Indians in America." [171]) to the recounting of her own battle for retention at the New School in New York City ("For almost a year, I had experienced that odd kind of alienation that results from being positioned as an onlooker in the usurpation of my own identity." [153]). In the process, she seeks to interrupt

> inherited boundaries of geography, nation, episteme, and identity that distort vision so that they can be replaced with frameworks and modes of being that enable an understanding of the dialectics of history, enough to assist in navigating the terms of learning and the fundamentally pedagogic imperative at its heart: the imperative of making the world in which we live intelligible to ourselves and to each other—in other words, teaching ourselves. (6)

Ultimately, teaching for justice would seek to undermine epistemic frameworks and practices that are simply unable to explain those itineraries of violence that gain their political force through "names such as democracy and civilization" (3).

In section 3 of *Pedagogies*, "Dangerous Memory: Secular Acts, Sacred Possession" (chapters 6–7), Alexander continues this pedagogic initiative by showing us how the personal is political and how the spiritual is political as well. She illustrates how one might go about constructing oppositional knowledges and practices by reconsidering the conventional relations between the secular and the sacred that would decidedly split the latter from the former in modernity's self-narration of development. Here, she refuses to yield the space of the spiritual to religious fundamentalists, whose vision of sinners in the hands of an angry God sets the conceptual limits to the functions of the spiritual in social debate today. At the same time, she resists the notion that "no self-respecting postmodernist would want to align herself (at least in public) with a category such as the spiritual, which appears so fixed, so unchanging, so redolent of tradition" (15). Working against these traditions of sanctioned knowledge and practice, Alexander observes that while "humans made the Crossing, traveling only in one direction through Ocean given the name Atlantic[,] Grief traveled as well" (289).

Alexander draws on this history of grief—exemplifying the recent affective turn in queer studies—through her experiences with Santeria and Vodou. Such experiences lead her to commune with a slave woman named Kitsimba, who made her own Atlantic Crossing in the eighteenth-century, as well as with other sisters of color, ancestrally recalled in *This Bridge Called My Back*.[3] "In the realm of the secular," Alexander remarks, "the material is conceived of as tangible while the spiritual is either nonexistent or invisible. In the realm of the Sacred, however, the invisible constitutes its presence by a provocation of sorts, by provoking our attention" (307). We may choose to ignore the Sacred. However, attuned to its effects, and to its affective valences, the spiritual promises to lead us elsewhere, yielding forms of knowledge and practice that evade the instrumental radar of empiricism and scientific rationality, the cornerstones of Enlightenment thinking.

Understanding that ghosts and spirits do not depend on our collective acknowledgment to validate their existences provides a new way to approach Bruno Latour's insistence that "we have never been modern"—or, at least, quite as modern as we would like to believe. Even more, it allows those left out of modernity's instrumental reason to make better sense of a social world that outsources them as collateral damage. Alexander summarizes,

> I wish to examine how spiritual practitioners employ metaphysical systems
> to provide the moorings for their meanings and understanding of self—in
> short, how they constitute or remember experience as Sacred and how that
> experience shapes their subjectivity. Experience is a category of great

epistemic import to feminism. But we have understood it primarily as secularized, as if it were absent Spirit and thus antithetical, albeit indirectly, to the Sacred. (295)

By queering the Black Atlantic in these provocative ways, Alexander offers bold ways to reimagine and rethink the intersectional and interdisciplinary relationships among queer studies, area studies, diaspora studies, postcoloniality, transnational feminism, ethnic studies, Marxism, and globalization. Indeed, such a queering of the Black Atlantic is long overdue. Alexander's specific attention to the postcolonial Caribbean highlights issues of sovereignty, citizenship, immigration, and social belonging, placing Afro-diaspora and African American studies in more immediate conversation with Asian/Asian American studies as well as Latin/Latin American studies, whose long-time engagements with these categories have helped fuel the critique of hetero- and homonormativity, kinship, and elective affiliation in the field of queer diasporas. Alexander's methodology draws sustained attention to different and uneven histories of slavery, coerced migration, and indentureship that construct these legal and social formalizations. Furthermore, her focus on the queer Caribbean supplements the more cosmopolitan emphases of Afro-diaspora in the Black Atlantic (which connect, for example, the metropolitan capitals of New York, London, and Paris). As Alexander notes:

> There is a great deal of urgency for us to map . . . some crucial analytic shifts that will prompt postcolonial studies to engage more strategically with the "here and there," to position immigration, for instance, as an important site for the local reconfiguration of subalternity and the local reconfiguration of race. . . . As certain strands of queer studies move to take up more centrally questions of political economy and racial formation, and of transnational feminism and immigrant labor, the analytic vise in the discipline will be sharpened between those who hold on to a representational democratic focus within U.S. borders and those who espouse an antipathy toward the links between political economy and sexuality. (253)

In bringing together all these various and distinct fields, Alexander's project provides a compelling account of what Lisa Lowe describes as the "Intimacies of Four Continents" — the material as well as philosophical dialectic of African slave and Asian indentured labor, of which the Caribbean is a prime exemplum, subtending the dialectic of Euro-American modernity. This crucial but disavowed

correspondence provides an alternative history to the affirmation of human freedom and the forgetting of race in the Americas, a "perverse modernity."

Attention to questions of the visible and invisible are also central to Gopinath's
Impossible Desires. Her study, consisting of six chapters and an epilogue, draws
together a diverse set of cultural texts—from South Asian diasporic film, literature, music, and photography—to construct an archive of "impossible desires"
whose erotic itineraries are linked to a queer female subjectivity that is often made
to disappear in the epistemological protocols of the various fields with which she
is engaged. In Gopinath's book, attention to this queer female subjectivity reworks
a number of dominant perspectives across several fields. For example, *Impossible
Desire* contests the insistent and asymmetrical attention to gay male agency and
desire that defines much of GLBTQ studies. As she puts it, "How do we clear the
theoretical and representational space to imagine a queer subjectivity that is not
always already male, or a female subjectivity that is not always already heterosexual" (78)? In this manner, Gopinath also shifts consideration from dominant analyses of *gender* in transnational feminism by considering what is at stake in focusing
critical attention on the category of transnational *sexuality* developed by a queer
diasporic (and queer of color) critique of family, kinship, and nation. "The failure
of feminist scholars of South Asia and the South Asian diaspora," she observes,
"to fully interrogate heterosexuality as a structuring mechanism of both state and
diasporic nationalisms makes clear the indispensability of a queer critique" (10).
Despite powerful analyses of "woman" as "emblematic of the concept of home
and nation, as feminized domestic space, and as a site of chaste and unsullied
spirituality," postcolonial feminism is "marked by a curious lack of attention to the
production of heterosexuality and homosexuality within these discourses" (136).
From a slightly different perspective, Gopinath refuses a heteronormative logic
of postcolonial sovereignty that would situate "the terms 'queer' and 'diaspora' as
dependent on the originality of 'heterosexuality' and 'nation' " (13).

Locating a queer South Asian female subject as the starting point for theorizing queer diasporas narrates "a different story of how global capitalism impacts
local sites by articulating other forms of subjectivity, culture, affect, kinship, and
community that may not be visible or audible within standard mappings of nation,
diaspora, or globalization" (12). These are communities that lack social power but
nevertheless have presence. Throughout her analyses, Gopinath emphasizes that
within "the patriarchal logic of an Indian immigrant bourgeoisie, a 'nonhetero-
sexual Indian woman' occupies a space of impossibility, in that she is not only
excluded from the various 'home' spaces that the 'woman' is enjoined to inhabit

and symbolize but, quite literally, simply cannot be imagined" (18). Gopinath proceeds to imagine these figures of impossibility and how they pose an insistent challenge to the logics of South Asian patriarchy at home and abroad. Her readings unfold along a terrain of the unimaginable, the ephemeral, and the invisible, invoking a range of "dissident and non-heteronormative practices and desires that may very well be incommensurate with the [Western] identity categories of 'gay' and 'lesbian'" (11).

The book's careful attention to an archive of female desire embodied in a host of domestic figures — mothers, daughters, wives, in-laws, maids, and courtesans — is spread across a wide spectrum on both sides of the "Brown Atlantic" and (largely) the global North: in the United States, Canada, the Caribbean, the United Kingdom, and India; in mainstream, Bollywood, and independent cinema (such as Gurinder Chadha's *Bend It Like Beckham* [2002], Girish Karnad's *Utsav* [1984], Deepa Mehta's *Fire* [1996], Mira Nair's *Monsoon Wedding* [2001], Damien O'Donnell's *East Is East* [1999], and Pratibha Parmar's *Khush* [1991]); in literature (including works by Ismat Chughtai, Shani Mootoo, V. S. Naipaul, and Shyam Selvadurai); in music (bhangra, new Asian dance music); and in photography (by Parminder Sekhon). Throughout, Gopinath attends to how the space of the "domestic" — defined here as both "home" and "nation" — is reconfigured by queer diasporas.

Unlike the developmental trajectories of gay and lesbian coming-of-age narratives in the West, which culminate with the rejection of home and the confines of the closet, Gopinath's archive insistently holds on to and reclaims the space of the domestic, working and reworking its sexual protocols and its private-public boundaries for its own purposes. In her analysis of the director Ian Iqbal Rashid's *Surviving Sabu* (1998) and O'Donnell's *East Is East*, Gopinath observes that "home" is

> not simply or necessarily the place from which the queer subject is evicted or exiled. Rather, "home" is a space that is ruptured by and imaginatively transformed by queer diasporic subjects even as they remain within its confines. This queer transformation of the diasporic "home" constitutes a remarkably powerful challenge to dominant ideologies of community and nation in ways that may very well escape intelligibility within a logic of visibility and "coming out." (79)

Notably, the "stars" of Gopinath's domestic dramas are not cross-dressers or butch lesbians. Rather, female homoeroticism is consistently signaled in the films and writings she analyzes by a hyperbolic and spectacularized femininity detached from its heterosexual moorings. The South Asian femme suffuses the space of the home, and rather than exist in an exilic relationship to it, she challenges the Western tendency to imagine gays and lesbians as primarily located in the space of the public sphere ("We're here, we're queer, get used to it!"). At the same time, she reworks the dominant epistemic tropes of visibility and invisibility, public and private, that "may exist outside, or indeed, within a Euro-American context" (145). In Gopinath's *Impossible Desires*, home might be described as delineating an alternative public sphere. Home is not private, as theorized under liberalism. Instead, it is a crucial public site of labor within the global restructuring of capitalism. Here, the femme's queer desire exceeds the male state lineages that define conservative notions of nationhood and diaspora as the privileged zone of filial prerogative, challenging South Asian native as well as immigrant patriarchy (such as Hindu nationalism).

In a spectacular reading of the Urdu writer Ismat Chughtai's 1941 short story "Lihaf" ("The Quilt"), Gopinath extends this analysis by rethinking the "will-to-see" that attends the politics of the closet, the emergence of female same-sex relations, and the demands for visibility in the West. Chughtai's narrator, a young girl visiting the upper-class Muslim household of her aunt, witnesses some sort of relationship between the sequestered aunt and her female maidservant. Each evening, the little girl is drawn to the energetic contortions emanating from the two figures under the quilt. Yet when all is revealed, when the quilt is ultimately lifted, the narrator curiously refuses disclosure: "What I saw when the quilt was lifted, I will never tell anyone, not even if they give me a lakh of rupees." Contesting the Western logics of the "will-to-see," Gopinath writes that the "quilt can be read not so much as a kind of concealing device beneath which the 'truth' of visual 'proof' of sex and desire lie, as much as a kind of mediating and constantly shifting surface that negotiates and marks the borders between different economies and organizations of erotic pleasure" (150). Here, her careful attention to this reworking of the boundaries of domestic space and knowledge extends beyond the epistemology of the closet in the West to offer new spaces and critical approaches in theories of transnational feminism, postcoloniality, and globalization.

Feminist theory has done much to denaturalize the artificial boundaries separating public and private in liberal society that facilitate gendered domination in political, economic, and social life. For instance, the conflation and confusion of two different private spheres—the home and the market—subtending the public sphere make possible the uncompensated exploitation of female domestic labor in the "private" space of the home. Transnational feminists have rightly extended this critique to consider how the hyperexploitation of domestic labor from the global South inserts Third-World women (as well as men) into this gendered equation, a reconfigured disparity between home and work as well as two other forms of the "domestic" — that is, the domestic nation-states of the North and those of the South under neoliberal globalization. Gopinath's attention to queer female desire's reformulation of these indeterminate boundaries points to how public and private, home and market, kinship and corporation, and home and nation-state do not easily map onto South Asian and South Asian diasporic political economies through such binaries. Furthermore, it also stresses how categories of female sexuality are insistently deployed and regulated to stabilize these precarious distinctions in the homeland and the diaspora.

In sum, Gopinath, like Alexander, boldly charts a history of the present in which heteronormativity and contemporary nationalisms are neither a natural nor an inevitable result of neoliberal globalization marching across the world. In both books, queer diasporas place South Asian and Caribbean perspectives at the center of transnational feminism, postcolonial studies, and critical race theory to consider the numerous ways by which attention to female sexuality in the global South presents us with histories of the past and present that do not march to the beat of enlightened liberalism's deafening drums. To the contrary, the field of queer diasporas provides a compelling account of how a turn to queer circuits of desire might interrupt the dominant itineraries of globalization and the current ascension of queer liberalism as one of its regnant effects. Ultimately, it works to keep queer studies queer.

Note

1. Hannah Arendt, *The Origins of Totalitarianism* (New York: Harcourt, 1968), 296.
2. Louis Althusser, "Ideology and Ideological State Apparatuses (Notes towards an Investigation)," in *Lenin and Philosophy and Other Essays* (New York: Monthly Review Press, 1971), 132, 143.
3. Moraga, Cherríe and Gloria Anzaldúa, eds., *This Bridge Called My Back: Writings by Radical Women of Color* (New York: Kitchen Table Press, Women of Color Press, 1984).

ONE NATION UNDER GAY

Greg Youmans

Gay Rights and Moral Panic:
The Origins of America's Debate on Homosexuality
Fred Fejes
New York: Palgrave Macmillan, 2008. x + 280 pp.

In an early scene of Gus Van Sant's *Milk* (2008), Harvey Milk approaches the "top gays" of San Francisco to see if their way of doing politics can make room for his own. The film suggests that Milk's populism and sexual frankness are incompatible with the don't-rock-the-boat, crypto-homophile stance of the other men. An hour later, Milk's Bay Area–based efforts against the Briggs Initiative have changed the hearts and minds of a majority of state voters, including those in conservative Orange County, as if by magic. Fred Fejes's important book complicates and deromanticizes this history. At the book's center is a detailed account of the major U.S. struggles over gay rights in 1977 and 1978, from the battle against Anita Bryant in Dade County, Florida, to six other local contests that followed in its wake, including the statewide struggle in California. Fejes clarifies the difference between the Religious Right's success at repealing gay civil rights ordinances like the one in Dade and its concurrent failures in passing proactively antigay measures, such as Briggs's Proposition 6, which would have made it legal to fire any public school teacher who spoke favorably of homosexuality. Fejes also makes it clear that the "top gays," such as the *Advocate*'s publisher, David Goodstein, did not fade away during these struggles. Goodstein and others used their money and connections to steer media framing of the issue from homosexuality to privacy and to harness support from powerful organizations and individuals, such as the teachers' unions and ex-governor Ronald Reagan. Fejes's book clarifies the shift toward a desexualized, privacy-rights understanding of "gay rights" in the late 1970s, an important dynamic that Van Sant's movie obscures with its rhetoric of sexual freedom and coming out.

Though the core of Fejes's book is local, its frame is national. It is concerned with the role of mainstream media channels in shaping popular conceptions of homosexuality. Widespread media attention transformed Bryant's countywide referendum into an unprecedented national debate over the definition, role, and legitimacy of homosexuality in the United States. Fejes argues that the ensuing series of nationally mediated contests fostered a new national identity among U.S. gays and lesbians. "Emerging during these months was what political scholar Benedict Anderson described as 'an imagined community,' a community defined not by physical space and boundaries or the actual physical contact among its members but by the mental image of affinity — 'the image of communion' — that each held in their minds" (215). As they sought ways to support unprepared and beleaguered local activists in Miami, St. Paul, Wichita, and elsewhere, gay activists in more-established urban communities formed and reinforced national fundraising campaigns and political organizations. Fejes's book is thus a history of the "origins of America's debate on homosexuality," a history of the rise of a national gay and lesbian movement, and (though less explicitly so) a history of the rise of U.S. gay nationalism.

The book chronicles the political efforts of the two major camps in the late-1970s struggle over gay rights: gay liberal activists and the Religious Right. It devotes many pages to the effort by the main group of Miami gay activists to establish a neutral, Carter-era "human rights" framework that would downplay the homosexual, and by extension sexual, specificity of their cause. But the book also discusses the competing insistence by some gay activists on a sexual-liberationist framework. Moreover, Fejes presents his history in a way that does not boil down to a simple matter of gay versus straight. The attitudes and experiences of Miami's black, Cuban, white, and Jewish populations become central to the story of the Dade County campaign and vote. Along the same lines, Fejes refuses to allow Bryant's particular inflection of Southern Baptist faith to stand in for the entirety of the "Religious Right," and he also counters the misperception that all religious voters voted against gay rights. Throughout, the book explores the media and demographic strategizing behind the competing get-out-the-vote campaigns. This approach is one of the book's strengths, though a few sections uncritically reproduce the blanket group characterizations that are a hallmark of demographic thinking. Moreover, the voting blocs and media sources that Fejes presents are more diverse than the pool of activists he interviews and discusses, which is composed mainly of the gay white men who had access to high-profile positions in the movement. The book also offers little discussion of contemporaneous critiques of mainstream gay politics emanating from further on the left.

Oddly, despite the book's title, the term *moral panic* seldom appears in the text, and Fejes does not engage at length with the critical literature on the concept. Where the term does appear, Fejes applies it to mass-mediated public anxiety around homosexuality. However, the antigay actions of Bryant and Briggs were intimately bound up with another moral panic of the late 1970s, an orchestrated state and media campaign around child pornography, sexual abuse, and prostitution, replete with dubious claims and inflated statistics. Fejes discusses this concurrent development, but not as a "moral panic." He seems interested in these parallel events only to the extent that they provided political ammunition to the Religious Right. I believe there is a missed opportunity here. In a book so focused on the relationship between mass-media framings and gay activist self-presentations, it seems vital to attend to the interplay of these two moral panics. What role did the late-1970s panic over intergenerational sex and child sexual endangerment play in the consolidation and accomplishments of gay liberalism?

Today, as the mainstream movement strives to reduce the complexity and contradictions of queer politics to a "gay rights" movement, and beyond this to a "marriage rights" movement, it is likely that the electoral and legislative battles of the late 1970s will continue to supplant the Stonewall riots as our dominant origin story — a phenomenon already witnessed in *Milk*. For this reason, Fejes's book arrives just in time. With its wide-ranging yet meticulous attention to detail and difference, the book offers a history of the late 1970s that is, one hopes, irreducible and difficult to romanticize.

Greg Youmans is a lecturer in the film and digital media department at the University of California, Santa Cruz.

DOI 10.1215/10642684-2010-030

(UN)LIMITED INTIMACY

Douglas Dowland

Unlimited Intimacy: Reflections on the Subculture of Barebacking
Tim Dean
Chicago: University of Chicago Press, 2009. 237 pp.

Tim Dean's latest book is a remarkable exploration of what is arguably the greatest taboo in contemporary gay men's culture: the act of condomless anal intercourse. His claim that barebacking is not just an errant sexual practice but an emotional and cultural practice for many of its participants may strike some readers as audacious. And his interpretation of nonmonogamous barebacking as an act of kinship will provoke. But the most meaningful and productive shock of reading *Unlimited Intimacy* comes from its constant reminder that barebacking did not appear suddenly or randomly. Even if we are not practitioners, the discourses of our own sexual practices have helped construct condomless anal intercourse as the site of maximized intensity and "unlimited intimacy."

"Barebacking," Dean reminds us, is a relatively new term to describe the contemporary meanings of a very old act. As such, barebacking is an invention birthed in the wake of other inventions. He writes that "gay men invented safer sex and risk-reduction guidelines, but now we have invented Barebacking. Unprotected anal sex between men has become something different than it once was: Barebacking does not represent a 'relapse' or misguided return to what gay sex before AIDS used to be" (5). For many, barebacking is an attempt to modulate risk with intimacy, to create and maintain affective bonds to help one emotionally cope (and possibly thrive) with the imminent threat of infection and death. As Dean puts this rather compactly, "Bareback subculture reclaims gay sex as *sexuality* by relegating epidemiological concerns to secondary status" (11, emphasis in original).

This is important to consider because we so often presume that barebackers are in denial of, or ignorantly disregard, the mortality and seriousness of HIV/ AIDS. But Dean interprets barebacking as just one of many strategies for having a sexual life in the presence of the virus. "Paradoxically bareback subculture institutionalizes risk as a permanent condition of existence, embracing and eroticizing it, while promulgating the idea that seroconversion renders moot one particular risk" (69). From this, it could be argued that the rhetoric of "safe sex" is replete with its own paradoxes that it too embraces and eroticizes.

To me, the second chapter of *Unlimited Intimacy* bears this point out: it is possibly the best close reading of pornographic film to date, a complex study of the work of pioneering "bareback" pornographer Paul Morris. Adopting the strategy formulated by Linda Williams in her classic *Hard Core* (1989), Dean argues that the invisibility of HIV creates a quandary for bareback pornography similar to the impossibility of the filmed female orgasm in heterosexual pornography.[1] Bareback pornography attempts to assuage this invisibility with carefully constructed visibilities: an emphasis on group sex and demarcating (in Morris's work, often through subtitles) the precise moment of internal climax. In fact, Dean goes so far as to suggest in the third chapter that straight pornography has taken to mimicking gay pornography with a renewed interest in condomless intercourse, even adopting some of the slang that was once solely in the barebacker's argot.

Dean's final chapter is a puzzling jeremiad on the search for casual sex online, which he argues privatizes public life and makes "cruising" a purely sexual endeavor, reducing its potential to generate friendships, feelings of community, and ultimately, one's sense of self. He writes that "the ethics of cruising is a matter not of how many people one has sex with or what kind of sex one has with them (bareback or otherwise) but of how one treats the other and more specifically, how one treats his or her own otherness" (177). Certainly one can arrive at the same conclusion without making a straw man out of the Internet, claiming that it reduces "the contact sport of cruising to a practice of networking" (194).

Also, I wish that Dean had more thoroughly explored the boundaries of barebacking as "unlimited intimacy": the paradoxes he masterfully locates are often disregarded in lieu of anecdote and confession. Dean is truly brave to continually remind readers that he engages in the practices that are the focus of his study, but such bravery fosters a reliance on "experience" that scholars such as Joan Wallach Scott have successfully questioned.[2] The academic discourse on barebacking is really just beginning, and it will take many more voices before the practice attains the full range of scholarly attention that it deserves. *Unlimited Intimacy* advances this emergent discourse by leaps.

Note

1. Linda Williams, *Hard Core: Power, Pleasure, and the "Frenzy of the Visible"* (Berkeley: University of California Press, 1999)

2. Joan Wallach Scott, "The Evidence of Experience," *Critical Inquiry* 17, no. 4 (1991): 773–98.

Douglas Dowland is a visiting assistant professor of English at Ohio Northern University.

DOI 10.1215/10642684-2010-031

INTERSEX IN AMERICA: A CULTURAL HISTORY OF UNCERTAINTY

Jana Funke

Bodies in Doubt: An American History of Intersex
Elizabeth Reis
Baltimore: John Hopkins University Press, 2009. xvii + 216 pp.

How does culture deal with bodies that fail to conform to the norms of sexual dimorphism? And what is at stake in managing these bodies? Focusing on the last three hundred years of American cultural and medical history, Elizabeth Reis's study reveals the different strategies employed to make sense of intersexual bodies. Often viewed as monstrosities up until the eighteenth century, these bodies were subject to a range of different medical explanations over the following two hundred years. The changing understanding of intersex was characterized by the tension between a focus on the gonads as the true marker of sex and the competing consideration of secondary sex characteristics, as well as what we would nowadays define as the individual's sexual orientation and gender identity. At the same time, the increased availability of medical technologies opened up the possibilities of elective and nonelective surgical alteration of genital appearance and the construction of allegedly normal male and female bodies. Drawing on a large num-

ber of historical cases, Reis describes the relation between these developments
and reveals how cultural understandings of intersex evolved. In doing so, she also
exposes the contradictory nature of cultural constructions of sexual difference.

Taking the reader up to the present day, *Bodies in Doubt* concludes with a
consideration of recent attempts to replace intersex with the alternative term disorder of sex development (DSD) or, as Reis suggests, the less stigmatizing "diver-
gence of sex development" (153). Reis illustrates that we have come a long way
from delegating sexually ambivalent bodies to the sphere of the fantastic, mon-
strous, or humanly impossible; however, the concluding discussion of the nomen-
clature controversy reminds us that the uncertainties evoked by the intersexual
body are not history but continue to be negotiated today. If the emergence of the
intersex movement in the past fifteen years and the growing academic interest in
intersex studies have resulted in a new focus on intersex as a human reality, the
very meaning of sexually ambivalent bodies as well as how we should speak about
these bodies remains, as the book's title suggests, *in doubt*.

Reis's study is of particular interest as it illustrates that this uncertainty
not only concerns the construction of sexual dimorphism but also affects more
general understandings of what counts as normal, natural, and human in a specific historical moment. The history of intersex, Reis suggests, is not only a history
of changing figurations of physical sex but also a history of the cultural figura-
tion of human experience and identity as such. Throughout *Bodies in Doubt*, for
instance, Reis points to the close relationship between intersex and homosexuality. She explains how the desire to safeguard the norms of heterosexuality and
marriage would influence the decisions doctors made when trying to signify the
sexually ambiguous bodies of their patients. At the same time, there were anxieties that "hermaphroditism [could be] just a cover for a same-sex sexual relationship" (68). Convincing doctors that such individuals were members of the opposite
sex, patients could potentially gain the right to change sex and thus fraudulently
claim a social and legal identity that legitimated an otherwise illicit relationship
between members of the same sex. The fear of deception also forged an association between sexual changeability and racial instability in nineteenth-century
America where "the unnerving possibility that individuals could suddenly change
sex paralleled early national preoccupation with race, racial categories, and the
possibility of changing racial identity" (36). Pointing to the interrelation of sex and
sexuality as well as sex and race, *Bodies in Doubt* is at its strongest when it reveals
how far-reaching cultural norms were implicated in managing sexually ambivalent
bodies.

Unfortunately, at times, the analysis of the intersections between the medical treatment of intersex and the wider cultural context breaks off all too soon. The relation between the mutable sexual and racial body, for example, remains isolated and is not taken up in later chapters. Another oversight regards the changing cultural relationship between America and Europe as rival centers of sexual knowledge production. Reis focuses primarily on American sources, but she also draws on European texts without reflecting on the changing nature of transatlantic relations. More generally, because of the book's large scope, attention to detail sometimes yields to a more wide-ranging survey of historical development. As a result, Reis misses a few opportunities that would have allowed her to further develop her argument and add to her study's originality.

Nevertheless, *Bodies in Doubt* undoubtedly deserves a prominent place in the growing body of literature on intersex history and politics. One of Reis's main achievements is that she places present-day intersex politics in the context of a long and complex cultural history. Moreover, her discussion sheds light on the American history of intersex before the 1950s, a period that has not yet received much critical attention. Thus Reis's research complements Alice Dreger's seminal *Hermaphrodites and the Medical Invention of Sex*, which deals mainly with British and French sources in the late nineteenth and early twentieth centuries.[1] Reis has unearthed a wealth of new American case histories that not only make for interesting reading but also offer fresh insight into the cultural construction of intersex bodies. *Bodies in Doubt* is an excellent and highly engaging introduction to the medical and cultural history of intersex. In addition, by raising awareness of the multiple ways in which intersex relates to other markers of human experience such as sexuality, race, or class, Reis invites further investigation and opens up a set of questions that might well prove central to intersex studies in the future.

Note

1.   Alice Domurat Dreger, *Hermaphrodites and the Medical Invention of Sex* (Cambridge: Harvard University Press, 2000).

Jana Funke is an associate research fellow in the Centre for Medical History at the University of Exeter.

DOI 10.1215/10642684-2010-032

UNCLOSETING THE SOUTH

Lisa Hinrichsen

Sweet Tea: Black Gay Men of the South
E. Patrick Johnson
Chapel Hill: University of North Carolina Press, 2008. 565 pp.

In *Sweet Tea: Black Gay Men of the South*, E. Patrick Johnson assembles a variety of oral histories that collectively explore the range of codes and practices that emerge from the intersection of southern, queer, and black identities, and examines how these seemingly conflicting ideological positions are mediated and negotiated within what he terms the "diverse (and perverse) social fabric of southern living" (1). Building on earlier groundbreaking work by John Howard and James T. Sears while more directly focusing on questions of race and masculinity, Johnson assertively challenges the myth that to be gay in the South is to live a life marked by silence, invisibility, and isolation.[1] The voices collected here not only dispute the idea that gay subcultures flourish primarily in northern, secular, urban areas but also attempt to deconstruct myths about black male sexuality and rework stereotypes about southern identity.

Johnson foregrounds this tripartite mission early on: "Not only does the history of southern black gay men demand a reconsideration of what constitutes a 'vital' subculture; it also necessitates a reconsideration of the South as 'backward' and 'repressive,'" when clearly gay community building and desire emerge simultaneously within and against southern culture" (3). Toward these ends, Johnson collected the oral histories of sixty-three men from fifteen different states across the South between August 2004 and October 2006. While he consciously attempts to represent a range of occupations and class backgrounds, he also acknowledges upfront that he has largely relied on his own networks of friends and acquaintances to provide sources. While this gives an intimacy to the project—and ensures Johnson's safety—it also, at times, provides too narrow a range of black gay experience. Most of the oral histories come primarily from men born in the late 1940s to the early 1960s, and those of the under-thirty set, who have had a radically different experience of both queer sexuality and southern identity, are noticeably underrepresented.

Over seven lengthy chapters organized by overarching themes and shared stories, Johnson tackles numerous aspects of gay black life in the South. Chapter 1 is about growing up; chapter 2 considers and challenges the "closet" as a model of black homosexuality in the South and explores the ambivalence of many of these men's identification with a politicized and public sexuality; chapter 3 centers on the role of religion and the black church in the expression of gay male sexuality; chapter 4 examines sexual activity; chapter 5 focuses on the extended narratives of four non-gender conforming men; chapter 6 concentrates on stories of love and loss; and chapter 7 examines queer identity across generations, comparing the lives of two men who are eighty-six and ninety-three years old with the youngest in the study, who were twenty-three and twenty-one years old at the time of the interviews. While this thematic framework emphasizes the shared stories that draw these men together, it ends up ultimately blurring the geographic and demographic diversity that Johnson carefully tried to cultivate, making it difficult to follow each recurring narrator.

As a black gay southerner himself, Johnson's study is also a negotiation of his own identity, and he foregrounds this quite consciously, framing his research as an act of "critical performance ethnography" (8) that relies on a "co-performance" whereby "both the researcher and the narrator are performing for one another" (8). Yet it is unclear how these statements in his introduction play out in the text itself: Johnson provides short framing sections within each of the text's seven chapters, but shies away from making these brief preludes adequately reflective. Likewise, he holds back from probing his subjects in the interviews, instead providing only occasional interjections into their stories.

Curiously, of all the facets of identity that he examines here, the role of regional belonging is the thorniest for Johnson to negotiate, and he frequently rehashes stereotypes about southern identity as he seeks to revise them, noting, for example that "southerners tend to be great bearers of gossip" (110) and that when "people think of the South, after foodways and hospitality, religiosity is often what comes to mind" (182). These generalizing statements are set in striking contrast to the oral narratives themselves, which reveal a much more ambivalent, contradictory, and fascinating perspective on black gay southern existence. The oral narratives reveal southern gay men's relationship to the performative codes of being southern and underscore how these men "employ southern culture itself, which produces its own codes and practices that mediate conflicting ideological positions, to speak to the complicated realities of their own lives" (19). Notably, Johnson's retention of the performative nature of southern speech also nods toward the importance of oral tradition and the vernacular in African American culture.

Many of the men in the study speak only under a pseudonym, and their stories do not always reveal the liberated narrative Johnson seems to be seeking, but rather identities shot through with ambivalence. Both the introduction and the epilogue to this study underscore the ongoing violence — even death — associated with being gay in the South and form testimonies to the efforts still needed to ensure equality. Overall, however, Johnson performs important work in *Sweet Tea* for gay and lesbian studies, gender studies, African American studies, and southern studies. Indeed, the richness borne out in this study begs for a companion volume on black gay women in the South.

Note

1. See John Howard, ed., *Carryin' On in the Lesbian and Gay South* (New York: New York University Press, 1997); and James T. Sears, *Lonely Hunters: An Oral History of Lesbian and Gay Southern Life, 1948–1968* (Boulder, CO: Westview, 1997).

Lisa Hinrichsen is assistant professor of English at the University of Arkansas.

DOI 10.1215/10642684-2010-033

BACKWARD STANCES

Colin Carman

Anachronism and Its Others: Sexuality, Race, Temporality
Valerie Rohy
Albany: State University of New York Press, 2009. xvi + 178 pp.

Anachronism has long vexed those historians of sexuality wishing to avoid projections of the present onto the past. Referring, for example, to anachronism as a significant "difficulty" at the outset of his foundational *Christianity, Social Tolerance, and Homosexuality* (1980), John Boswell warned that "one must be extremely cautious about projecting onto historical data ideas about gay people inferred from modern samples."[1] Meanwhile, in the preface to their *Premodern Sexualities* (1996), Louise Fradenburg and Carla Freccero challenged the norm that "modern desires and perspectives" must be repressed to read and represent history faithfully. For them, the disavowal of anachronism demands the "renunciation, the *ascesis*, of 'self,'" and since this renunciation tries to "hide its own narcissistic investments, it begs for queer scrutiny."[2] With *Anachronism and Its Others: Sexuality, Race, and Temporality*, Valerie Rohy has joined Heather Love's *Feeling Backwards* in supplying just the sophisticated sort of "queer scrutiny" that anachronism, backwardness, and regression truly deserve, this time with attention to American literature and culture.[3] Contending that queer and black subjects have anachronism in common, she grapples with the pseudoscientific analogy between the imagined arrested development of the former and the putative primitivism of African Americans. As Rohy herself boldly declares at the start of this slim and compelling study, "this book traces the temporal analogy between race and sexuality to its limits" (xv). Anachronism emerges as an ideologically charged formation paradoxically outside, yet integral to, the heteronormative time lines of personal development and human history. Rohy's *Anachronism* no doubt confirms and promotes the current interest in the relationship between sexuality and temporality, refining the view, best articulated by Judith Butler in *Bodies That Matter* (1993), that "'sex' is an ideal construct which is forcibly materialized through time."[4]

The basis for Rohy's major claim, that the race-sexuality analogy is a temporal problem with lasting effects on cultural politics, can be found in the annals of nineteenth-century evolutionary and sexological research. The first of six chapters foregrounds three discourses — history, psychoanalysis, and literature — to show how the earliest theorizations of homosexual identity borrowed from racist evolutionary models. On the heels of Rohy's preface, in which she reads *Diana: A Strange Autobiography* (1939) as reliant on scientific theory to diagnose lesbianism as aberrant, she turns to a surprising and useful source: Theodore Roosevelt's speech, from 1910, on the "Biological Analogies in History" (another linkage between racialized notions of cultural evolution and temporality). Sigmund Freud was similarly invested in evolutionary analogies, and Rohy's meticulous close reading of his footnotes from 1905 to 1920, particularly his ceaseless revisions and lack of periodization, yields this axiom: "The *text itself* must evolve and mature, however stubbornly and materially writing also preserves the past" (11).

Chapter 2 combines *The Narrative of the Life of Frederick Douglass, An American Slave* with Harriet Jacobs's *Incidents in the Life of a Slave Girl* to show

how predominant notions of anachronistic blackness were replaced by representations of homosexuality as equally archaic and how such abolitionist works construe same-sex desire as merely a symptom of slavery's perverse power to feminize its masters and masculinize white women. Denied the right to marry and barred from knowing their own ages, the enslaved came to privilege marriage as a symbol of freedom in an effort to reclaim time, but in ways that further subordinated homosexuality as a woeful thing of the past. Chapter 3 argues that while the regionalist writings of Sarah Orne Jewett and Willa Cather were at odds with American nationalism at the close of the nineteenth century in dually literary and sexual ways, a gay-positive novel like Cather's *Sapphira and the Slave Girl* reconnects the love between women with futurity and progress. Chapters 4 and 5 examine Pauline Hopkins's 1903 novel, *Of One Blood: or, the Hidden Self* and Ernest Hemingway's *Garden of Eden*, respectively; Rohy's reading of Hemingway's posthumously published Africa narrative is especially progressive as both a corrective to Toni Morrison's reading that, Rohy writes, "omits the central role of homosexuality" in Hemingway's "Africanism," and as a convincing use of Freudian oedipality to show how Hemingway's veneration of heteronormative masculinity is actually a screen for a much queerer substrate (115).

Rohy's final chapter, which is titled "Ahistorical" and appeared in these pages in 2005, would have made more conceptual sense at the book's beginning rather than at its end, but perhaps this reversibility is intentional, supporting, like the larger work itself, a transference of ideas from the present into the past. There is a similarly minor objection to be made. Beyond slavery, the force with which sex/uality and race are materialized is most apparent, for Rohy, in the rhetorical violence of "gay is the new black," a slogan sufficiently criticized in chapter 3 for first, resuscitating the race-sexuality analogy by the "embalming" of black history "in the service of queer politics," and second, "making blackness *merely* historical, a museum exhibit and no longer a vital site of contestation" (70). Perhaps Rohy underestimates the degree to which social conservatives see homosexuality as undeserving of public approval, much less marriage equality, and how the admittedly rough logic of "gay is the new black" actually forces such opponents to think of sexuality not simply in terms of sex but in terms of civil rights; the analogy, after all, is a teleological one, positing that sexual minorities are destined for the same equality won by black Americans in the twentieth century, and such a view shouldn't be so summarily dismissed. In light, however, of Rohy's theoretical deployment of the future perfect tense throughout this inquiry to denote a combination of anticipation and retrospection, it is fitting to say that Rohy's *Anachronism and Its Others* is nearly perfect as it presently stands.

Notes

1.   John Boswell, *Christianity, Social Tolerance, and Homosexuality: Gay People in Western Europe from the Beginning of the Christian Era to the Fourteenth Century* (Chicago: University of Chicago Press, 1980), 24.

2.   Louise Fradenburg and Carla Freccero, *Premodern Sexualities* (New York: Routledge, 1996), viii.

3.   Heather Love, *Feeling Backward: Loss and the Politics of Queer History* (Cambridge, MA: Harvard University Press, 2007).

4.   Judith Butler, *Bodies That Matter: On the Discursive Limits of "Sex"* (New York: Routledge, 1993), 1.

Colin Carman teaches English at Colorado Mountain College and has published extensively in the *Gay and Lesbian Review*.

DOI 10.1215/10642684-2010-034

About the Contributors

Lisa Duggan is professor of social and cultural analysis at New York University. She is author of *Sapphic Slashers: Sex, Violence, and American Modernity* (2000) and *Twilight of Equality: Neoliberalism, Cultural Politics, and the Attack on Democracy* (2003). She is coauthor with Nan Hunter of *Sex Wars: Sexual Dissent and Political Culture* (1995, 2006), and coeditor with Lauren Berlant of *Our Monica, Ourselves: The Clinton Affair and National Interest* (2001).

David L. Eng is professor of English, comparative literature, and Asian American studies at the University of Pennsylvania. He is author of *The Feeling of Kinship: Queer Liberalism and the Racialization of Intimacy* (2010) and *Racial Castration: Managing Masculinity in Asian America* (2001). In addition, he is coeditor with David Kazanjian of *Loss: The Politics of Mourning* (2003), with Alice Y. Hom of *Q & A: Queer in Asian America* (1998), and with Judith Halberstam and José Esteban Muñoz of a special issue of the journal *Social Text*, "What's Queer about Queer Studies Now?" (2005).

Steven Epstein is the John C. Shaffer Professor in the Humanities and professor of sociology at Northwestern University. He is the author of *Impure Science: AIDS, Activism, and the Politics of Knowledge* (1996) and *Inclusion: The Politics of Difference in Medical Research* (2007). He studies the contested production of biomedical knowledge, with an emphasis on the interplay of social movements, experts, and health institutions, and with a focus on the politics of sexuality, gender, and race.

Lisa Henderson is associate professor and chair in the Department of Communication at the University of Massachusetts, Amherst. She is author of numerous essays on sexuality and culture and of *Love and Money: Queers, Class, and Cultural Production*, forthcoming from New York University Press.

Neville Hoad is associate professor of English at the University of Texas at Austin. He is the author of *African Intimacies: Race, Homosexuality, and Globalization* (2007) and coeditor, with Karen Martin and Graeme Reid, of *Sex and Politics in South Africa: The Equality Clause/Gay and Lesbian Movement/the Anti-apartheid Struggle* (2005).

Sharon P. Holland is an associate professor of English, African and African-American studies, and women's studies at Duke University. She is the author of *Raising the Dead: Readings of Death and (Black) Subjectivity* (2000), which won the Lora Romero First Book Prize from the American Studies Association (ASA) in 2002. She is also coauthor of a collection of trans-Atlantic Afro-Native criticism with Tiya Miles entitled *Crossing Waters/Crossing Worlds: The African Diaspora in Indian Country* (2006). Holland was also instrumental in the republication of Lila Karp's novel *The Queen Is in the Garbage* (2007), one of the first second-wave feminist novels.

Dredge Byung'chu Käng is a PhD/MPH candidate in anthropology and global epidemiology at Emory University. He is conducing ethnographic research in Bangkok on gender pluralism, social status, and Asian regionalism, with a focus on transnational relationships. He is also involved in community and HIV organizing with transgender women and sex workers in Thailand.

Regina Kunzel is a professor of gender, women, sexuality studies, and history at the University of Minnesota. She is author of *Criminal Intimacy: Sex in Prison and the Uneven History of Modern American Sexuality* (2008) and *Fallen Women, Problem Girls: Unmarried Mothers and the Professionalization of Social Work, 1890 to 1945* (1993), and coedited, with Jeffrey Escoffier and Molly McGarry, a special issue of *Radical History Review*, "The Queer Issue: New Visions of America's Lesbian and Gay Past," in 1995. Kunzel is working on a book on the encounter of psychiatry and sexual and gender nonconformity.

Heather Love is associate professor of English at the University of Pennsylvania and the author of *Feeling Backward: Loss and the Politics of Queer History* (2007). She is currently at work on a book on the source materials for Erving Goffman's 1963 book *Stigma: On the Management of Spoiled Identity*.

Robert McRuer is professor and deputy chair of the Department of English at George Washington University. He is author of *Crip Theory: Cultural Signs of Queerness and Disability* (2006) and coeditor, with Abby L. Wilkerson, of "Desiring Disability: Queer Theory Meets Disability Studies," which appeared as a special issue of *GLQ* in 2003. With Anna Mollow, he is coeditor of the forthcoming anthology *Sex and Disability*.

Joanne Meyerowitz is professor of history and American studies at Yale University. She is author of *How Sex Changed: A History of Transsexuality in the United States* (2002) and *Women Adrift: Independent Wage Earners in Chicago, 1880–1930* (1988) and editor of *History and September 11th* (2003) and *Not June Cleaver: Women and Gender in Postwar America, 1945–1960* (1994). Her most recent article is "'How Common Culture Shapes the Separate Lives': Sexuality, Race, and Mid-Twentieth-Century Social Constructionist Thought," *Journal of American History* 96, no. 4 (2010): 1057–84.

Gayle Rubin is assistant professor of anthropology and women's studies at the University of Michigan. She is author of a number of canonical essays on sexualities and genders, sexological theory, durable inequalities, gay and lesbian ethnography, and urban North America. She is author of two books, both forthcoming from Duke University Press: *Deviations: Essays in Sex, Gender, and Politics* and *Valley of the Kings: Leathermen in San Francisco, 1960–1990*.

Susan Stryker is associate professor of gender studies at Indiana University, Bloomington, and the author, most recently, of *Transgender History* (2008).

Carole S. Vance is an anthropologist at Columbia University in New York City. She writes on sexuality, human rights, policy, representation, and, most recently, trafficking and teaches in many international academic and advocacy settings. She coordinated the Barnard College Sexuality Conference and edited *Pleasure and Danger* (1984), the collection of conference papers in which Gayle Rubin's essay "Thinking Sex" first appeared.

JOURNAL OF THE

HISTORY

OF

SEXUALITY

Mathew Kuefler, Editor
San Diego State University

Volume 19, Issue 2, May 2010

SUBSCRIPTION RATES:
Individuals: $51 • Institutions: $207• Student: $36
Canada: add $11.50 • Other foreign: add $19.50
Single Copy Rates: Individuals: $22 • Institutions: $72
Canada: add $6.00 • Other foreign: add $10.50

UNIVERSITY OF TEXAS PRESS
Journals Division • Box 7819 • Austin, Texas 78713-7819
Phone: 512-232-7621 • Fax : 512-232-7178
journals@uts.cc.utexas.edu • www.utexas.edu/utpress